THE HISTORY OF THE NATIONAL TRUST

FOR HISTORIC PRESERVATION, 1963–1973

THE HISTORY OF THE

NATIONAL TRUST FOR HISTORIC PRESERVATION

1963–1973

By Elizabeth D. Mulloy

FOR THE NATIONAL TRUST FOR HISTORIC PRESERVATION
IN THE UNITED STATES

THE PRESERVATION PRESS

NATIONAL TRUST FOR HISTORIC PRESERVATION IN THE UNITED STATES

Washington, D.C.

1976

International Standard Book Number: 0-89133-033-x

Library of Congress Catalogue Card Number: 65-4705

The National Trust for Historic Preservation
740–748 Jackson Place, N.W.
Washington, D.C. 20006

Printed in the United States of America
by The John D. Lucas Printing Company, Baltimore, Md.

Designed by Gerard A. Valerio

Cover art: The Shadows-on-the-Teche, New Iberia, La., a property of the National Trust. The view from the Bayou Teche (front) and the street view (back) were painted by Adrian Persac in 1961. The watercolors hang in The Shadows dining room (see p. 49). Figures in the foreground are prints from the Godey's Lady Book pasted on by the artist.

Endpapers: Adaptation of endpapers used in 1972 in the redesigned Historic Preservation, *the quarterly magazine of the National Trust. The endpapers were created exclusively for* Historic Preservation *by Colonial Williamsburg, Inc., E. N. Crain, bookbinder, using the traditional "Dutch swirl" motif.*

To the Trust staff, whose dedication helped guarantee a future for the past, and especially to Helen Duprey Bullock. Her example helped involve many persons in preservation, both as volunteers and professionals.

Contents

Preface

In 1963, David E. Finley, a founder of the National Trust for Historic Preservation and chairman of its Board of Trustees for the first 15 years, wrote the history of the Trust from 1947 through 1963, a record of its activities and achievements in those formative years. At the end of a tenure full of remarkable accomplishments he wrote, "Preservation of historic and significant sites and buildings was never needed more than it is today, when so much that is important from an architectural, scenic or historic point of view is being destroyed for temporary convenience or monetary gain."

As true as that statement was in 1963, it is even more true today. Apathy, ignorance and greed still threaten valuable products of our culture. Fortunately, preservation, accomplished through the Trust and the many organizations it represents, has since been significantly aided by federal, state and local governments. In 1966, the year of the "Preservation Congress," the national commitment to preservation was reinforced and expanded; more important, legislation provided workable tools and authorized funds for achieving the goals of preservation. Thus, the years in which I had the privilege of serving as David Finley's successor have been most exciting and challenging, filled with both frustrations and rewards.

In the last months of my chairmanship, it occurred to me that his history should be brought up to date. I therefore asked the Department of Publications, which has recently been reorganized as the Preservation Press, to undertake this project. A number of people should be recognized for their work on the book: Before her retirement, senior editor and historian Helen Duprey Bullock developed an outline for the book, and Terry B. Morton, vice president and editor for the Preservation Press, directed the project. Patricia E. Williams, who served as archivist from 1966 to 1974 and who is community education coordinator, Office of Preservation Services, helped assemble the necessary research materials and provided information on past Trust activities. Elizabeth D. Mulloy reviewed these materials, gathered additional data and wrote the history. Sharon W. Timmons, associate editor for special projects, edited the manuscript. In addition to current Trust executive staff, the manuscript was reviewed by Helen Duprey Bullock, David E. Finley, Robert R. Garvey, Jr., Charles B. Hosmer, Richard H. Howland, William J. Murtagh, Joseph Prendergast, Frederick L. Rath, Jr., Robert M. Utley and Tony P. Wrenn. Jennie B. Bull, associate editor, edited the final manuscript and supervised production.

The book is divided into two parts. Part One summarizes the material in Finley's history and also covers the succeeding three years, 1963–66, including the passage of the National Historic Preservation Act of 1966. The reason for this division is that the passage of the 1966 legislation marked a turning point in the preservation movement, for the federal government then officially committed itself to a policy of preservation. Part Two deals with the unprecedented growth of the Trust after 1966 and the increasing involvement of the federal government in preservation.

Readers should note that this is not an evaluative history of the Trust. It is instead a written record of Trust achievements. An objective assessment of the place of the Trust in the history of the preservation movement awaits evaluation by a historian not directly associated with the Trust.

I could not conclude anything I have to say about the Trust without expressing my indebtedness to all the Trustees with whom I have been fortunate to serve and my deep appreciation of the efforts of a dedicated and able staff. I would especially like to mention Robert R. Garvey, Jr., who was serving as executive director when I became chairman and continued in that capacity until he was succeeded by Joseph Prendergast who then served for the remainder of my time as chairman. Both of these men were indispensable to the orderly growth and increasing influence of the Trust. I wish particularly to commend the outstanding leadership of James Biddle who became president of the Trust in 1968. He brought not only youth, vigor and imagination to the Trust but also a hunger for work and a remarkable dedication to his responsibilities. Many of the most valuable programs of the Trust are due to his initiatives and his confidence in the ability of the Trust to move forward.

Finally, I consider it a privilege to have been associated with the Trust in a leadership capacity.

GORDON GRAY, chairman emeritus
National Trust for Historic Preservation

Foreword

If America forgets where she came from,
if the people lose sight of what brought them along,
if she listens to the deniers and mockers,
then will rot and dissolution begin.

CARL SANDBURG, *Remembrance Rock*

The story of the historic preservation movement in America is not a long one. Since the birth of the United States, there have been those who have understood the need to save some tangible evidence of our cultural and historical heritage, but only recently has the critical need to remember "where we came from" become obvious to many of us. Only now are we beginning to see how greatly our future depends on an awareness of our past.

Once the term *preservation* meant saving and restoring buildings of national historical significance, turning them into museums where citizens could come for inspiration. Once preservation was regarded solely as the work of historians and antiquarians or a diversion of the well-to-do. Too often the idea of preservation was misunderstood entirely—and was either tolerated as a harmless eccentricity or cursed as an obstacle to "progress."

The founders of the National Trust understood many years ago the implications of losing our national heritage. They recognized that the postwar building boom, symbolized by wrecking ball and bulldozer, threatened more than just a few irreplaceable structures. They foresaw more far-reaching consequences of an "out-with-the-old, in-with-the-new" philosophy.

Perhaps because they were familiar with the past, they could predict a future in which America found itself without roots, without a sense of identity, with nothing to lose. To prevent such a future, the Trust pledged its efforts to two primary goals: (1) to save those things of cultural and historical value (2) in order to instill in the American people full appreciation of their legacy.

In the quarter century since its inception, the Trust has remained true to its original mission. One reason that it has remained so, and at the same time developed and advanced its mission and goals, is that the Trust had outstanding leadership. David E. Finley, former director of the National Gallery of Art, whose vision and drive played a major role in the establishment of the Trust, served as chairman of the Board of Trustees for 15 years before stepping down from that position in 1962. Since that time, he has continued to devote much time and talent to the preservation movement and especially to the National Trust, serving as chairman emeritus and honorary Trustee.

Gordon Gray, Finley's successor, likewise made a significant contribution to the preservation movement. He was recognized for this leadership a number of times. One of the first awards presented to Gray was the George McAneny Medal for Historic Preservation, given in 1967 by the American Scenic and Historic Preservation Society; and in 1973 the U.S. Department of the Interior presented Gray with the Conservation Service Award, in part for his testimony in behalf of the National Historic Preservation Act of 1966. During his 11-year tenure as chairman of the Board of Trustees, the Trust grew from fewer than 4,000 to 42,000 members, the operating budget increased from less than $250,000 to almost $3.5 million and assets grew from less than $4 million to almost $7 million. But these figures reflect only the surface of Trust accomplishments under Gray's leadership. During the period from 1962 through 1973, Trust influence reached from isolated rural areas to giant urban centers, from city and state councils to the White House, from Maine, to Alaska, to Hawaii, to Puerto Rico to countries abroad.

Through the years, as the Trust worked to bring the need for preservation into public awareness in this country—and abroad—it helped expand the meaning of the term *preservation*. Preservationists today recognize aesthetic and architectural values along with historical and patriotic values as legitimate criteria for preservation efforts. In addition, attention is focused on structures and sites of local and state, as well as of national, significance. The scope of things to be saved has likewise broadened considerably. To notable sites, buildings and objects, the categories under the Trust charter, have been added districts and structures, two additional categories specified in the National Historic Preservation Act of 1966. This emphasis in the national legislation has helped highlight concern for such landmarks as neighborhoods, gardens, town squares, engineering and industrial structures, entire towns, rural areas and open space in urban areas.

Ways of educating the public and of instilling appreciation have also expanded far beyond the historic house museum and historic village concept. Most significant is the growing acceptance of a concept the

Trust has actively fostered from its beginning—the idea of continuing use. No longer are buildings simply "embalmed as architectural freaks," as *New York Times* architectural critic Ada Louise Huxtable once described museum use. Today many are renewed and used: lived in, worked in, played in, learned in. They are regarded no longer merely as monuments or shrines, but as landmarks, in the total sense of the word. They tell us where we are, both culturally and geographically. They are beginning to be valued as integral parts of the full fabric of our communities.

Charged in its congressional charter to "facilitate public participation," the Trust has also aided in broadening the meaning of the term *preservationist*. Today planners, architects, bankers, realtors, writers, developers, artists, public officials, craftsmen, homemakers and students have joined with traditional preservationists—museologists, genealogists, archaeologists, historians and other professionals; all are citizens who care about preserving the integrity of their surroundings. The preservation movement has truly become a grassroots crusade, an avocation as well as a vocation. In addition, there are more preservation professionals, applying their special skills daily in preservation work, as opportunities for employment in the field have increased.

Most important, and most difficult to measure, is the influence the preservation movement has had on the national consciousness of the environment. To be sure, there are those who value quantity above quality and size over significance, who see change (any change) as progress, who define price solely in terms of dollars. But now there is also a growing awareness that our future depends on how wisely we manage the rich resources, both natural and built, we have inherited. Preservationists were among the first to point out the fact that we depend on a total environment, made up of intricately entwined elements, for our spiritual and mental as well as our physical sustenance. Today, more and more of us are realizing that the total environment is fragile and must be treated with respect.

This final point—that protection of the environment must include concern for our cultural heritage as well as for the natural beauty of our land—was reemphasized in the report of a Special Study Committee appointed by Gordon Gray in October 1972. The committee, composed of 20 outstanding leaders in preservation whose interests and activities covered a cross section of related fields, was charged by Gray to review current Trust programs and to chart new goals for the future. The chairman, with typical concern and farsightedness, gave the committee a broad mandate to investigate possibilities for improvements and expansion of Trust programs. He stressed his conviction that preservationists must find new ways to make common cause with environmentalists. Because of the importance of the study, the Ford Foundation provided support for the undertaking.

Obtaining the expert services of a study director, four assistants and consultants for special studies, the committee communicated with a wide variety of people: Trustees; Trust staff members; members of the Board of Advisors, Trust committees and property councils; representatives of government agencies and private conservation and preservation organizations; friends of the Trust; critics; even persons who were unfamiliar with Trust work. More than 100 interviews were conducted; other comments were solicited in meetings or by correspondence. Besides traveling throughout the United States, the staff director also went to England with a study group sponsored by the Oatlands Council to get a fresh look at preservation from the British perspective.

Out of these efforts came a number of imaginative concepts. Some were already being implemented in Trust programs. Others could be realized immediately with slight revisions. Still others would require years of planning and increased funding. All showed that foresight and long-range thinking were imperative if the "common cause" were to be successful.

In 1973, after the Board of Trustees had voted approval, the committee report was published as *Goals and Programs*. Assessing the mood of the nation, the committee found that a major public concern was for the lowered quality of life that had developed even while the nation grew in population and in technological skills. It therefore urged the Trust to continue to conduct its programs in the context of "the broad environmental and land-use movement aimed at the overall improvement of the quality of life." It advised the Trust to stress the "amenity" value of preserving America's historical and cultural heritage in order to continue to attract a wider commitment from the American public. The increasing role of public decision makers in locating public utilities, in assessing taxes, in zoning and land use planning, the committee decided, would also necessitate both broad educational programs and ongoing negotiations by preservationists if government leaders (especially those on the local level) were ever to see preservation as an integral part of community development.

Specific recommendations for the Trust in its role as the national leader of the preservation movement included broadening its constituency by adapting more programs to the needs of inner-city dwellers and rural inhabitants and by continuing to focus its services on local levels. The committee also urged the expansion of Trust services in such areas as research, publications, in-service training in building crafts and the use of easements, revolving funds and other preservation mechanisms. In the operation of its properties, the Trust was called upon to maintain the highest standards of preservation. Through its own acquisitions and in its role as an adviser to property owners, the Trust could set examples by broadening the range of structures to be preserved, and through demonstration projects it could pioneer innovative methods of acquisition and use. Implicit in its recommendations was a mandate to the Trust to maintain the quality of its past leadership.

Approval of the study committee report was one of the many steps taken by the Trust to accomplish that goal. To succeed Gordon Gray as chairman of the board, the Trustees elected Carlisle H. Humelsine, president of the Colonial Williamsburg Foundation and a former member of the Trust Board of Trustees from 1961 through 1972. Another former Trustee (1969–72) and former administrator of the U.S. General Services Administration (1965–69), Lawson B. Knott, Jr., was named executive vice president of the Trust in 1974. Besides their dedication to the cause of preservation, both men brought wide experience in business and government to the Trust.

In November 1973, shortly after Gordon Gray relinquished his chairmanship, it was announced that matching grant funds from the U.S. Department of the Interior for fiscal year 1974 would total $10.5 million, an increase of approximately 57 percent over the $6.7 million in grants allocated for fiscal year 1973. The Trust allocation was raised from $1.31 million to $1.75 million. As he resigned the active chairmanship to take on other duties, Gray could be sure that the Trust would continue to grow in new directions.

Addressing a group of preservationists in the spring of 1974, he reminded them of the critical need for their efforts:

> Today we cannot help but be deeply concerned about the malaise among our people. We do not seem to have any heroes any more. There has been a loss of faith in and respect for our institutions. We express little confidence in our future. For this, we must all share the guilt.

> At the same time, we genuinely yearn to regain faith in our country and confidence in its stability. Notwithstanding our many faults, we are still one of the greatest societies in the world, built—in history's reckoning—in a very short time indeed. It is not just because we have the oceans, the rivers, the mountains and the plains, but because of what we, in our best moments, have done with the abundance provided by God.

> But unless our people, especially our young, understand how and

why we have developed as we have, they will not have the wisdom, the understanding nor the incentive to carry on for the future.

I am not suggesting that historic preservation can in itself bring about this understanding, but I do submit that it is a very important aspect of what needs to be done. If we are to bring about the best in our institutions and among our people, we must preserve the best of our tangible heritage. If we succeed, our people can continue with pride and with stability of mind and purpose.

I believe that every blow struck for historic preservation is a blow struck for the survival of our society as we have been fortunate enough to know it.

Gordon Gray's words ring especially true today, as we celebrate the 200th anniversary of our nation's founding. In fact, this book, which was written at the encouragement of Gray, is one of the Bicentennial projects of the Trust. It is an especially appropriate one, too, for the Trust is an organization concerned with history, and, as such, it recognizes that documentation of the past is an invaluable aid in assessing the present and planning for the future. What better way to honor our heritage and affirm our future than by reviewing our preservation efforts to date and rededicating ourselves to the task ahead!

JAMES BIDDLE, president

National Trust for Historic Preservation

PART ONE

1947-66

George Washington's residence, Mount Vernon, Va., in a state of disrepair, 1855. (Mount Vernon Ladies' Association of the Union)

Arlington House, Arlington, Va. Gen. Samuel P. Heintzelman, staff and women on east portico steps, c. 1861. (National Park Service)

CHAPTER ONE

Beginnings: The Trust Technique

In his *History of the National Trust for Historic Preservation, 1947–1963*, David E. Finley documented the beginnings of the National Trust, its organization and its accomplishments. In retrospect, the range of those early accomplishments is impressive, especially when it is remembered that the country was not then as attuned as it is today to the importance of the environment, nor had it begun to recognize natural and historic resources as essential to that environment. However, the dedicated persons who were responsible for Trust achievements in those days worked faithfully to make Americans aware that their past was being rapidly destroyed, and they assisted citizens in every way possible in taking action to stop destruction. The influence of these preservationists continues today. Through their creativity and perseverance, they laid the foundations for many current Trust activities.

To fully comprehend the contribution to historic preservation the Trust and its supporters made, and continue to make, it is necessary to understand how and why the organization was started. Trust history begins soon after World War II, when, in an era of optimism, the nation focused its attention on its own growth. In a rush to build a better present, the country was unwittingly wiping out portions of its cultural heritage, including urban neighborhoods as well as historic buildings and sites. There was a great threat in urban redevelopment programs and suburban growth. Increased construction was the result of the need for housing, highways and recreational facilities that was necessitated by the postwar baby boom, the new mobility of the population and the growing hours of leisure time available to the average American. While not opposed to construction and change, preservationists saw that if the public and the government did not value the nation's architectural legacy, little could be done to prevent the swift disappearance of many of its treasures.

Numerous historic areas were in jeopardy: Washington Square and Battery Park in New York City, Lafayette Square in Washington, D.C., Charleston, S.C., Natchez, Miss., Santa Fe, N.M., and many more were fated to be disrupted. Urban renewal programs threatened landmarks with demolition in Mobile, Ala., Portsmouth, N.H. and New London, Conn., to name but a few. Real estate developments, parking lots and souvenir stands were encroaching on landscapes surrounding the Civil War battlefields of Fredericksburg, Manassas and Gettysburg. Valleys rich with scientific artifacts from prehistoric times were scheduled to be flooded in water control projects, buried by agricultural practices or destroyed by land leveling. The War Department, considering 58 military installations as inefficient or unnecessary, had declared them surplus property. These sites and structures, including Fort Sumter and Fort Moultrie in Charleston Harbor, spanned the military history of the United States, and their fate was uncertain. From the preservationist viewpoint, provision had to be made for saving the many symbols of America's past.

It was evident that part of this responsibility would have to be borne by private citizens, because although some federal legislation and programs did exist, the government had traditionally taken only a partnership role with private interests in preservation efforts—and generally only in response to citizen demand. In the case of one of the first notable preservation efforts, the federal government had not responded at all. Public adoration of George Washington, the impetus for the creation of numerous shrines that still dot the eastern part of the nation, had prompted the New York state legislature in 1850 to save one of Washington's headquarters, Hasbrouck House in Newburgh, as a museum. But neither the Virginia state legislature nor the federal government acted to save his home, Mount Vernon. This task was left to a private group, the Mount Vernon Ladies' Association of the Union, which in 1858 after years of work succeeded in preserving the historic house. Its successful organizational network and fund-raising methods served as models for future private ventures.

Though Congress had appropriated funds for Revolutionary War memorials as early as 1777, the federal government had seemingly adopted a laissez-faire policy in regard to the preservation of historic sites, an attitude it maintained for many years. The government's first formal acquisition of a historic property was not until 1864. That year, federal officials purchased Gen. Robert E. Lee's Virginia home, Arlington House, informally known as the Custis-Lee Mansion. The government's motive for obtaining ownership was not, however, based on the desire to preserve one of the country's historic, architectural treasures, but rather on political considerations. Union Secretary of War Edwin M. Stanton, regarding the mansion and grounds as spoils of war, had sought to insure that the Lees would never again occupy the family estate. Among other maneuvers, Stanton initiated a public auction at which the U.S. government—predictably, the highest bidder—paid itself $26,800

Captain Barnes House, Portsmouth, N.H., in 1936 (above). The house converted to a filling station (below). (Library of Congress)

for the property. Not until 1883, when the Supreme Court ruled in favor of the family's rightful ownership, were the Lees properly reimbursed. In the meantime, the surrounding area had been established as the site of the Arlington National Cemetery.

The first significant government preservation effort grew out of federal concern for natural areas. An act of Congress in 1872 created Yellowstone National Park in Wyoming as the first national park, and in 1889 Casa Grande in Arizona was designated a national monument, the first park tract set aside for its historical value. Vandalism of Indian ruins in this latter region prompted demands for their protection. Several organizations, including the American Association for the Advancement of Science, the Archaeological Institute of America, the Past Exploration Society, the Society for the Preservation of Historic and Scenic Spots, the American Anthropological Association, the Smithsonian Institution and the General Land Office of the U.S. Department of the Interior, had expressed concern.

In response, Congress passed a general bill to protect nationally important historic, natural and scientific resources. The Antiquities Act (Public Law 59-209), signed by President Theodore Roosevelt in 1906, provided the mechanism whereby the President could proclaim as national monuments any landmarks, structures and objects of historical or scientific interest situated on federally owned or controlled land. It also provided that objects on privately owned land might be relinquished to the government and accepted by the Secretary of the Interior. Prescribing a penalty for unauthorized excavation on federal land, the law allowed archaeological research only by accredited educational or scientific institutions, with the stipulation that findings would be made accessible in public museums. One major drawback in the legislation was that it failed to consolidate jurisdiction in one agency, instead leaving each site to the purview of whatever department had first dealt with it. This led to the duplication of effort in some areas and no effort in others.

In 1916 the National Park Service, destined to become the leader in federal historic preservation, was created by an act of Congress (Public Law 64-235). As a bureau of the U.S. Department of the Interior, it was charged "to promote and regulate the use of the Federal areas known as national parks, monuments and reservations . . . to conserve the scenery and the natural and historic objects and the wildlife therein and to provide for the enjoyment of the same in such manner and by such means as will leave them unimpaired for the enjoyment of future generations." By 1933 the National Park Service had taken over sites previously administered by the War and Agriculture departments, thereby alleviating some jurisdictional problems.

Preservation legislation had been passed on the local and state levels by the 1930s. The first local legislation establishing a historic district was enacted in Charleston, S.C., in 1931, to be followed in 1937 by the Vieux Carré Commission in New Orleans, La. From 1924 onward the San Antonio Conservation Society devoted its energies to the preservation of the scenic and historical landmarks of the oldest surviving Spanish city in Texas. At first the society devoted its efforts to the maintenance of the original channel of the San Antonio River, but by the 1930s the conservation group had begun to restore portions of the buildings at San Jose Mission. In 1936 the Carnegie Institution of Washington undertook a historical research and preservation study of St. Augustine, Fla., which included the hiring of two staff historians and an archaeologist. This program, which consumed several years in the late 1930s, culminated in the purchase of one building and the publication of a major study on the fortifications of Spanish Florida. The local historical leaders in St. Augustine were not able to turn this outside assistance into a meaningful preservation program for a period of several decades. In Monterey, Calif., however, in 1937, the St. Augustine studies did have a profound effect, and the zoning ordinance and master plan for historic preservation worked out in Monterey were based on the St. Augustine research. Beginning in 1931 the garden club in Natchez, Miss., developed an annual garden pilgrimage that became a major source of tourism and a principal means of support for the large plantation houses in that antebellum community. Except for these southern beginnings, little progress was made in state and local preservation legislation until the end of World War II, when Alexandria, Va., Williamsburg, Va., and Winston-Salem, N.C., enacted historic district ordinances.

A number of state agencies developed historical programs that were to become functioning parts of their state parks systems by the 1930s. These developments permitted several of the state governments to take advantage of the New Deal employment programs. One of the first states that had become involved in the 1920s was Indiana, under the enlightened leadership of Col. Richard Leeber, culminating in the development of Spring Mill Village, a restored pioneer village in Mitchell, Ind. In California, a state bond issue in 1928 made possible a fund for matching grants for the purchase of historical properties in that state. During the 1930s these funds permitted the development of parks at La Purisima Mission, San Juan Bautista and the Vallejo home in Sonoma, Calif. The state of Pennsylvania became involved in historic preservation with the reconstruction of Pennsbury Manor in the late 1930s and Illinois, Ohio and North Carolina also had state historic sites by the late 1930s.

The status of preservation in the United States in 1935 was summarized in the *Report to the Secretary of the Interior on the Preservation of Historic Sites and Buildings,* requested by Interior Secretary Harold L. Ickes and funded by John D. Rockefeller, Jr. The report was initiated when President Franklin D. Roosevelt in 1933 began to formulate legislation for a federal preservation program that resulted in passage of the Historic Sites Act of 1935.

Pointing to the millions of visitors who annually toured some 500 historic house museums, the report established that public interest in preservation was great. It identified the leading private preservation groups and summarized activities of state and local governments, citing them for the acquisition and preservation of more than 60 historic houses for public benefit. It especially commended the Henry Ford Museum at Greenfield Village, Dearborn, Mich., one of America's first open-air museums, and Colonial Williamsburg, Va., the most extensive private restoration project in the country.

Federal activities, however, were found wanting. J. Thomas Schneider, author of the report, concluded: "In contrast to the growth of private interest and activity in the preservation of historic sites and buildings, the Federal Government has assumed very little responsibility." In the National Park System, for example, there were numerous parks and national monuments but only 23 historic buildings, some of which, said Schneider, "can hardly be classed among the first rank of historic houses of national significance." One problem was that the National Park Service was severely hampered by inadequate legislation. Since the government cannot prevent the destruction of historic sites on privately owned land, the lack of a broad national policy kept the government from planning, developing and promoting a well-rounded preservation program. (By 1975 the National Park Service administered about 170 historic buildings, monuments and sites in 231 historical areas, plus thousands of historic properties in natural and recreational parks.)

Also, a review of the preservation legislation and accomplishments in Great Britain, France, Germany, Sweden and Italy underscored the main thrust of the report: The United States was the only major nation in the western world that had not formally adopted a national preservation policy.

Congress passed the Historic Sites Act (Public Law 74-292) in August 1935, a legislative breakthrough that laid the groundwork for tangible preservation activities. Outlining programs for research and inventory, the act provided for the continuation of the Historic American Buildings Survey. (In 1933 HABS had been established, carried on through a tripartite agreement by the National Park Service, the American Institute of Architects and the Library of Congress.) The act also empowered the National Park Service under the Secretary of the Interior to purchase privately owned sites and buildings (with certain restrictions); to execute corporate agreements with private owners; to preserve, maintain and operate such sites and buildings for the benefit of the public; and to initiate public education programs. To implement these programs, the Park Service was authorized to establish technical advisory committees. Further, the act created the Advisory Board on National Parks, Historic Sites, Buildings and Monuments. For the first time, the United States government had committed itself to historic preservation as a national goal.

Research that would prove crucial to preservation began in the 1930s. As a part of President Franklin D. Roosevelt's New Deal, many projects were initiated to provide jobs for the nation's unemployed, among them writers, artists, historians and architects. With funds from various federal relief agencies, a series of cultural projects was begun. The Historic Records Survey, for example, was established to catalogue local records of American history. For the Index of American Design, artists rendered examples of native arts and handicrafts. Writers employed under the Federal Writers' Project of the Works Progress Administration (which later evolved as the Writers' Program of the Work Projects Administration) prepared state guides containing valuable geographical and historical information and local lore from communities across the nation. The Historic Sites Survey of the National Park Service, the first systematic classification of the nation's historic and archaeological monuments, was started in 1937. Perhaps most valuable to future preservation efforts was the work of architects on another Park Service project, the Historic American Buildings Survey, which represented the beginnings of an assembly of measured drawings, photographs and written data on early American architecture.

But most of these programs were born during the Depression and therefore restricted by economic crisis. Because there was no guarantee for their continuation, vast areas of data seemed destined to remain unexplored. For example, the inadequacy of research work and information dealing with such things as early American building design and materials had been noted by Schneider. In his report, he called for "a permanent research and reference library for both American and foreign works and publications in the field."

With the advent of World War II, however, federal preservation activity came nearly to a halt. Although the United States developed no policy for protection of its national cultural heritage during the war, it did pursue a policy of protection of arts, monuments and archives of other nations when fighting in Europe and attempted to return any such resources acquired during the war to their rightful owners. At home, the lack of personnel and pressing defense needs kept preservation work at a minimum. Thus by 1947, a major part of the responsibility for preserving the national heritage fell to the private sector.

Preservationists responded to this challenge with the resources they had built over the years. Hundreds of historical and patriotic organizations had worked for preservation on state and local levels and had accumulated much useful information. To their experience and the technical data amassed at such places as Colonial Williamsburg and the Henry Francis du Pont Winterthur Museum were added the enthusiasm and energy of ad hoc preservation groups. In 1950 preservationists had won the battle for Castle Clinton, a 140-year-old fortification in New York City, and citizen action had prompted the New Jersey state legislature to provide supplemental funds for the preservation of the Princeton Battlefield. Many other citizens, dismayed by the destruction of many of Europe's monuments during the war, began to join forces to prevent similar losses, although by other causes, in America.

These early preservationists came to believe that a national organization was needed to coordinate their efforts. To some, it was clear that preservation needed a national standard-bearer, an agency that could plan nationwide programs and set long-range goals while mustering resources for the immediate tasks at hand. A nongovernment organization was determined to be preferable, for a private organization would have several advantages. For one thing, the venture would depend largely on voluntary support and participation, which a private organization could enlist with greater success. Also, there were emergencies that would be difficult for a large government agency to handle. The National Park Service representatives, in particular, believed that a nongovernment body could act as a liaison between public and private agencies. It would have national prestige and it would be less hindered by regulatory restraints.

The formation of a national preservation organization was initiated when delegates met in 1947. They represented such organizations as the National Gallery of Art; the North Carolina Department of Archives and History; the American Scenic and Historic Preservation Society; the American Institute of Architects; the National Park Service; the American Association of Museums; the Advisory Board on National Parks, Historic Sites, Buildings and Monuments; the Society for American Archaeology; the American Historical Association; the Philadelphia National Shrines Park Commission; and the Society for the Preservation of New England Antiquities. These organizations later became charter members of the National Trust.

As originally planned, there were to be two interrelated organizations: the National Council for Historic Sites and Buildings, which would acquire members and increase interest in historic preservation throughout

Delegates gathered for the organizational meeting of the National Council for Historic Sites and Buildings at the National Gallery of Art, Washington, D.C., April 15, 1947. From left to right: Guy Stanton Ford, Turpin C. Bannister, Frank H.H. Roberts, Jr., David E. Finley, Solon J. Buck, Waldo G. Leland, H.E. Kahler, A.E. Demaray, Carroll L.V. Meeks, John L. Caskey, George A. McAneny, Francis S. Ronalds, U.S. Grant, III, Luther H. Evans, Christopher C. Crittenden, Ronald F. Lee, Milton L. Grigg, Ella Lonn, Kenneth Chorley, J.O. Brew, Mrs. Dwight F. Davis, Walter A. Taylor, Richard Koch, S. Fiske Kimball, Charles E. Peterson, Robert N.S. Whitelaw, Alexander Hamilton, Eric Gugler, Verne Chatelain, Charles Messer Stow, (?), Gardner Osborn, Laurence Vail Coleman. (National Trust)

the country, and the National Trust, a legal entity through which historic properties could be acquired and operated. The Council was incorporated in the District of Columbia on June 23, 1947. Gen. U.S. Grant, III, USA (Ret.) was elected Council president, and David E. Finley was named chairman of the Executive Board. Ronald F. Lee of the National Park Service was chosen secretary.

The Council immediately began work to obtain a congressional charter for the Trust. This was accomplished on October 26, 1949, when President Harry S. Truman signed Public Law 81–408, establishing the National Trust for Historic Preservation.

Be it enacted by the Senate and House of Representatives of the United States of America in Congress assembled, That, in order to further the policy enunciated in the Act of August 21, 1935 (49 Stat. 666), entitled "An Act to provide for the preservation of historic American sites, buildings, objects, and antiquities of national significance, and for other purposes," and to facilitate public participation in the preservation of sites, buildings, and objects of national significance or interest, there is hereby created a charitable, educational, and nonprofit corporation, to be known as the National Trust for Historic Preservation in the United States, hereafter referred to as the "National Trust." The purposes of the National Trust shall be to receive donations of sites, buildings, and objects significant in American history and culture, to preserve and administer them for public benefit, to accept, hold, and administer gifts of money, securities, or other property of whatsoever character for the purpose of carrying out the preservation program, and to execute such other functions as are vested in it by this Act.

In addition, the charter provided for a Board of Trustees comprising six Trust members and three ex-officio members—the attorney general of the United States, the secretary of the Smithsonian Institution and the director of the National Gallery of Art.

At first, the National Council was chiefly involved with enrolling members. These efforts were aided by the nearly 40 charter organizations. By 1952 Louise du Pont Crowninshield, later vice chairman of the Trust, using regional committees, had acquired more than 100 member organizations and nearly 500 individual members. However, the rate of growth was not increasing as rapidly as hoped and fund raising was difficult. Moreover, dual membership and overlapping functions made operations of the Council and Trust confusing. After careful study, the two organizations voted to merge. Bylaws were revised and on July 18, 1953, the Trust charter was duly amended by Public Law 83–160.

Administrative operations during this period were under the direction of David E. Finley, chairman of the Board of Trustees, and were the direct responsibility of director Frederick L. Rath, Jr., formerly of the National Park Service, and his assistant, Betty Walsh Morris. Initially, Trust headquarters were located in space lent by the National Park Service. Staff members used two rooms in the Lincoln Museum at Ford's Theatre, and furnishings and office equipment were borrowed.

In 1950 substantial funds for operating needs came in the form of two grants totaling $50,000, one from the Old Dominion Foundation, established by Paul Mellon, and the other from the Avalon Foundation, established by Ailsa Mellon Bruce. In May 1950 office space was placed at the Trust's disposal by the American Institute of Architects, a Trust charter organization, in its own headquarters, The Octagon, a historic neighbor of the White House. By 1951 the staff included Henry H. Surface as administrator and general counsel, Helen Duprey Bullock as historian and archivist and Virginia Nelson as fund raiser. That year, the headquarters were again relocated, this time at 712 Jackson Place on Lafayette Square. The Trust received additional income by leasing a majority of the townhouse space provided by the Andrew W. Mellon Educational and Charitable Trust.

National Trust activities at this time were geared to a wide range of goals. Primarily the Trust worked to inform the nation of the need to preserve its heritage, to arouse opinion and sentiment in favor of preservation and to mobilize the public to form preservation groups. While careful to avoid duplicating the efforts of organizations and programs already in existence, the Trust at the same time aimed at making both extant and newly formed organizations aware of the assistance it could give them.

Funds were, of course, critically needed, not only for the support of Trust programs but also to provide assistance to other organizations. In addition, it was necessary to build a permanent preservation fund that could be drawn on in case of emergencies. Preservationists had discovered that too often structures were lost because money was not readily available in a crisis and could not be raised in time to save them.

As an owner and preserver of representative historic structures and sites, the Trust planned to conduct research relating to the preservation and use of its properties and to make them models of preservation and intepretation. Technical information gained from such research and experience would be disseminated through on-site assistance, educational programs and journals and periodicals. Using the resources of the Historic American Buildings Survey and encouraging wider implementation of the HABS program, the Trust also hoped to encourage governmental units to save significant structures within their jurisdictions.

In 1948 the Trust developed a set of criteria for evaluating historic sites and buildings, which supplemented its acquisition policy and met the need for a national standard to determine what should be protected. Written by the Committee on Standards and Surveys under the chairmanship of Waldo G. Leland, the criteria were adapted from the National Park Service criteria for the Historic Sites Survey developed in the 1930s. They were revised and expanded in 1956 under the editorship of Guy Stanton Ford. As revised, they stated

> A structure or area should have outstanding historical and cultural significance in the nation or in the state, region, or community in which it exists. Such significance is found in:

Historic structures or sites in which the broad cultural, political, economic, or social history of the nation, state or community is best exemplified, and from which the visitor may grasp in three-dimensional form one of the larger patterns of the American heritage.

Structures or areas that are identified with the lives of historic personages or with important events in the main currents of national, state or local history.

Structures or areas that embody the distinguishing characteristics of an architectural type-specimen, inherently valuable for a study of a period-style or method of construction; or a notable work of a master builder, designer or architect whose individual genius influenced his age. Mere antiquity is not sufficient basis for selection of a structure for permanent preservation, but can be a factor if other more significant examples have disappeared or if the building forms part of an especially characteristic section of a given community. Smaller structures, such as the first squared-log cabins or the sod houses of the pioneers, may be as important relatively as the mansions of the past.

Structures or sites of archaeological interest that contribute to the understanding of aboriginal man in America.

Preference was to be given structures and sites where original building material had retained its integrity. In the words of the preservation "commandment" that was part of the criteria, "Generally speaking, it is better to preserve than repair, better to repair than restore, better to restore than reconstruct." Also important were accessibility to the public and the availability of fire and police protection and essential utilities. Whenever possible, the criteria stated, the property should be adaptable to a functional use—with education as the primary goal. According to the criteria, sponsors of a project should be able to bear the cost of preserving the property and should plan carefully for its endowment or for a program by which it could be self-sustaining.

In 1951, the Trust first became involved with a historic property that it would eventually own—Woodlawn Plantation in Mount Vernon, Va. The plantation had been the home of Eleanor Parke (Nellie) Custis Lewis, granddaughter of Martha Washington and ward of George Washington, and her husband, Lawrence Lewis, Washington's nephew. Woodlawn had been purchased in 1948 by a religious society. Its historical associations and architecture, however, made its preservation as a historical museum desirable, so the Woodlawn Public Foundation was organized for the purpose of purchasing the mansion. After considerable effort, the necessary funds were raised and the foundation acquired Woodlawn. The property was then offered to the Trust on a long-term lease basis, and in 1951 the Trust assumed its administration under the

Decatur House, Washington, D.C. South drawing room, with Beale furnishings.
A property of the National Trust. (Wm. Edmund Barrett for the National
Trust)

direction of a property committee composed of Trust members and curator Worth Bailey, though the foundation retained title. With a grant
from the Old Dominion Foundation, the Trust was later able to assume
financial responsibility for the estate, including a mortgage. It paid the
remaining indebtedness through gifts from the Avalon Foundation and
others, acquiring the title to Woodlawn in 1957.

Mrs. Truxtun Beale announced in 1953 that she was bequeathing to
the Trust her residence, historic Decatur House on Lafayette Square in
Washington, D.C. Designed by architect Benjamin Henry Latrobe, the

house was built in 1818–19 for naval hero Stephen Decatur and had been lived in by other illustrious citizens, including statesman and orator Henry Clay, former President Martin Van Buren and George M. Dallas, Vice President under James K. Polk. Mrs. Beale had written a history of the house, *Decatur House and Its Inhabitants,* which she published privately in 1954; she gave the book to the Trust for sale at the property. Upon her death in 1956, the Trust acquired Decatur House.

In 1954 Edith Bolling Galt Wilson, the second Mrs. Woodrow Wilson, stipulated that the Trust should, upon her death, receive the house on S Street in the capital where President Wilson had lived from 1921, after leaving the White House, until his death in 1924. The 26-room Georgian Revival structure, designed in 1915 by architect Waddy B. Wood for Henry Parker Fairbanks, was filled with mementos of Wilson's career. It became a Trust property upon Mrs. Wilson's death in 1961. Both Decatur House and Woodrow Wilson House were accepted by the Trust under its restriction that an adequate endowment be provided to assist in restoration.

In 1954, however, the Trust had found it necessary to make a departure from this policy in order to accept title to a historic property. Casa Amesti, an early 19th-century adobe and redwood house in Monterey, Calif., filled with French and Spanish furniture and surrounded by formal Italianate gardens, had been left to the Trust by Frances Adler Elkins, but no endowment had been provided to assure its maintenance. After careful study, a solution to the problem of making the property self-sustaining was reached: A men's group in Monterey, the Old Capital Club, was invited to use the house as a meeting place and luncheon club during the week. On Friday afternoons, it would be opened to the public. The Old Capital Club accepted the proposal and the property was saved. At Casa Amesti, the Trust put into practice an alternative to using historic properties as museums or educational facilities; this method of property operation and protection is, in fact, still developing. The success of this adaptive use of Casa Amesti has served as a model for preserving other properties owned by the Trust and those of other preservation groups.

One of the most valuable Trust services—the publication of *Historic Preservation,* which carried news of the national preservation movement —began in March 1949. Originally published as the *Quarterly Report* of the National Council for Historic Sites and Buildings, the first issue had opened, appropriately enough, with a plea for membership and money from Council President Gen. U.S. Grant, III. Subsequent issues of the quarterly included articles on preservation projects abroad, reprints of talks from Trust annual meetings, notices of recent books on preservation and a feature entitled The Passing Parade—headlines of lost

Woodlawn Plantation, Mount Vernon, Va. A property of the National Trust.
(Wm. Edmund Barrett for the National Trust)

Woodrow Wilson House, Washington, D.C. A property of the National Trust.
(Robert Oakes for the National Trust)

battles. By the spring of 1952, despite limited resources, *Historic Preservation* had become a full-fledged magazine, issued on a regular basis and complete with black-and-white illustrations and such features as reports on archaeological projects and legislative developments and listings of new members and job opportunities in the preservation field.

In 1953 the Trust, along with the National Park Service, the Library of Congress and the American Institute of Architects, became actively involved in an effort to establish the Historic American Buildings Survey Inventory. The inventory was intended to supplement the documentary

Casa Amesti, Monterey, Calif. Garden View. A property of the National Trust. (Morley Baer for the National Trust)

work of the Historic American Buildings Survey; survey documentation, which included measured drawings and extensive photographic coverage, was time-consuming and could be applied to only a selected number of buildings. Even so, more than 6,000 structures were recorded before 1941, when WPA funding for the survey ended. In reviewing the collection, it was recognized that many significant structures had yet to be recorded and that geographic and chronological distribution was uneven. A recording project that would be less scholarly and selective than HABS, but more broadly based, and that would speed up the effort to identify the nation's architectural heritage was needed. To accomplish this task a one-page inventory form (the Historic American Buildings Survey Inventory) had been adopted in 1952. Under the direction of preservation officers of local chapters of the American Institute of Architects, volunteers recruited in part by the Trust used this form to gather valuable supplemental information. By listing less data about more structures, the inventory was designed to provide a pool of information upon which preservation groups could draw and to establish priorities for more thorough documentation in the future.

To reach public and semipublic agencies, such as chambers of commerce, members of the staff and the Board of Trustees traveled thousands of miles speaking on behalf of the Trust and emphasizing the economics of "practical preservation." Radio and television appearances, plus newspaper and magazine articles written or aided by the staff, further spread the word, as did thousands of letters written in response to questions from private citizens.

Many trips were made in a purely advisory capacity to help preservation groups engaged in specific projects. From this nucleus of Trust service programs evolved the "Trust technique":

1. Making a brief personal consultation if circumstances permitted; otherwise, consulting by correspondence or by telephone.
2. Collecting material for a concentrated attack on the problem at hand.
3. Advising on the basis of cumulative experience in the field.
4. Stimulating the public consciousness—and its conscience.
5. Following through with guidance by correspondence.

By 1955 the Trust had aided the preservation of a variety of structures and sites, including the Adam Thoroughgood House, Norfolk, Va.; the Palace of the Governors, Santa Fe, N.M.; the Egyptian Revival–style First Presbyterian Church, Nashville, Tenn.; New Salem Village and the Abraham Lincoln Home, Springfield, Ill.; and the historic Scandinavian utopian community, Bishop Hill, Ill. The Trust had also provided advice on the restoration and interpretation of such historic structures as Andrew Jackson's Hermitage in Nashville and the Ulysses S. Grant House in Galena, Ill. Technical help in establishing historical zoning legislation had also been given to groups in Boston and Nantucket, Mass., Bethlehem, Pa., and Easton, Md. Services were provided to all who requested them, regardless of Trust membership. However, membership increased in areas where help had been donated.

In addition to this circuit-riding approach, the Trust began a series of preservation short courses that grew into a major part of its education program. In 1955, a course in Historic House Keeping was cosponsored by the Trust and the New York State Historical Association, a member organization, and *Antiques* magazine. This week-long course, held in Cooperstown, N.Y., was modeled generally after a summer school sponsored by the English National Trust for the Preservation of Places of

Historic Interest or Scenic Beauty held at Attingham in Shropshire; the course was designed to be broad enough for application in any locality. The faculty, including Frederick L. Rath, Jr., Helen Duprey Bullock and Trustee Mrs. Hermann G. Place, taught methods of receiving, preserving, and exhibiting and interpreting historic houses. The course was so successful that it continued for three more years and spawned similar courses thereafter.

Throughout its first years, the Trust gained continuing publicity for the cause of preservation. One of the most successful programs was its 1955 tour of historic houses of the Federal period in the District of Columbia. This first Trust walking tour featured Decatur House, Blair House, the John Marshall House, St. John's Church and Parish House on Lafayette Square, The Octagon and the Arts Club, once the residence of James Monroe. Directed by a local committee and Hardinge Scholle, former director of the Museum of the City of New York who in 1951 had joined the Trust staff as consultant, the tour attracted a near-capacity crowd of 1,500 visitors. Publicity preceding the tour was the most extensive the Trust had received in the Washington area, and net profits were $3,000.

The same year, a new program brought additional publicity and revenue to the Trust and some of its member organizations. Author of *The Williamsburg Art of Cookery* and a recognized authority on early American cooking, Helen Duprey Bullock was approached by the Dromedary Company, a division of the National Biscuit Company, and asked to assist in the collection of historic recipes suitable for adaptation to modern ready-mix products. Dromedary owned the rights to the gingerbread recipe used by Mary Washington, George Washington's mother, and the company was marketing it as a ready-mix product. Since Kenmore, Mrs. Washington's home near Fredericksburg, Va., was a National Trust member organization, the company sought Helen Bullock's help in locating other historic recipes. With the Trust acting as an intermediary, contracts were worked out between Dromedary and several member organizations. As new products were marketed, royalties helped not only the Trust and its Woodlawn Plantation, but also such member organizations as the Thomas Jefferson Memorial Foundation at Monticello; the Girl Scouts of America, which operated Juliette Gordon Lowe's home in Savannah, Ga.; and the Theodore Roosevelt Association at Sagamore Hill, Oyster Bay, Long Island.

Trust participation in yet another venture served as a persuasive example of the sound business possibilities in preservation. In 1951 a group of citizens in Georgetown in the District of Columbia had joined together to save from destruction a number of buildings of the early Federal period. Historic Georgetown, as the organization became known,

Property owned by Historic Georgetown on M Street, N.W., Washington, D.C. (John J-G. Blumenson)

restored and adapted them into shops, restaurants and apartments in a pioneering instance of historic preservation through business operations. The Trust, having been given gifts of stock in the organization, expected to benefit financially from its participation in the project, and staff members began to encourage others to think of preservation as a business investment.

By 1956 the Trust membership included 2 corporations, 182 organizations and almost 1,500 individuals. The groundwork for future programs had been laid, and the Trust was gaining recognition as a leader in the preservation field. Elling P. Aannestad, an analyst commissioned by the New York Community Trust to investigate the status of cultural and historic preservation, had found the Trust "a young but well-established national voluntary agency." The Aannestad report praised the accomplishments of the Trust, especially commending it for the high level of professional competence of its advisory services and for its development of national criteria by which buildings might be assessed. The report continued, "The fact that this agency now receives two-thirds of its income from member organizations and individual members is substantially indicative of the widespread feeling of need over the country for some form of central planning and advisory service."

The year 1956 was also a time of change for the Trust staff. Director

Federal construction around Lafayette Square, 1956, necessitated the Trust move from its Jackson Place headquarters. (National Trust)

Frederick L. Rath, Jr., left the Trust to become vice director of the New York State Historical Association, and Richard H. Howland, chairman of the Department of History of Arts at Johns Hopkins University, was appointed Trust president. Terry Brust (Morton) also joined the Trust as secretary to the president and within a few months became managing editor of *Historic Preservation*. When government construction work began around Lafayette Square, the Trust headquarters were moved from 712 Jackson Place to 2000 K Street, N.W.

At the same time, the Board of Trustees formed an Ad Hoc Committee on Planning composed of Trust members, Trustees and representatives of federal and other agencies engaged in preservation work. The committee consisted of Trust president Howland, Trustees David E. Finley and H. Alexander Smith, Jr.; Christopher Crittenden of the North Carolina Department of Archives and History; Ronald F. Lee of the National Park Service; Walter A. Taylor of the American Institute of Architects; and Charles Cecil Wall of Mount Vernon. The purpose of the committee was to review current preservation programs of the agencies represented and to plan the various programs more carefully so that efforts would not overlap or compete.

Out of the committee deliberations came a redefinition of the purpose of the Trust. It was decided that the Trust goal should be education, in the broadest sense of the term. The Trust function as an information clearinghouse was to continue, and, in the operation of its properties, it was determined that the Trust should set standards of professional integrity in preservation, administration and interpretation.

Among the important aspects of the education program outlined by the Committee on Planning were proposals to increase Trust assistance to national and local inventory programs; sponsor university courses and fellowships for the training of preservation architects, administrators and research workers; organize seminars, forums, institutes and lectures; build up a wide and representative membership; enlarge the present advisory service rendered by the Trust; and operate a publications program that would issue monographs, books and special publicity pieces in the field of historic preservation and that would increase the scope and influence of the quarterly *Historic Preservation*.

A donation from the Robert Lee Blaffer Trust enabled the National Trust to change its graphic image during 1956. At its founding, the Trust adopted as an emblem the national eagle, symbolizing the mission "Safeguarding America's Heritage." Though still apropos, the design had begun to look old-fashioned; under the direction of graphics designer Leonard Rennie, the emblem was refined. The new one featured an adaptation of an eagle designed by 18th-century architect and craftsman Samuel McIntire of Salem, Mass. In the design, which was to typify the nationwide character of the Trust, the eagle represented the North. To symbolize the South, a wreath of garland oak leaves and acorns adapted from a carved ornament on the Hammond-Harwood House in Annapolis, Md., was added. An Ionic capital adapted from a column on the U.S. Treasury Building symbolized Washington, the national capital and the location of Trust headquarters.

The original Trust colors, orange and gray, had been borrowed by General Grant from his alma mater, West Point. Upon the approval of the Board of Trustees, these colors were replaced by terra-cotta, the color of earth, from which all building material and eventually all architecture spring. The new emblem and the use of terra-cotta color with black on Trust stationery and on the cover of *Historic Preservation* made Trust correspondence and publications as distinctive in appearance as they were in content.

The following year, 1957, was one of expansion in all the aforementioned categories. As the Historic House Keeping course entered its third year, the Trust began conducting regional conferences addressed to specific preservation problems in a particular locality. The first was held in Lexington, Ky.: The Blue Grass Preservation Short Course, an intensive three-day program, was cosponsored by the Trust, the Foundation for the Preservation of Historic Lexington and Fayette County. Through

The National Trust eagle emblem interpreted on a silkscreen fabric print designed by Janis Newton, 1957 (above). (Capitol Photo Service) The original Trust symbol and 1957 revision (left above and below). The original Louise du Pont Crowninshield Award, used from 1960 to 1973 (right). (National Trust)

panel sessions at the conferences, lectures and field trips, the Trust encouraged public participation in preservation programs, while at the same time striving to set high standards of professionalism in the field. Funds for travel expenses and printed conference materials and compensation for a small faculty were supplied by the Eli Lilly Foundation.

To fulfill its function as a central source of information on preservation trends, especially legal developments, the Trust began to collect pertinent legal enactments, especially federal, state and municipal ordinances that protected both historic and architectural monuments and historic districts. This material provided the basis for the first edition of Jacob H. Morrison's *Historic Preservation Law*, for which Helen Duprey Bullock wrote the preface. Using some of the funds remaining from the Lilly Foundation grant for the short courses, the Trust was able to reprint and distribute a range of information to preservationists at a nominal cost. Reprints included legislative ordinances; John Codman's chronicle of the preservation of the Beacon Hill area in Boston, *Preservation of Historic Districts by Architectural Control* (first published in the newsletter of the American Society of Planning Officials); the Trust criteria for evaluating historic sites and buildings; advice on seeking foundation support; and a model constitution for a tax-exempt preservation organization. These were often sent with letters in response to questions from members and the public. When a problem obviously required more than "do-it-yourself" publications, however, the staff scrupulously avoided giving push-button answers. Instead, the questioner was furnished with bibliographies and reprints of articles by professionals and was assisted in seeking solutions.

As a part of its continuing support of the Historic American Buildings Survey Inventory program, the Trust served as one of the repositories for the HABS inventory forms. In addition, in 1957–1958 the Trust sponsored an inventory of the architecture of Virginia prior to the Civil War. Grants totaling $16,000 from the Old Dominion and Avalon foundations made it possible for the Trust to send 24 architectural students from the University of Virginia into the state's 100 counties in search of examples of early Virginia architecture. Aided by volunteers from the Garden Club of Virginia, these students, under the direction of Frederick D. Nichols, professor of architecture and fine arts at the University of Virginia, recorded 3,078 structures on HABS Inventory forms.

Through correspondence and on-site advice, the staff in 1957 aided preservation efforts in many communities, including, for example, Bethlehem, Pa.; the Church Hill district and St. John's Church, Richmond, Va.; the Greater St. Louis Project, Mo.; Historic Savannah, Inc., Ga.; the Providence Preservation Society, Providence, R.I.; Portsmouth, N.H.;

Philadelphia and Germantown, Pa.; Baltimore, Md.; the San Francisco Mint, Calif.; the Robie House, Chicago, Ill.; and Chalmette Battlefield, La.

To create incentives for preservation, the Trust sought ways to focus national attention on superlative achievements. In 1957 it began making plans to establish the Louise du Pont Crowninshield Award, a memorial to one of its charter members, a vice chairman of the Board of Trustees and a dedicated preservationist. The award, designed by Italian sculptor Albino Manca, featured the Trust eagle in bronze, plated with gold, on a polished green stone base. The honor includes a scroll citation and a cash stipend of $1,000. The first award, presented in 1960, appropriately honored one of the first preservation groups active in the country, the Mount Vernon Ladies' Association of the Union.

The Aannestad report had noted in 1956 that the Trust budget (at that time, a little more than $50,000) "bears no evident relation to the problems of national leadership for voluntary participation in a preservation program." Finally in 1957 an endowment was received that would help assure the future operation of the Trust. Impressed by Trust accomplishments, growth in membership and potential effectiveness, the Old Dominion and Avalon foundations made grants to the Trust totaling $2.5 million. Ailsa Mellon Bruce, chairman and founder of the Avalon Foundation, stated, "While governmental programs deserve support, a special need exists for an expanded private preservation agency. The National Trust is the single voluntary organization at the national level devoted exclusively to the broad field of cultural preservation and merits our support and that of other foundations and individuals."

The financial security enabled the Trust to expand and initiate new programs in the following years, under the chairmanship of David E. Finley and the direction of Trust president Richard H. Howland. Educational programs were coordinated by the assistant to the president, William J. Murtagh, formerly with Historic Bethlehem, Pa., who joined the staff in 1958. Regional preservation conferences were held that year in St. Louis, Mo., Newport and Providence, R.I., and New York City, where leading preservationists presented technical papers on a variety of subjects, including architectural preservation standards and integrity in furnishing and interpreting historic properties. Using funds supplied by the Lilly Foundation, the Trust awarded five scholarships to enable midwesterners to attend the Seminar on Early American Culture, sponsored by the New York State Historical Association, at Cooperstown, N.Y. In 1959 the Trust cosponsored the New Jersey Preservation Forum at Cape May, and staff members participated in conferences sponsored by member organizations.

The acquisition in 1958 of the Shadows-on-the-Teche, built in the 1830s and an outstanding example of southern Louisiana antebellum architecture, provided the place and the opportunity for another type of educational experience. Preservationists could learn how a master plan for restoration is developed by observing its evolution at The Shadows. Bequeathed to the Trust by William Weeks Hall, great-grandson of the builder, David Weeks, the mansion in New Iberia, La., came not only with an endowment but also with a valuable collection of furniture and manuscripts. In addition to a study of these items, Trust historian Helen Duprey Bullock made an intensive study of the Hall and Weeks family papers at Louisiana State University, out of which came information for use in drawing up the master plan for the restoration of the mansion and grounds. In 1961, with a grant from a special committee of the American Institute of Decorators, the Trust sponsored a series of three educational conferences at The Shadows. At the first, held in February, participants from Louisiana and other states joined for discussions on the theme "Integrity in Restoration." The second, held in May, concentrated on the preparation of a master plan for the conversion of a private residence into a public museum. In October, the third conference and final program centered on the dedication of the house and gardens, restored by architects Richard Koch and Samuel Wilson, Jr., of New Orleans. Through this series of conferences, the Trust had offered an on-site learning experience, rewarding to professionals working in the preservation field and other interested persons.

Public awareness of the Trust and its services grew. Many programs helped make the Trust known, but one in particular drew a great deal of attention. This was a 1958 traveling exhibit entitled "Architecture Worth Saving," which was cosponsored by the Museum of Modern Art in New York City, *Architectural Forum* magazine and the National Trust. Not only did the display alert the public to threats to the national architectural heritage, but its joint sponsorship (called by a *New York Times* art critic "strange bedfellows") demonstrated the concern for preservation that was shared by all persons and groups involved in the arts and humanities.

While it continued to encourage the participation of every person in preservation efforts, the Trust also saw the crucial need for recruiting and training professionals for careers in preservation. Beginning in 1958, it cosponsored with Colonial Williamsburg, the American Association for State and Local History and the American Association of Museums a six-week-long seminar in historical administration. This was the first coordinated effort by these organizations to attract qualified young graduate students to careers in historic preservation. Fellowships for the course, which was held in Williamsburg, were offered to 12 students

*The Shadows-on-the-Teche, New Iberia, La. A property of the National Trust.
(James K. Mellow)*

with at least a year of graduate study in American history, American studies, American art and architectural history or allied fields. Six auditors could also attend at their own expense. Seminar participants met and learned from experts, including Trust staff members, studying case histories, attending lectures, conducting laboratory work and participating in field trips to area historic museums. A final examination covered material on a comprehensive reading list. The course thus gave a complete and realistic overview of the opportunities and problems in administering historical organizations.

Also in 1958, an anonymous donation of $10,000 was given to the Trust for educational use as the nucleus of the Walden Fund. In 1960, the fund paid expenses for Trust staff participation in preservation seminars in New Jersey, Maryland, Iowa, Virginia, New York and Pennsylvania. Money from the fund also enabled the Trust to sponsor a regional conference in Springfield, Ill. During the year, the staff gave more than 100 lectures and provided advice from headquarters in more than 6,000 letters.

With growing demands on the small staff, the Trust required additional administrative direction and in 1960 created the position of executive director. Robert R. Garvey, Jr., former director of Old Salem, a Trust member organization in Winston-Salem, N.C., was appointed to fill the position and began work in September. Richard H. Howland, first Trust president, resigned to become head curator of the Department of Civil History at the Smithsonian Institution. During the year, in addition to carrying on its regular programs, the Trust staff underwent a comprehensive reorganization. On January 1, 1961, five departments were established: Administration and Finance, Membership and Public Relations, Education, Property and Information. Each department had a counterpart advisory committee, made up of Trustees and individual members, who could participate actively in Trust affairs and keep in touch with preservationist groups around the country.

In addition to his executive duties, Garvey directed the Administration and Finance Department and administered the Department of Membership and Public Relations. Gordon Gray served as chairman of the advisory committee for the Administration and Finance Department, while Ronald F. Lee was chairman of the advisory committee on membership and public relations. The Department of Administration and Finance handled all purchasing, expenditures and financial reporting, in addition to administering Trust properties. The Finance Committee of the Board of Trustees had review of Trust financial matters except the management of endowment funds, which was handled by the Investment Committee headed by H. Alexander Smith, Jr.

The Education Department was directed by William J. Murtagh. The

Four staff leaders of the National Trust attend reception at Smithsonian Institution during January 1973 meeting of state historic preservation officers. From left to right: James Biddle, president 1968—present; Robert R. Garvey, Jr., executive director 1960—67; Richard H. Howland, president 1956—60; Frederick L. Rath, Jr., director 1949—56. (Carleton Knight, III)

committee assigned to assist that department was led by Henry N. Flynt. The committee assisting the Information Department, which was directed by Helen Duprey Bullock, was under the chairmanship of Trustee Walter Muir Whitehill. Robert G. Stewart, formerly planning consultant for the St. Louis County Historic Buildings Commission, St. Louis, Mo., joined the Trust as director of the Department of Properties; the properties advisory committee was headed by Carl Feiss. In addition to the staff reorganization, committees at each Trust property were reorganized as property councils. The expanded staff necessitated yet another move, to the Transportation Building at 815 17th Street, N.W.

By 1961 the Trust was able to fulfill the need to publish more scholarly information and devote more extensive coverage to such topics as legislative developments. *Historic Preservation* became the vehicle for this function. To continue providing information about current preservation projects and fast-developing trends, the monthly four-page newsletter *Preservation News* was initiated. Assembled from the growing files of Trust correspondence and press clippings and the publications of Trust member and related organizations, *Preservation News* kept members up to date on happenings in the preservation field. It called attention to endangered buildings and featured new preservation projects. In the beginning, there was little or no editorial comment in the newsletter; news articles only were presented. In the magazine, however, controversial subjects were covered in articles and in editorials. Issues of the magazine were made available in quantity at cost to the organizations involved. Neither the magazine nor the newsletter was copyrighted, so that greater distribution could be obtained through other publications reprinting articles, giving the Trust credit.

The Trust had made a good start in many programs and its growth was good for an organization of its kind. But progress also had to be measured against the forces of destruction, which were gaining momentum. Trust members likened their work to a man trying to ascend a descending escalator while it increased speed. For every building saved, hundreds were being threatened, destroyed by intent or demolished by neglect.

The Trust sought to dramatize both sides of the situation in a 1961 traveling exhibit entitled "Preservation: Heritage of Progress." The photographic display, prepared under the direction of the departments of Information and Education, chronicled the preservation and loss of buildings in America and Europe. It was first shown in New York City at the Cooper Union Museum for the Arts of Decoration in October 1961, coinciding with the Trust annual meeting. The exhibit was so popular that in the next four years it traveled to 23 cities in the U.S. and two in Canada under the auspices of the American Federation of Arts.

To supplement the photographs and to symbolize the forces destroying the country's architectural heritage, the Trust had commissioned drawings by artist Miles Rolph. Using Gustave Dore's *Four Horsemen of the Apocalypse* as his inspiration, Rolph created *The Four Horsemen of Destruction*. War was shown as a grim figure brandishing a sword, Disaster wielding a scythe and Fire shooting a flaming arrow. The fourth figure, Man, beckoned toward the future. Superimposed on this fourth horseman was the spectre of a bulldozer. The goal of the exhibit was to show that other than in such natural disasters as earthquakes, man bears the chief responsibility for the destruction of his own heritage.

Large crowds in cities around the country saw the exhibit; others read about it in a special 1961 issue of *Historic Preservation* (vol. 13, no. 3), which also served as the exhibit catalogue, including representative photographs. By showing examples of buildings lost and saved, the Trust hoped to make the American public aware of the crisis.

At the Williamsburg Seminar for Historical Administrators, students continued to be prepared for careers in preservation. The Trust also provided for the training of part-time volunteer workers in the field. In February 1962, the first Conference for Historic Museum Associates was offered at Woodlawn Plantation. Through lectures and workshops, participants learned how to deal with problems related to museum display and interpretation and were given a behind-the-scenes look at acquisition and restoration work. Faculty members for the conference were drawn from the Trust, the Smithsonian Institution, the National Park Service, the National Gallery of Art and other museums in the Washington area. Fourteen volunteers and professionals from historic house museums in 12 states and the District of Columbia participated in the initial workshop.

In addition to these educational programs, the Trust, each October, held its annual meeting and preservation conference. The meetings served not only as opportunities to handle organizational business but also as educational experiences. At these gatherings, Trust members could benefit from panel discussions featuring international experts in preservation-related fields, seek individual consultation on preservation efforts in their own communities and learn from the experiences of fellow Trust members. Exhibits assembled by member organizations featured a wide range of preservation projects.

The Trust scheduled the annual meeting and preservation conferences in various parts of the country, for there was no other nationwide forum of this kind and the Trust wanted to make the meetings accessible to as many people as possible. Annual meetings had been held in Chicago, Nashville, New York City, New Orleans, Pittsburgh, Washington,

"The Four Horsemen of Destruction," designed for a Trust exhibit by Miles Rolph, 1961, symbolizes the forces threatening the landmarks of America, as illustrated on the opposite page. (National Trust)

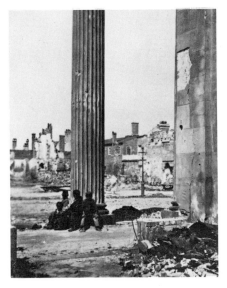

WAR! Ruins of Charleston, S.C., in April 1865. (Library of Congress)

FIRE! Belle Grove Plantation, White Castle, La., after a fire in March 1952. (Clarence John Laughlin)

DISASTER! Hurricane Carol's destruction of the Old North Church steeple, Boston, Mass., in August 1954. (Reprinted with permission of Boston Herald American.)

MAN! Razed Detroit City Hall, Detroit, Mich., in October 1961. (Reprinted with permission of Detroit Free Press.)

Encroachment on surroundings of a Jackson, Miss., mansion. (Marion Cost Wolcott, Library of Congress)

D.C., and Swampscott, Mass. Usually meeting places were chosen because of outstanding preservation work being carried on in the area.

The 1962 meeting in San Francisco marked the end of David E. Finley's chairmanship of the Board of Trustees. Finley believed strongly that the Trust would benefit from the periodic rotation of leadership, so at the meeting he submitted his resignation. The board, after voting to confer on Finley the title of chairman emeritus, unanimously elected Trustee Gordon Gray as his successor. The new chairman was a lawyer, publisher, corporation director, former president of the University of North Carolina, former Secretary of the Army and special adviser on national security to Presidents Dwight D. Eisenhower and John F. Kennedy. Thus Gray brought to the chairmanship a wide range of governmental, academic and business experience.

CHAPTER TWO

To Encourage Public Participation

In little more than a decade since its founding, the National Trust had established or assisted in organizing a number of practical educational programs that were invaluable to preservationists. Among them were the Williamsburg and Woodlawn seminars, regional conferences, periodical and technical publications and consultation services. Four of the five Trust properties were open to the public and were drawing substantial numbers of visitors each year. From a sponsoring group of fewer than 40 organizations and a handful of individual members, Trust membership had grown to 3,250 individuals, 410 organizations and 5 corporations. However, Trust leaders realized that if service and property programs were to continue to grow, it was imperative that Trust membership be increased and the base of financial support expanded.

As a nonprofit organization, the Trust depended on the voluntary time and efforts of its supporters; moreover, its programs were financed primarily by membership dues and donations. In 1963 foundations and individuals responded to the need for funds, and that year, Trust operating finances totaled approximately $270,000. But expansion of Trust programs was limited; the Trust needed an increased income and an increased membership in order to grow.

In June 1963 Glenn E. Thompson, former history consultant with the American Association of Museums, joined the Trust staff as director of the Department of Membership and Public Relations. The department revised membership policies, prepared new membership brochures and application forms and issued certificates to member organizations. The staff also began preliminary planning for a corporate membership drive.

At this time, new members were recruited primarily on a person-to-person basis. Trustees and property council members, as well as the staff and individual members, were asked to increase personal recruiting efforts within their communities. Gifts of membership were urged at Christmastime and for birthdays and graduations. Meanwhile, Trustees and staff members continued to cross the country, telling about the work of the Trust and soliciting membership and support.

Such recruitment resulted in less than satisfactory growth rates, however. From 1962 to 1963, for example, the membership increased by only 23 percent. In 1964, the Board of Trustees investigated the possibility of employing such promotional marketing techniques as direct-mail solicitation. As a result of the investigation, the board voted to initiate a direct-mail membership campaign. The first mailing was made possible by Trustee Mrs. W. Randolph Burgess, who provided what she termed a "grubstake" for the venture. In its direct-mail campaign, the Trust reached thousands of potential preservationists and convinced them of the importance of the Trust mission. Within a year from the initiation of the membership campaign, the total individual membership grew from approximately 5,000 to 8,000.

There was, however, much to be done to increase the financial resources of the Trust. In 1964 opportunities for support were expanded by creating new membership categories. In addition to regular memberships, new levels of life membership (donations of $1,000 to $5,000) were established: sponsors, donors, patrons, benefactors and fellows. The categories were to be cumulative so that contributors would be appropriately acknowledged and given special recognition as their support grew. Also, a Memorial Endowment Fund was created for contributions in memory of Trustees and members.

Indicative of this new aggressive attitude of the Trust was the statement of purpose adopted by the Board of Trustees in May 1964. In it, the Trust defined itself as "a militant, independent organization, not opposed to necessary and constructive change." The program expansion in all departments during the period 1963–66 reflected the attempt by the Trust to translate that definition into reality.

The annual meetings held during this period, planned and managed by the Education Department, reflected both the growth and nationwide character of the Trust membership. The San Francisco meeting in 1962, the first Trust meeting on the West Coast, drew 450 participants; at the 1966 meeting in Philadelphia, registrants numbered more than 800. In the intervening years, conferences were held in Washington, D.C., San Antonio, Tex., and Raleigh, N.C.

Added to the regular agenda of workshops, lectures, panel discussions and field trips were postmeeting tours. The first, after the 1962 annual meeting in San Francisco, was to Hawaii, where preservationists reviewed preservation projects in the new state. After the San Antonio meeting in 1964, 51 members traveled to Mexico to view efforts there. As part of the 1965 postmeeting tour, cosponsored by Old Salem and the Moravian Church, preservationists toured Moravian settlements in Winston-Salem, N.C., and some continued abroad to view Moravian communities in the Netherlands, West Germany, East Germany, Czecho-

Anna-Catherina House, Winston-Salem, N.C. Moravian settlement visited by preservationists on 1965 post–annual meeting tour. (William J. Murtagh)

slovakia and Switzerland. William J. Murtagh, director of the Education Department, served as educational coordinator and architectural commentator for the tour.

Regional conferences were increased as communities realized the importance of preserving their architectural heritage and called on the resources of the Trust. The success of previous conferences in Cooperstown, N.Y., and Lexington, Ky., prompted the Trust to schedule 1963 conferences in Auburn, Ala.; Winston-Salem, N.C.; Cape May, N.J.; Sewanee, Tenn.; Concord, N.H.; Lewes, Del.; and the District of Columbia. Four conferences were held in 1964—in Mobile, Ala.; San Diego, Calif.; Columbus, Ga.; and Minneapolis, Minn. The 1965 conference schedule included meetings in Hilton Head, S.C.; Columbus, Ohio; Lexington, Ky.; and Trenton, N.J. In 1966 meetings were held in Tallahassee, Fla.; Tarrytown, N.Y.; Clemson, S.C.; and Austin and Houston, Tex. These programs, planned and executed by the Education Department, provided information and support to local preservation societies, as well as attracting new members to the Trust.

In 1965 the Trust cooperated, on an experimental basis, with The Catholic University of America on a Field Seminar on American Traditions. The seminar, designed for teachers, concentrated on the pre–Revolutionary War period, with lectures and a six-day tour of historic sites in Maryland and Virginia. Teachers taking the course for credit

Documentary photograph of St. Louis Cathedral, Presbytere (left) and Cabildo
(right) on Jackson Square, Vieux Carré, New Orleans, La. Protected by
preservation legislation since 1936. (Library of Congress)

were required to write research papers on some facet of their experience.
The course was repeated the following year.

The number of applicants to the Woodlawn Seminar for Historic
Museum Associates increased greatly, for the seminar remained one of
the few training courses dealing with problems of museum functions
designed for both museum professionals and volunteers. The Williamsburg Seminar for Historic Administrators continued to provide a worthwhile learning experience for current and future professional preservationists. By 1966, in its eighth year, the Williamsburg seminar had
graduated 96 fellows and 46 museum professionals already at work in
the field. Of the fellows, 24 percent had continued graduate work,
while 62.2 percent were teaching or working for historical agencies or
museums. Geographically, seminar alumni were active in Alberta,
Canada, and in 33 states, including Hawaii, and were involved in such
diverse agencies as the Jazz Museum in New Orleans, the Metropolitan
Museum of Art in New York City, the Tennessee State Library and
Archives in Nashville, the Architectural Survey of Texas in Fort Worth,
Historic Bethlehem in Pennsylvania and the Stuhr Museum of the
Prairie Pioneer in Grand Island, Neb.

While conferences grew in number and scope, the Education Department also developed the Trust library and visual aids collections. Books

on preservation topics came as gifts and review copies as well as by purchase, and as the library grew, a card catalogue was begun. In response to the increasing demand for visual aids, the Trust photographic collection was also expanded; in 1963 indexing and cataloguing of the collection was begun. In 1965, the Walden Fund, which had been designated for educational programs, made possible the creation of the National Trust Slide Lecture series for use by classroom teachers, other educators and lecturers. The series covered a variety of preservation projects, including the renovation and restoration of the White House and the preservation of properties owned and administered by the Trust. By 1966, 7,000 slides of buildings in the United States and abroad were available to Trust staff members and researchers.

Of equal value to researchers were the Trust archives, managed by the Department of Information. The local and state preservation legislation collection had grown quickly and was expanded and updated in 1962. The effort secured preservation legislation from 250 cities, including such laws as zoning ordinances establishing historic districts and general ordinances providing for the preservation of historic sites, buildings or objects. This information was catalogued and indexed, and a bibliography of preservation laws was assembled and distributed. In addition, a reference list naming all areas that had adopted architectural controls was compiled and made available to communities that sought to institute such controls. Through the list, the Trust hoped to share with communities contemplating the adoption of preservation legislation the experience of those that had already taken similar actions.

By collecting national publications, comprehensive files of correspondence and legislative data, the Trust began to develop a major preservation reference center for use by students, city planners, Trust members, writers, historians and other researchers. The archives also served as a resource center for such agencies as the U.S. General Services Administration, the U.S. Commission of Fine Arts, the U.S. Urban Renewal Administration, the National Capital Planning Commission and the American Institute of Architects.

The Information Department also amassed comprehensive material from which to draw solutions for technical or general preservation problems. This information was available to the public at no cost, and the demand for it was great. In 1964, for example, the Trust helped 24 municipalities in 17 states begin architectural surveys; it answered inquiries for general information from 168 communities in 43 states and numerous foreign countries. Letters from the general public, urgent telephone calls from worried preservationists, postcards from school children asking for "all you can send me on American history"—in 1964 the Information Department staff responded to approximately 6,000 such requests.

Sometimes the response was simply an expression of moral support and encouragement. For others, more technical research assistance was required. In 1964 James C. Massey, supervisory architect for the eastern office of the Historic American Buildings Survey, wrote the Trust-published monograph on the importance and techniques of conducting architectural surveys. In 1965 New Orleans attorney Jacob H. Morrison used Trust material in preparing a revised edition of his earlier study, *Historic Preservation Law.*

Other books prepared for publication with assistance from the Information Department included David E. Finley's *History of the National Trust for Historic Preservation, 1947–1963* (published by him and given to the Trust in 1965), Charles B. Hosmer's *Presence of the Past* (G.P. Putnam's Sons, 1965) and *Great Houses of America* (G.P. Putnam's Sons, 1966) by Lionel and Ottalie K. Williams, which featured two Trust properties.

In 1964 archivist Tony P. Wrenn coauthored with Robert L. Montague, III, the book *Planning for Preservation* (American Society of Planning Officials), which covered the basic economic and legal aspects of preservation. Helen Duprey Bullock, director of the Department of Information, served as consultant for the five-volume *National Treasury of Cookery* (Heirloom Publishing Company, 1966) by Mary and Vincent Price. The books contained illustrations of the restored kitchens and dining rooms of 29 properties administered by Trust member organizations.

The staff also contributed numerous articles to professional and special-interest magazines such as *Charette*, the American Institute of Architects *Journal, Midwest Museums Quarterly, Museum News, Wisconsin Magazine of History, Antiques* and *American Archivist.* In addition, articles about the Trust appeared in 10 popular magazines: *American Heritage, American Home, Atlantic Monthly, Better Homes and Gardens, Changing Times, House and Garden, Interiors, Life, Reader's Digest, Time* and *Woman's Day.* Some of the articles were made available to Trust members as reprints or tearsheets at nominal cost.

In 1965, a bonus book program was established, making new titles available to the Trust membership at a discount. Under this arrangement *American Gardens*, featuring Trust property gardens and those of many member organizations, and *Lee In His Own Words*, published by the Eastern National Park & Monument Association (a Trust member organization), were sold in substantial quantities. The Trust also distributed a special edition of President Woodrow Wilson's last published writing, *The Road Away from Revolution.*

Preservation News, the prime source of information about develop-

Helen Duprey Bullock, Trust historian and editor 1950-73, in Blue Dyers House kitchen, New Harmony, Ind. (James K. Mellow)

ments in the preservation field, was expanded in 1964 to 14 issues, with the extra issues covering the annual meeting. The illustrated magazine *Historic Preservation* was also expanded; six issues instead of the usual four were published. The distribution of *Preservation News* and *Historic Preservation* increased appreciably every year as the membership increased and as members put in pre-publication orders on special issues of the magazine.

The Information Department also handled publications and filing for other Trust departments. It organized, cross-referenced and indexed all departmental files and prepared lists of both international and domestic preservation organizations. The latter list was first published in 1962 and three years later was revised and redesigned as the *Geographical Directory* of Trust member organizations and their properties. During this time, the Information Department staff also conducted research on Trust properties and classified and identified the property photographic collection. From this material, staff members wrote and produced leaflets and booklets on all Trust properties.

To expand public identification of the Trust, the Information Department issued press releases on major Trust activities and staffed press desks at various preservation meetings. In 1965 staff members aided in the preparation of articles in 23 newspapers, including the *National Observer*, the *New York Times* and the *Wall Street Journal*, and they assisted the Columbia Broadcasting System, the National Broadcasting Company and Screen Gems in the production of various shows. In 1965, with encouragement from the U.S. Urban Renewal Administration, the Information Department developed an application for a demonstration grant from the agency to produce a motion picture that would show the ways in which the urban renewal program could assist in preservation undertakings.

Throughout 1963–66, the Trust senior staff and board members still found time to travel, proselytizing and consulting with preservationists from coast to coast, their travel expenses shared by area organizations on the tour. The following is a typical example of the strenuous schedules often maintained by preservation "missionaries."

Saturday, April 2	Easton, Md. Field trip with Columbia University School of Architecture
Sunday, April 3	Easton, Md. Field trip with Columbia University School of Architecture. Leave for New York City by car
Monday, April 4– Tuesday, April 5	New York City. Columbia University, public lectures on "Post-Revolutionary Kitchens" and "Pre-Revolutionary Kitchens"

Wednesday, April 13– Friday, April 15	Columbia, Tenn. Fifth Tennessee Preservation Conference
Saturday, April 16	Smyrna, Tenn. Consultation on Sam Davis Home with local chapter of APTA [Association for the Preservation of Tennessee Antiquities]
Friday, April 22	Dayton, Ohio. Arrive that evening in Dayton. Dinner at 6:30 p.m.—lecture to follow
Saturday, April 23	Leave Dayton for Hudson and Peninsula by car. Stay in Peninsula for night
Sunday, April 24	Twinsburg, Ohio. Arrive by 7 or 8 p.m. that evening
Monday, April 25	Strongsville, Ohio. Meeting at 8 p.m. with the Women's City Council (open to Legislative Commission members)
Tuesday, April 26	Lancaster, Ohio. Arrive by 1 p.m. Fairfield Heritage Association, 6 p.m. dinner, 8 p.m. public slide lecture at Lancaster High School
Wednesday, April 27	Akron, Ohio. Stan Hywet Hall Foundation, 10 a.m. lecture at Carriage House Auditorium (open to members and public)
Thursday, April 28	Perrysburg, Ohio. Maumee Valley Historical Society, 12 noon luncheon meeting with subsequent tour and conferences
Friday, April 29	Leave from Toledo, Ohio, to go to either Washington, D.C., or Henry Ford Museum and Greenfield Village, Dearborn, Mich.
Saturday, April 30	In Washington or at Greenfield Village
Sunday, May 1	Return from Greenfield Village to Washington

Staff and Trustees were assisted by Trust members in these pursuits, but the geographical range of Trust outreach efforts was, of course, limited. It was determined that a formal system was needed through which the needs of each region could be communicated to the Trust. To this end, the Trust in 1966 established the Board of Advisors, with a goal of two representatives from each of the 50 states, the District of Columbia and all U.S. territories and possessions.

The years from 1963 to 1966 were equally productive for the Trust property program. Policies relating to properties were reviewed in 1963, and long-range decisions were made. The Trust maintained its support of preservation through local trusteeship, whereby historic buildings were preserved and maintained by local groups. Simultaneously, it emphasized the functional aspect of historic buildings. It encouraged people to live in old houses and to use old public buildings so that they might serve as "living" landmarks. Evaluation of bequest proposals and plans for acquisitions were developed, and policies regarding loan objects (paintings, furniture and other decorative arts loaned to and by the Trust) were also reviewed.

Two goals were uppermost in the new property policies. First, the Trust wanted to increase the number of its properties when adequate means of support could be found for preservation and maintenance. Second, the Trust renewed its pledge to make its properties outstanding examples of preservation and interpretation. Basic to the attainment of these goals was the gearing of present properties to be more useful to their neighborhoods and communities, because Trust leaders believed their familiar equation "more use = more interest = more visitors = more revenue = more and better programs" applied to Trust properties as well as to membership. Based on this equation, the Trust had a right to be optimistic about the future, for in 1963 its properties—Casa Amesti, Woodlawn Plantation, Decatur House and The Shadows—had attracted more than 48,000 visitors.

Special events at the properties attracted many of these visitors and resulted in increased publicity for the Trust and preservation. Because Decatur House and Woodlawn Plantation were located, respectively, in and near the national capital, they were frequently engaged for special Trust events or for use by other groups. In 1964, a typical year, Decatur House was the scene of 16 Trust meetings and conferences. Forty-three other groups met there for lectures, and official entertainments were held for more than 3,600 persons. Among the guests and hosts were First Lady Mrs. John F. Kennedy, King Mohammed Zahar of Afghanistan, a presidential scientific adviser and, appropriate to the legacy of a naval hero's home, Paul B. Fay, Jr., the Under Secretary of the Navy.

Woodlawn, too, was used by the community. The Trust rented the plantation's pasture and stables to the Belvoir Polo Club, thereby reducing maintenance costs of the "amenity lands" surrounding the property. Woodlawn also served as a repository for furniture and objects on loan to the Trust. Among the special events held there—in addition to the annual Seminar for Historic Museum Associates—were club meetings, luncheons, teas and receptions sponsored by garden clubs, the American Institute of Architects, the Daughters of the American Revolution and the Philadelphia Museum of Art. Traditional events included a Christmas-time carol sing by candlelight, polo benefits, tours during the Garden

Club of Virginia's Garden Club Week, a Salvation Army benefit, a needlework exhibit and the Fall Flower Show. Another annual event, later discontinued, was the Completion Day Celebration. It was held in September, usually around Labor Day, to celebrate completion of construction of the mansion; the time of the event was based on a date found inscribed on a beam in the attic. Although researchers have been unable to verify that the date September 9, 1805, is when construction was completed, it is known that in the 1800s, when Woodlawn was constructed, builders sometimes inscribed somewhere within the building the date on which the new house was turned over to its owner.

Not only was Woodlawn the scene of adult and family activities, it was also, because of its availability and convenient location, a popular destination for field trips by nearby school classes. In 1966, with resources from the Walden Fund, the Trust sought to relate field trips to the property more closely to school curricula by developing follow-up activities for the classroom. A sample program for fourth-graders included both follow-up activities and a pretour orientation session. Upon arrival at the property, the children were shown slides and told specific things to look for during the tour. As they were taken through the house, they could then be more alert to evidence showing the life-style of the Lewis family. For continuing study, the Trust developed tests and vocabulary lists for the fourth-graders; they were used in conjunction with lessons on Virginia history. Especially popular were activity kits— bird books adapted from the illustrations and written observations of Lorenzo Lewis, son of Lawrence and Nellie Custis Lewis, and needlework kits modeled after a sampler made by his mother.

Maintenance and repair of Trust properties were priorities during the early 1960s. The Woodrow Wilson House was cleaned and recarpeted in time for the 1963 Washington, D.C., annual meeting, after which the property was officially opened to the public. Woodlawn, however, demanded the most attention. The historic plantation, which because of circumstances had been accepted without an adequate endowment, had been operated on a restricted budget for years. Repairs had been made to the roof of the main house and to the roadway. Tree surgery and landscaping had also been carried out with the help of the Garden Club of Virginia, but there were no long-range plans for restoration and maintenance of the house and gardens. Despite the fact that Woodlawn was the most visited Trust property, income from admissions did not cover the costs of capital improvements, so many repairs had to be delayed. In 1966 badly needed support came in the form of a $100,000 gift from the Harriet Pullman Schermerhorn Charitable Foundation. Because of this endowment, the Trust was finally able to initiate long-range restoration and maintenance programs at the historic plantation.

President Woodrow Wilson's typewriter on display at Wilson House. (Robert Oakes for the National Trust)

At the Shadows-on-the-Teche in New Iberia, La., a three-year program of tree surgery and landscaping was completed in 1963. In less than a year, however, Hurricane Hilda smashed into the Louisiana coast, inflicting extensive damage to the bayou mansion and, consequently, substantially decreasing visitation to the property. A special appeal was made to the Trust membership to secure financing for the necessary repairs.

At Decatur House during 1965 and 1966, the kitchen wing and the third floor were adapted for office space to accommodate the Trust staff, while the wine cellars and other basement areas provided archival and curatorial storage space and facilities for a mail room. Staff members undertook an extensive historical and archaeological investigation in preparation for restoration of the exhibit area within the house.

The staff move to Decatur House in the fall of 1966 brought to an end what had been a nomadic existence. Trust headquarters had been moved four times since staff members had first begun work in borrowed offices in historic Ford's Theatre. The first two moves brought the Trust to locations of historical interest—The Octagon and 712 Jackson Place on historic Lafayette Square just across from the White House—but the

Dining room of the Shadows-on-the-Teche, New Iberia, La. (The watercolors reproduced on the cover of this book hang in this room.) (James K. Mellow)

Malcolm Simmons probes for artifacts in 1966 excavation of Decatur House garden. (Elwood Baker, Washington Star-News)

others were to modern office buildings. These latter moves were the result of the Trust eviction from 712 Jackson Place during government construction around Lafayette Square.

The eviction came during the presidency of Dwight D. Eisenhower as a result of the growth of the executive branch. Government workers were moved into several buildings adjacent to the White House. In January 1957, following congressional approval of plans for the construction of public buildings on Lafayette Square, the government took title to nine parcels of land on Jackson Place, at the west side of Lafayette Square including the building at 712 and several others next to Decatur House. Although this historic house and Blair House, which is around the corner on Pennsylvania Avenue, were to be spared, their 19th and 20th-century neighbors were to be demolished. In 1958 Congress voted to construct a new Court of Claims and a Court of Customs and Patent Appeals on Madison Place, at the east side of the square, where Dolley Madison once lived.

The original government plans called for the destruction of all buildings on Jackson Place, with the exception of the Decatur House complex at one end. Following criticism of the plan by the Trust and others, the government modified the proposal, suggesting the reconstruction of a 19th-century–style townhouse at the other end of Jackson Place in order "to provide balance." The new six-story federal office building would be built between the new townhouse and Decatur House, occupying most of the land in the block formed by Jackson Place, Pennsylvania Avenue, H and 17th streets.

The Trust had publicly expressed dismay at the original plan but realized that arguing for retention of the integrity of the historic area would be difficult: Of the 14 plots fronting Jackson Place, five were occupied by fairly new office buildings, ranging in height from five to nine stories, so there already existed an inharmonious mixture of old and new. Of the remaining 19th-century townhouses, three were scheduled for demolition by private developers. Thus, the government could not be charged with destroying the character and scale of the area. The Trust decided to channel its energy into influencing the evolution of the government architectural design so that as much harmony as possible would be achieved.

By 1962 President and Mrs. John F. Kennedy had taken a personal interest in the proposed development. At the President's suggestion, the San Francisco architectural firm of John Carl Warnecke and Associates was selected in 1963 to redesign the Lafayette Square project and to landscape Lafayette Park. Warnecke's design, endorsed by the Trust, called for the retention of most of the historically significant buildings on the east and west sides of the square. Further, to preserve the scale

Lafayette Square federal construction project, completed in 1966, integrated the Trust-owned Decatur House (right) with existing and reconstructed townhouses and placed the new federal office building behind them. In 1973 Trust headquarters were located on the third floor of Decatur House, its servants wing, two adjoining townhouses and a nearby office building. (John J-G. Blumenson)

of the facades fronting the park, reconstructed townhouses would replace the modern office buildings. The taller federal buildings were to be placed behind them. Decatur House was credited with being a substantial factor in the effort to provide a harmonious blend of old and new architecture in the area.

The use of Decatur House as the new Trust headquarters not only removed the financial drain of rent payments, but its use as both a historic house museum and an office was considered by Trust leaders, staff and members to be a fitting symbol of the Trust mission.

The acquisition of four properties during the period 1963–66 strengthened Trust leadership as an owner and administrator of representative structures and sites. Each of the properties was in itself significant historically and architecturally. Together they dramatically expanded the range of the Trust collection of historic houses.

Belle Grove, Middletown, Va. A property of the National Trust. (Sabin Robbins)

In 1964 the Trust received Belle Grove, a late 18th-century farm near Middletown, Va., in the Shenandoah Valley. Belle Grove was bequeathed to the Trust by Harvard University botanist Francis Welles Hunnewell of Wellesley, Mass., who, after seeing the farm during a search for botanical specimens, bought and restored it. Received in good condition, Belle Grove was opened to visitors in the spring of 1967.

The farmhouse spans several eras. It was built about 1794 under the direction of Maj. Isaac Hite, an aide-de-camp to Gen. Peter Muhlenberg during the Revolutionary War, and its design was directly influenced by Thomas Jefferson. Major Hite had married Eleanor Conway Madison, sister of the future President James Madison in 1783. A decade later, as the house was being planned, Madison sent his brother-in-law's builder to visit Monticello for inspiration, writing to Jefferson, "In general, any hints which may occur to you for improving the plan will be thankfully accepted." Research has shown that Jefferson did suggest some elements of the design. During the Civil War, Belle Grove served as Gen. Philip Sheridan's headquarters and was severely damaged during the Battle of Cedar Creek, fought on October 19, 1864, when Confederate soldiers led by Gen. Jubal Early made a predawn raid on sleeping Union soldiers.

Two other properties acquired by the Trust in 1964—Lyndhurst and the Pope-Leighey House—are polar opposites on the architectural spectrum. Lyndhurst, built in 1838 near Tarrytown, N. Y., for Gen. William Paulding, one-time mayor of New York City, is perhaps the finest example in the country of the Gothic Revival mansion, a style that flourished in the 19th century. Designed by Alexander Jackson Davis, the mansion echoes others like it that were built along the Hudson River during an era of unrestricted capitalism. The structure was enlarged by Davis for its second owner, George Merritt, and in 1880 was purchased by railroad magnate Jay Gould. Gould filled the mansion with paintings, screens, bronzes, sculpture, tapestries, brocades, rugs, porcelain, rare books and manuscripts. (As a benefactor of Mount Vernon, Gould also contributed to the beginnings of historic preservation in America.)

He also refitted a mammoth greenhouse on the property, stocking it with plants from all parts of the world. Interestingly, the railroad tycoon built a pier on the river from which he commuted to New York City on his yacht, the *Atalanta*. Lyndhurst, along with its art and its furniture, meticulously designed by Davis to match the Gothic architecture, was bequeathed to the Trust by Gould's daughter Anna, the Duchess of Talleyrand-Perigord.

The Pope-Leighey House, a 20th-century middle-class residence, is a striking contrast to Lyndhurst. Perhaps the only thing it has in common with the Gothic mansion is that it, too, was designed by a master architect—Frank Lloyd Wright. In 1938 Wright expressed his belief that "the house of moderate cost is not only America's major architectural problem but it is the problem most difficult for her major architects. As for me, I would rather solve it with satisfaction to myself and Usonia, than build anything I can think of." *Usonia* was British writer Samuel Butler's term for the United States; Wright borrowed it to describe the series of moderately priced houses he designed to be built in the East in the 1940s. The Pope-Leighey House, second of Wright's Usonian

Second Lyndhurst greenhouse as rebuilt by Gould c. 1884 after fire. (Dwyer Funeral Home, Tarrytown, N.Y.)

Lyndhurst, Tarrytown, N.Y. Dining room, with Alexander Jackson Davis furnishings. A property of the National Trust. (Louis H. Frohman)

Master carpenter Howard C. Rickert supervises dismantling of the Frank Lloyd Wright–designed Pope-Leighey House in Falls Church, Va., October 1964. (Jim McNamara, Washington Post)

series, was built in Falls Church, Va., for *Washington Evening Star* newspaper reporter Loren B. Pope, who had written to Wright requesting the architect's services after reading his *Autobiography.*

The structure embodies many of the principles Wright made famous in 20th-century architecture. In a small building (just four main rooms), Wright created an illusion of space in a number of ways. For example, the use of rough cypress and brick, inside and out, and the expanses of glass incorporated into the design help make the house blend organically into its natural setting. Built-in furniture, also designed by Wright, makes maximum use of every square foot. The building epitomizes Wright's belief in "simplifying" by allowing the occupant to enjoy an easy, dignified relationship with nature. Mr. and Mrs. Robert A. Leighey, second owners of the house, keenly felt this relationship. Mrs. Leighey wrote, "I think you become a better person by living here. Little by little your pretensions fall away and you become a more truthful, a more honest person."

Mrs. Leighey brought the house to the attention of the Trust and the

*Pope-Leighey House, Mount Vernon, Va., after reassembly at Woodlawn
Plantation site. A property of the National Trust. (Wm. Edmund Barrett)*

U.S. Department of the Interior in February 1964 when plans for Interstate 66 threatened its destruction. A classic example of highway construction versus preservation, the Pope-Leighey cause was personally
espoused by Secretary of the Interior Stewart L. Udall, a longtime con-
servationist. In March Udall initiated talks with federal and state highway officials in hopes of having the highway rerouted. But right-of-way
acquisition and road alignment plans had gone too far by the time to
permit such a change. The only alternative to destroying the house was
relocating it.

To insure that the house would be relocated in a proper setting, a site
review committee was established, including Joseph Watterson, editor of
the American Institute of Architects *Journal*, and Robert R. Garvey, Jr.,
executive director of the Trust. After inspections of several sites and
careful deliberation, it was agreed that the best choice was a 1½-acre
wooded site at Woodlawn Plantation.

Although Trust policy was generally not in favor of moving a property away from its original setting, the Executive Committee of the

Board of Trustees adopted a motion to accept the house, move it to the Woodlawn estate and assume the responsibilities of its maintenance.

In July 1964 Mrs. Leighey accepted payment for her property from the commonwealth of Virginia and then turned the money over to the Trust to help finance relocation of the house. Anonymous donors met the remaining costs. With the supervision of the National Park Service and consultation by the Taliesin Associated Architects, Wright's architectural firm, the house was carefully dismantled, moved to Woodlawn and reassembled out of sight of the mansion so that each structure retained scenic integrity.

These two acquisitions (Lyndhurst and the Pope-Leighey House), opened to the public in 1965, helped give a new dimension to popular thinking about the purposes of preservation. For one thing, the preservation of many colonial and Federal houses had given rise to the belief that only 17th and 18th-century architecture was worth saving. Many people failed to appreciate products of either the last or the present century. Similarly, many had come to think that the term *historic structure* referred only to Revolutionary War–vintage buildings where George Washington might have slept. In preserving Lyndhurst and the Pope-Leighey House, the Trust could show that architecture can make its own history, giving the term *historic* a wider definition. Trust involvement with these structures reflected its belief that excellence in architectural design and craftsmanship is a criteria for preservation.

The notion that only lavish estates are significant enough to be saved was likewise contradicted by the preservation of the Pope-Leighey House. Moreover, its relocation at Woodlawn Plantation provided a lesson in contrasting life-styles. As William Wesley Peters, chief architect of the Taliesin Associated Architects and vice president of the Frank Lloyd Wright Foundation put it, "The Pope-Leighey House is to the citizen of today's democratic society every bit as appropriate as the elegant mansion was to the aristocrat of the pre-war South."

At this time, an investigation of the situation in Fairfax County, where Woodlawn Plantation and the Pope-Leighey House are located, revealed the lack of a historical survey and the legal means for saving historic structures. This led to action from several quarters: In the fall of 1964, the Bureau of Public Roads, then under the U.S. Department of Commerce, announced a new policy to protect historic resources. Local progress was made, too. Fairfax County established a staffed Landmarks Commission and a countywide architectural and historical survey was initiated. By 1968 the county had also passed legislation authorizing historic district zoning; the law allowed property lines to serve as boundaries around which buffer zones of a quarter mile could be established. Any adjacent development plans would be subject to review. The Trust

Oatlands, Leesburg, Va. A property of the National Trust. (Marler)

properties in Fairfax County were among the first to receive this protection.

In 1965 the Trust acquired its ninth property, Oatlands, a late Federal–style mansion and estate near Leesburg, Va. The historic mansion, built over the first third of the 19th century by George Carter, features a wealth of decorative detail and fine craftsmanship. Along with the mansion, the Trust received its first historic formal gardens, also designed by Carter. The gardens had been restored and developed by Mr. and Mrs. William Corcoran Eustis after they purchased the estate in 1903. One of Eustis's reasons for acquiring Oatlands was his keen interest in fox hunting and other equestrian sports, which could be enjoyed in the surrounding Virginia hunt country.

The Eustis family was not only prominent in Virginia; they were also well known in the nation's capital. William Corcoran Eustis was the grandson of William W. Corcoran, founder of the Corcoran Gallery of Art in Washington, D.C. His wife, Edith Livingston Morton Eustis, was the daughter of Levi Parsons Morton, who served as Vice President in Benjamin Harrison's administration. Oatlands was given to the Trust in memory of William and Edith Eustis by their daughters, Mrs. Eustis Emmet and Mrs. David E. Finley.

In 1965, Brinton Sherwood succeeded Robert G. Stewart as director of the Properties Department. With the recent acquisitions and the need to develop plans for their interpretation and use, the Trust also hired a full-time curator, John N. Pearce. Master plans for research and interpretation of the new properties were drawn up by the staff under Pearce's direction.

The program expansion that had taken place between 1962 and 1966 again necessitated reorganization of the Trust staff. This time, the Trust was divided into three departments: Program, Public Affairs and Administration. The Department of Program, headed by William J. Murtagh, included the Membership and Training Services Office, directed by Glenn E. Thompson; a newly established Publications Office, headed by Terry B. Morton; and a Properties Office, now headed by John N. Pearce, who replaced Brinton Sherwood after his resignation from the Trust in July. Ellen Beasley, as a curator, helped organize several Trust properties for their operation as historic house museums. In the Department of Public Affairs, directed by J. William Bethea, Eleanor N. Hamilton served as press officer. The Department of Administration was headed by George E. Newstedt. Members of Executive Director Robert Garvey's staff included Helen Duprey Bullock, senior editor and historian, and Pierre G.T. Beauregard, who served as a liaison with the property councils.

In October 1966 at the 20th Trust Annual Meeting and Preservation

Gordon Gray (left), chairman of the Board of Trustees 1962-73, receives U.S. Department of the Interior Conservation Service Award from Secretary of the Interior Rogers C.B. Morton, June 1973. (Carleton Knight, III)

Demolition of the Panamanian legation, Washington, D.C., April 1972. "Don't it always seem to go, you don't know what you've got till it's gone. They pave paradise and they put up a parking lot." From Joni Mitchell song "Big Yellow Taxi." (John J-G. Blumenson)

Conference, held in Philadelphia, Gordon Gray noted in a dinner address that the 10 years preceding the Bicentennial would be a "decade of decision" for the Trust. He urged the membership to ponder what effect the future would have on America's landmarks in order to plan for their preservation.

Gray pointed out that it was estimated that there would be more construction between 1966 and 1976 than there had been in the preceding 200 years. The projections of a building boom at the rate of about $60 billion per year threatened a tide of destruction of historic landmarks and areas. Gray noted that national programs geared to solving the pollution of the environment and promoting responsible stewardship of the nation's natural resources would demand heavy investments in science and technology. Efforts to cure social ailments of the country would also call for a great deal of time, money and human resources.

"We must be sure," Gray said, "that an adequate percentage of these resources is spent on culture, conservation and recreation." He reminded Trust members that the preservation of landmarks served all three of these needs. He stressed that preserving landmarks and recycling these tangible reminders of the nation's cultural heritage by living and working in them was not only sane economics but also a solution to some of the country's other ills.

The first four years of Gordon Gray's chairmanship of the Board of Trustees were marked by significant progress. Membership recruitment resulted in a growth from fewer than 4,000 members to more than 11,000. Service and property programs likewise expanded. So too did Trust awareness that the development of protective legislation and programs on federal and state levels would be a critical element if the Trust were to fulfill its mission. Thus, while the Trust carried on its regular programs, it also grew more aggressive in its role as a standard-bearer for preservation.

Drawing by Paul R. Hoffmaster.
(Preservation News, *December 1967*)

CHAPTER THREE

The Preservation Congress

The National Trust not only carried on its domestic preservation responsibility from 1947 to 1966, it also became involved in the international preservation movement. Concern for the cultural heritage of the world was a natural outgrowth of the congressional charge to the Trust to protect and encourage appreciation of America's cultural heritage. In fact, the example of national preservation policies and legislation in other countries was to help provide the impetus for federal involvement in preserving the U.S. cultural heritage, resulting in congressional enactment of the National Historic Preservation Act of 1966.

Since its establishment, the Trust had enjoyed a mutually beneficial relationship with preservation groups in a number of foreign countries. Advice by correspondence had been given by Trust staff to groups in Canada, Spain, Scotland, New Zealand, West Germany, the British West Indies, Bermuda, Australia and Mexico. Trustees and staff, by invitation, had lectured and studied in Japan, West Germany and other European countries, and on several post–annual meeting tours Trust members had viewed preservation outside the United States.

The closest relations had been with the English National Trust for the Preservation of Places of Historic Interest or Scenic Beauty. In fact, when the English Trust was established in 1895, it modeled its charter and its programs on an American antecedent, the Massachusetts Trustees of Public Reservations, a National Trust sponsoring organization that had been established in 1891. In 1900, Charles R. Ashbee, a member of the English Trust, came to America to report on British preservation activities and to encourage the establishment of a similar nationwide trust in the United States. Financed only by his lecture fees, Ashbee traveled from city to city, dismayed to find that while Americans were saving some of their country's natural wonders, they were obliterating architectural and historical monuments at an alarming rate. He also discovered that fierce regionalism had delayed the establishment of cooperative efforts. A trust was formed, but it died soon after, and a scrupulous committee returned to donors their share of the treasury—$134.28, after postage costs. One of the few who supported the idea (even volunteer-

Restoration work at Beegenhof, Amsterdam, The Netherlands. (William J. Murtagh)

ing to serve as the organization's secretary) was a young Chicago architect who was to become a giant of 20th-century architecture— Frank Lloyd Wright.

Later, cognizant of the damage caused by two world wars, preservationists came to realize that parochialism such as the American communities had exhibited at the turn of the century was a luxury no longer affordable. Isolated national action, no matter how extensive, would not assure survival of the world's cultural heritage. In 1945 the United Nations Educational, Scientific and Cultural Organization (UNESCO) was established; one of its programs was to unite preservation efforts internationally, just as the Trust would attempt to do a few years later in the United States.

The first step UNESCO took toward fulfilling these goals was the preparation of a series of international instruments. Drawn up were conventions, which are proposals that require ratification by United Nations members, and recommendations, which serve as patterns for national legislation or programs. For example, at an intergovernmental confer-

Guild Hall at Lavenham, Suffolk, England. Restored half-timbered landmark in 15th-century center of wool industry. (Letitia Galbraith)

ence at The Hague in 1954, UNESCO members prepared an international convention for the protection of cultural property in the case of armed conflict. Recommendations issued by UNESCO have dealt with such matters as principles that should govern archaeological excavation, the preservation of landscapes and the preservation of cultural property endangered by public or private works.

In 1958 UNESCO created the International Centre for the Study of the Preservation and the Restoration of Cultural Property. The function of the Rome Centre, so called because of its headquarters location, is to insure the international exchange of technical information concerning preservation, to stimulate further research on a cooperative basis and to assist countries applying to it for help. Today the Rome Centre provides consultation, publications and educational and training programs for the general public and for professionals involved in preservation-related fields. (In 1972 the centre abbreviated its name to the International Centre for Conservation in order to reflect its broad range of interests and to become known simply as the International Centre.) It has also sought to insure a reservoir of funds for preservation through the establishment of an International Fund.

In 1963 UNESCO designated the following year as International Monuments Year, called in this country the American Landmarks Celebration. The U.S. State Department asked the Trust to assume leadership of the celebration, and the Trust responded immediately by sponsoring a preparatory conference from which came some significant contributions to worldwide preservation. The Seminar on Preservation and Restoration was convened in early September 1963, when the Trust, along with Colonial Williamsburg as a cosponsor, assembled 160 persons active in the American preservation movement at Williamsburg. The purpose was to review the history of American preservation, including its European background; to analyze its philosophical basis; to examine its present effectiveness; and to discuss ways to shape its future. This was the first review of such magnitude of preservation efforts in the United States, and from it came comprehensive guidelines and principles that could be applied in other countries.

In designing the conference, the sponsors recognized the value of drawing on European experience. Invitations were extended to U.S. scholars Charles B. Hosmer, Jr., of Principia College, Christopher Tunnard of Yale University and Stephen W. Jacobs of Cornell University, as well as to scholars from abroad: Jacques Dupont, inspector general of historical monuments, Paris; Raymonde A. Frin, editor of *Museum* and a UNESCO program specialist, Paris; Stanislaw Lorentz, director of the National Museum, Warsaw; Peter Michelsen, director of Frilandsmuseet, Copenhagen; and Sir John Summerson, curator of Sir John Soane's Museum, London. The essays presented by these speakers dealt with such topics as the historical basis and philosophy of preservation, the influence of government participation and private philanthropy and the practical and educational uses of sites and buildings. Papers were distributed prior to the conference to provide time for the preparation of comments by colleagues, and lively debate characterized some discussions.

The seminar participants identified major areas of concern to preservationists: the shortage of architects and craftsmen to meet the requirements demanded by preservation and restoration; the future of historic districts in relationship with an increasing number of urban renewal projects; the changing character of central cities; the need for more basic information, especially architectural histories and handbooks on preservation techniques; and the proper role of government in preservation. The last area highlighted the greatest contrast between U.S. and European preservation methods. While the vast majority of European preservation efforts were government operated and financed, more than two-thirds of American efforts were privately financed and administered, with the result that preservation in America on the whole had been less comprehensive and less systematic than in Europe.

In a formal report on the seminar findings, "A Report on Principles and Guidelines for Historic Preservation in the United States," which was included as an appendix to the published conference proceedings, *Historic Preservation Today* (National Trust and Colonial Williamsburg, Inc., 1966), the preservationists emphasized the responsibility of local citizens in the preservation movement but also called on the federal government to share in the effort. "As federal legislation evolves in many related fields, such as urban renewal, housing, highway and dam construction, official recognition should be given to the preservation of recognized historical and aesthetic values, particularly whether at the national, state or local levels." Furthermore, the report said, the United States has "a national obligation to cooperate in international efforts to encourage preservation of important monuments wherever they may be situated."

But predictions about the future role of the government were gloomy. According to the report,

> All levels of American government prefer to be drawn as little as
> possible into historic preservation and, where it is unavoidable, only
> as a partner. In some notable instances federal control has arisen from
> the magnitude of a preservation project or has been exercised in
> default of local or state interests. The likelihood seems to be that this
> "hands off" policy will continue and that future governmental
> involvement will increase only in the direction of legislation for the
> protection of historic districts.

Throughout 1964, National Trust Board of Trustees chairman Gordon Gray and Interior Secretary Stewart L. Udall, working together as co-chairmen of the committee in charge of planning the American Landmarks Celebration, coordinated all aspects of American participation in the UNESCO program. The Trust continued to encourage a renewal of the national commitment to preserve the country's heritage by focusing attention on ongoing programs. Gray was named a member of the Joint Committee on Landmarks for the nation's capital. The committee, an organization appointed by the National Capital Planning Commission and the U.S. Commission of Fine Arts, included representatives from the Trust, the National Archives, the Library of Congress, the Smithsonian Institution, the U.S. General Services Administration and the District of Columbia Public Library. One goal of the committee was to prepare an inventory of significant landmarks in Washington, D.C., the first step in a program to identify and preserve landmarks in the nation's capital. The committee found that just 30 years after the beginning of the Historic American Buildings Survey, about half of the original 550 area structures recorded by HABS were gone. It hastened to begin a new effort to assemble a list of buildings in the District worthy of preservation and to make the public aware of the need for saving them.

In August, First Lady Mrs. Lyndon B. Johnson, honorary chairman of the Landmarks Celebration, officially opened the nationwide observance at a reception at the Woodrow Wilson House, presenting the Trust with a certificate designating the building as a National Historic Landmark. Culmination of the year-long celebration was American Landmarks Week, September 28 to October 4, 1964. Directed by a steering committee made up of representatives of some 55 organizations, American Landmarks Week was promoted by more than 350 civic, fraternal and commercial associations throughout the country. A presidential proclamation, 34 gubernatorial proclamations and the formation of numerous municipal action committees also aided in publicizing the week-long observance.

The Trust continued to actively underscore the need for international efforts in preservation. In April 1965, along with the Pan American Union and the National Quadricentennial Commission (a special committee that had been appointed by President John F. Kennedy), the Trust cosponsored the first Pan American Conference on Historic Monuments in St. Augustine, Fla. Official government delegates from the U.S. State Department and the National Park Service, as well as from most Latin American countries and Spain, reviewed Hispanic architecture and its modification in the New World. Following a study of such total-environment restoration projects as those in Cuzco, Peru, and in Chichén Itzá, Mexico, the conferees reviewed protective legislation throughout the Americas and developed recommendations for new legislation. These recommendations were forwarded to the Organization of American States for transmission to member governments.

That same month, the Trust took the initiative for another American activity in the international preservation movement by choosing three representatives to attend the organizational meeting of the International Council on Monuments and Sites (ICOMOS), held in Warsaw in June 1965. (The need for an organization such as ICOMOS had been discussed by participants at the UNESCO-sponsored Second International Congress of Architects and Technicians of Historic Monuments, held in 1964 in Venice, where the Trust was represented by Trustee Mrs. W. Randolph Burgess.) At the 1965 Constituent Assembly, delegates from 26 nations discussed and adopted organizational statutes and chose officers. Trust executive director Robert R. Garvey, Jr., was elected a vice president at the meeting.

The purposes of ICOMOS were defined in its statutes: "to promote the study and preservation of monuments and sites" and "to arouse and cultivate the interest of the authorities, and people of every country in their monuments and sites and in their cultural heritage." ICOMOS was to represent administrative departments, institutions and persons interested in the preservation and study of monuments and sites throughout the world. The organization, which was to have its headquarters in Paris, planned to initiate a program of publications, information and collaboration at the international level.

To foster its own growing role in international preservation activities, the Trust formed a Committee on International Relations, made up of Trustees and individual members, with Mrs. Burgess serving as the committee leader.

The primary concern of the Trust, however, was not international preservation. Trust leaders recognized that preservation was still low on the list of priorities of their fellow Americans—and of their government. They believed that only when America's leaders focused attention on historic preservation could the continuing tide of destruction of the nation's landmarks be stemmed. Because much of the destruction was the result of federally initiated or financed projects, they recognized that it was critical to make concern for preservation an integral factor in decision making at the federal level. Fortunately for America's landmarks, "the moon was right," as Gordon Gray put it, for a comprehensive reassessment of the situation, this time by public officials as well as by private preservationists.

In 1964, Congress had passed legislation of special interest to preservationists, for it signaled a change in the nation's awareness of its cultural heritage. The *Report of the Commission on the Humanities*, transmitted in 1964 to its sponsoring organizations—the American Council of Learned Societies, the Council of Graduate Schools in the United States and the United Chapters of Phi Beta Kappa—urged financial support for the humanities from the federal government. In stating the position of the Society of Architectural Historians, J.D. Forbes of the University of Virginia and former Trust president Richard H. Howland specifically urged federal financial support for the Trust, writing, "Architectural history differs from many other scholarly disciplines in that its primary raw materials are a rapidly diminishing resource. The high toll of architectural monuments from onslaughts carried on under what Lewis Mumford calls 'the soiled banner of Progress' is apparent on every hand." The Commission on the Humanities report called for the establishment of an independent agency, the National Humanities Foundation, to administer funds.

Following the issuance of this report, also in 1964, the National Arts and Cultural Development Act, creating the National Council on the Arts, became law. It was followed in 1965 by the National Foundation on the Arts and Humanities Act, which established an agency charged to encourage and support national progress in the arts and humanities. Although arts legislation had come before Congress periodically since 1877, this was the first to become law. The passage of this legislation was significant to the preservation movement, because it reflected a new, receptive climate for preservationists' concerns.

The way for this receptive climate had also been paved by U.S. Supreme Court decisions affirming the environmental "right to be beautiful." Associate Justice William O. Douglas, in particular, in 1954 wrote a majority opinion *(Berman* vs. *Parker)* stating, "The concept of the public welfare is broad and inclusive. The values it represents are spiritual as well as physical, aesthetic as well as monetary. It is within the power of the legislature to determine that a community should be beautiful as well as healthy, spacious as well as clean."

Other activities emphasized to the public that preservation was a vital factor in the quality of the total environment. In February 1965, following the submission of the report of the Task Force on the Preservation of Natural Beauty, President Lyndon B. Johnson expressed the need for massive preservation efforts in his message to Congress on the natural beauty of the country. Defining the "new conservation," he said, "Our conservation must not be just the classic conservation of protection and development, but a creative conservation of restoration and innovation. Its concern is not with nature alone, but with the total relation between man and the world around him. Its object is not just man's welfare, but the dignity of man's spirit." The President specifically cited the work of the Trust in his message and urged support for Trust programs.

A few months later, in May 1965, the preservation message again gained national attention through the White House Conference on Natural Beauty. Serving on the Townscape panel of the conference, Board of Trustees chairman Gordon Gray presented Trust recommendations for government action. Recommendations included the establishment of a national program for expansion of the existing inventory of landmarks of national significance to include landmarks of state and local significance and a certification system to provide legal protection to such landmarks, the creation of historic districts, the creation of a system by which private owners in any way injured or deprived by landmarks preservation and conservation activities might be compensated, the establishment of tax incentives for preservation activities and the creation of scenic easement policies and programs.

Also suggested were the use of restrictive covenants on historic properties, increased public ownership of significant properties, a revision of the bank loan system of the Federal Housing Authority in order to stimulate preservation, the expansion of municipal zoning for conservation purposes, the creation of machinery to veto government expenditures that would result in the destruction of landmarks and the use of federal loans and matching grants to encourage historic preservation.

Gray recommended further that eminent domain be used for the acquisition of significant structures and sites rather than for their destruction and that there be a codification of existing governmental administrative policies that favored preservation. These policies should, after codification, be translated into legislation, he added. The board chairman also suggested that better coordination of and communication about preservation activities be established within the federal government and between the government and private groups. Finally, it was proposed that private philanthropies be encouraged to support preservation endeavors and a program devised to guide those interested in adaptive uses of historic properties. Federal support for the Trust was again endorsed.

In the fall of 1965, a Special Committee on Historic Preservation was formed under the auspices of the U.S. Conference of Mayors with a grant from the Ford Foundation and a generous anonymous donation. Not only did the committee membership reflect a variety of fields of expertise, it also represented a cooperative effort between the private sector and all levels of government.

Congressman Albert Rains of Alabama, former chairman of the Housing Subcommittee in the U.S. House of Representatives, was the committee chairman. Members were Sen. Edmund S. Muskie, Maine; Rep. William B. Widnall, New Jersey; Gov. Philip H. Hoff, Vermont; Raymond R. Tucker, professor of urban studies, Washington University, St. Louis, Mo.; Laurance G. Henderson, director of the Joint Council on Housing and Urban Development; and Gordon Gray.

Ex-officio members were Stewart L. Udall, Secretary of the Interior (alternates: Walter I. Pozen, special assistant to the Secretary, and George B. Hartzog, Jr., director of the National Park Service); John T. Connor, Secretary of Commerce (alternate: Rex M. Whitton, federal highway administrator, Bureau of Public Roads); Robert C. Weaver, Secretary of Housing and Urban Development (alternate: William J. Slayton, commissioner of urban renewal); and Lawson B. Knott, Jr.; administrator of the U.S. General Services Administration (alternate: William A. Schmidt, deputy commissioner, Public Buildings Service). The technical director for the committee was Carl Feiss. Named as committee consultants were Trust executive director Robert R. Garvey, Jr.; John J. Gunther, executive director of the U.S. Conference of Mayors; Patrick Healy, executive director of the National League of

Cities; Casey Ireland, a member of the professional staff of the U.S. House of Representatives; Ronald F. Lee, regional director of the Northeast Region, National Park Service; and Gillis Long, assistant to the director of the Office of Economic Opportunity.

In order to prepare recommendations for developing a national policy for preservation, members of this committee studied current efforts in the United States and spent nearly a month abroad studying policies, techniques, methods and legislation in Great Britain, France, the Netherlands, West Germany, Poland, Czechoslovakia, Austria and Italy. Like participants at the 1963 Williamsburg meeting, they found that in Europe the protection of each nation's patrimony had been accepted as the rightful concern and responsibility of the government.

They concluded that a workable preservation program in the United States required the widest possible participation by government and nongovernment agencies and groups from the federal to the local level. The committee recommended that the following steps be taken.

1. A comprehensive statement of national policy be prepared to guide the activities and programs of all federal agencies.

2. An Advisory Council on Historic Preservation be established to provide leadership and guidance for the direction of interagency actions and to provide liaison with state and local governments, public and private groups and the general public.

3. A formal National Register be established in order to more thoroughly and systematically inventory and catalogue the nation's historic communities, areas, structures, sites and objects; a federal program of assistance to states and localities for companion programs formulated; and a strong federal public information program, based on material in the Register, established.

4. Added authority and significant funds be provided for federal acquisition of threatened buildings and sites of national historical importance and the urban renewal program expanded to permit local noncash contributions, including historic buildings in the National Register, both within and outside the project area.

5. Provision be made for federal loans and grants and other financial aid to support preservation activities and for the expansion of state and local programs of historic preservation.

6. Federal financial aid be given to and through the Trust to assist private interest and activity in the preservation field. (Such funds were to be for educational purposes and for direct assistance to private property holders.)

The committee made detailed recommendations for federal legislation applicable to the National Park Service and to the U.S. Department of Housing and Urban Development.

Gordon Gray, chairman of the Board of Trustees; Sen. Edmund S. Muskie,
from Maine; and Albert Rains, chairman of the Special Committee on Historic
Preservation (left to right), attending London conference during 1965 European
fact-finding tour. (Robert R. Garvey, Jr.)

The complete report of the committee, entitled *With Heritage So Rich*, was published by Random House in January 1966. The 230-page book, well illustrated and documented, told the American preservation story as the study committee had seen it; it contrasted the minimal federal support for historic preservation in the United States with the long tradition of government support for preservation in Europe.

Assembled and produced by Trust director of information Helen Duprey Bullock and Joseph Watterson, the volume included full-color photographs and commentary by poet George Zabriskie that showed vividly the diversity and beauty of the nation's cultural heritage. Essays by experts in various fields—historian and author Sidney Hyman, planner and educator Christopher Tunnard and library director and historian Walter Muir Whitehill—measured the scope of the destruction and the resulting crisis. Contributors associated with the Trust included Helen Bullock; Trust executive director Robert R. Garvey, Jr.; former Trust president Richard H. Howland; and Trustee Carl Feiss, who was also technical director of the committee.

With Heritage So Rich was made available to the public, and copies were distributed to President Lyndon B. Johnson and to Cabinet officers, members of Congress, governors of states and mayors of large U.S. cities.

The preservationists at the 1963 Williamsburg meeting, the Task Force on the Preservation of Natural Beauty, the President in his messages to Congress, the White House Conference on Natural Beauty and the Special Committee on Historic Preservation had agreed that the most crucial preservation needs were

1. An inventory of landmarks and the maintenance of a comprehensive National Register.
2. Federal grants to state and local governments for surveys.
3. Protection of landmarks from federally funded construction programs.
4. Revision of urban renewal legislation.
5. A review of various tax devices which, if implemented, would encourage preservation rather than demolition.
6. Further implementation of Trust programs.

Some of these needs could be fulfilled by expanding existing programs or strengthening extant legislation. For others, new laws had to be drafted before programs could be developed and funded. In the fall of 1966, the 89th Congress earned itself the title "The Preservation Congress" by passing a series of laws that essentially followed the recommendations of the Special Committee on Historic Preservation. These laws reiterated the national commitment expressed in the Historic Sites Act of 1935 and reemphasized the role of the private sector in historic preservation, specifically that of the Trust. An important impact of the legislation lay in the responsibility and power it gave to the federal government, the restrictions it placed on federally funded projects and the assistance it pledged to private, state and local groups. With the passage of this preservation legislation, the national policy expressed in the Historic Sites Act of 1935 could be more fully implemented, especially on the state and local level.

On October 15, 1966, President Lyndon B. Johnson signed into law the National Historic Preservation Act (Public Law 89-665), which declared "that the historical and cultural foundations of the Nation should be preserved as a living part of our community life and development in order to give a sense of orientation to the American people." In order to accomplish this, the act said,

> it is . . . necessary and appropriate for the Federal Government to accelerate its historic preservation programs and activities, to give maximum encouragement to agencies and individuals undertaking preservation by private means, and to assist State and local governments and the National Trust for Historic Preservation in the United States to expand and accelerate their historic preservation programs and activities.

In regard to federal programs, the act directly affected activities of the National Park Service. Title I of the act called for the expansion of maintenance of the existing inventory of districts, sites, buildings, structures and objects significant in American history. The nucleus of this new, formal National Register of Historic Places was the 150 historic and archaeological properties within the National Park System and those sites and buildings already designated National Historic Landmarks because of their "national significance in the historic development of the United States." By 1966, the registry of National Historic Landmarks, which had begun in 1960, consisted of 800 entries, three of which were Trust properties—Decatur House, Lyndhurst and the Woodrow Wilson House.

The National Historic Landmarks Program did not cease with the establishment of the National Register. It continues today, administered by the U.S. Department of the Interior. Potential additions to this registry are evaluated for designation under historical themes. Originally, the list of themes comprised 22 categories. In 1970 the list was revised, and nine thematic headings, with subthemes, were adopted.

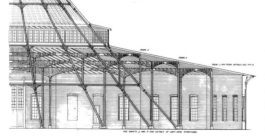

Historic American Engineering Record measured drawing of West Roundhouse, Martinsburg, W. Va. Prepared for B & O Railroad survey project, Summer 1970. (Jeffrey Jenkins for HAER)

THE ORIGINAL INHABITANTS

Subthemes:
The Earliest Americans
Native Villages and Communities
Indian Meets Europeans
Living Remnant
Native Cultures of the Pacific
Aboriginal Technology

EUROPEAN EXPLORATION AND SETTLEMENTS

Subthemes:
Spanish
French
English
Other

DEVELOPMENT OF THE ENGLISH COLONIES, 1700–1775

MAJOR AMERICAN WARS

Subthemes:
The American Revolution
The War of 1812
The Mexican War
The Civil War
The Spanish-American War
World War I
World War II

POLITICAL AND MILITARY AFFAIRS

Subthemes:
1783–1830
1830–1860
1865–1914
After 1914
The American Presidency

WESTWARD EXPANSION, 1763–1898

Subthemes:
Great Explorers of the West
The Fur Trade
Military-Indian Conflicts
Western Trails and Travelers
The Mining Frontier
The Farmers' Frontier
The Cattlemen's Empire

AMERICA AT WORK

Subthemes:
Agriculture
Commerce and Industry
Science and Invention
Transportation and Communication
Architecture
Engineering

THE CONTEMPLATING SOCIETY

Subthemes:
Literature, Drama and Music
Painting and Sculpture
Education
Intellectual Currents

SOCIETY AND SOCIAL CONSCIENCE

Subthemes:
American Ways of Life
Social and Humanitarian Movements
Environmental Conservation
Recreation in the United States

Frederick Douglass Home, Washington, D.C. A National Historic Landmark owned by the National Park Service. (Museum of African Art)

Mummy Cave, Canyon de Chelly National Monument, Chinle, Ariz. (Myra Borchers for the National Park Service)

Two committees—a special consulting committee and the Advisory Board on National Parks, Historic Sites, Buildings, and Monuments, established by the Historic Sites Act of 1935—carefully study all properties proposed for landmark designation. After deliberation, committee recommendations are forwarded to the Secretary of the Interior, who is empowered to designate eligible National Historic Landmarks. Following announcement of a property's eligibility, those who administer it are invited to apply for official landmark designation, and participate in the program by agreeing to preserve the historical integrity of the site or structure, to use it for a purpose consistent with its historical character and to allow periodic inspections by the National Park Service. In return, the property owners receive a certificate of landmark designation and, if desired, a bronze plaque indicating the landmark status of the property.

Properties brought to the attention of the National Park Service through the Federal Inter-Agency Archeological Salvage Program, directed by the Park Service Division of Archeology, are also considered for listing in the National Register. Under this program, when such structures or sites or their environments are to be altered or destroyed by federal or federally licensed projects, actions are to be taken to minimize the loss.

However, the importance of the new National Register lay not so much in the listing of those places of national importance, which had formerly received designation, but in its recognition of places of local and state significance. To identify and record significant local and state properties, the 1966 act called for the initiation of statewide surveys. The act also provided for the Secretary of Interior to set standards for expansion. To assist in this work, the secretary called for the establishment of official state review agencies whose function it was to evaluate properties for nomination to the Register. Actual nominations would be made by state liaison officers (who later acquired a more descriptive title, state historic preservation officers). The National Park Service was given the responsibility to make the final decision concerning the inclusion of any property in the Register. To administer the National Park Service overall historic preservation program, the Office of Archeology and Historic Preservation was created within the National Park Service, under the direction of Ernest A. Connally of the University of Illinois. This new office also assumed the administration of other programs formerly directed by the Park Service divisions of History, Architecture and Archeology.

Another significant provision in the National Historic Preservation Act of 1966 was the creation of the Advisory Council on Historic Preservation. An independent agency, the council was designed as a forum

Advisory Council on Historic Preservation, established by National Historic Preservation Act of 1966, sworn in at first meeting, July 1967, by Secretary of the Interior Stewart Udall (left). (Advisory Council on Historic Preservation)

of experts whose chief function would be to mediate between federal agencies to assure a coordination of construction and preservation interests. Using the National Register criteria, the council would determine the effects of federal projects on historic places listed in the Register.

Other council responsibilities included advising the President and Congress on administrative and legislative matters; recommending measures to coordinate activities of federal, state and local agencies and private institutions and individuals; disseminating information pertaining to such activities; encouraging, in cooperation with the Trust and appropriate private agencies, public interest and participation in preservation; sponsoring studies on such questions as the adequacy of legislative and administrative statutes and regulations pertaining to historic preservation activities of state and local governments and the effects of tax policies at all levels of government; suggesting guidelines to assist state and local governments in drafting legislation; and promoting, in cooperation with appropriate public and private agencies and institutions, training and education in the field.

As originally proposed, the Advisory Council was made up of 17 members: 10 presidential appointees from outside the federal government and the secretaries of the Interior, Commerce, the Treasury and Housing and Urban Development; the administrator of the U.S. General Services Administration; the Attorney General; and the chairman of the National Trust Board of Trustees. The creation of this review body, along with the expansion of the National Register, represented the nation's first attempt to control the future of its cultural heritage by providing a degree of federal protection for its historic landmarks.

To fulfill the federal pledge to support private and state preservation efforts, the National Historic Preservation Act provided for a program of matching grants to the Trust and to the states. Fifty percent matching grants made available to the states were designed to assist in making statewide surveys of historic resources, formulating the state historic preservation plans required by the act and, ultimately, assisting in the preservation of individual properties listed in the National Register.

The National Trust not only had a major role in framing and explaining the purposes of the National Historic Preservation Act, but it also provided some of the key personnel to implement the responsibilities delegated to the National Park Service under the act. Robert R. Garvey, Jr., Trust executive director since 1961, was named executive secretary of the Advisory Council on Historic Preservation. William J. Murtagh, former director of the Trust Department of Education and recently named head of its new Department of Program, was appointed first keeper of the National Register after a brief period as acting executive director following Garvey's departure. Parodying Nathan Hale's famous last words, Gordon Gray remarked that he regretted having "but one staff" to give to his country.

In addition to the National Historic Preservation Act, two other pieces of legislation provided benefits to the cause of preservation. The Transportation Act of 1966 (Public Law 89-670) established the U.S. Department of Transportation. The act brought under the jurisdiction of the new department five agencies: the Federal Aviation Administration, the Federal Rail Administration, the Coast Guard, the St. Lawrence Seaway Corporation and the Federal Highway Administration, which now included the Bureau of Public Roads that had formerly been a part of the U.S. Department of Commerce. These agencies were directed to observe the national policy declared by the act, "that special effort should be made to preserve the natural beauty of the countryside and public parks and recreation lands, wildlife and waterfowl refuges and historic sites."

The highway program, established under the Federal-Aid Highway Act of 1956, had stimulated the construction of some 41,000 miles of highway in the National System of Interstate and Defense Highways. Provisions had been made for archaeological salvage, with the federal government paying 90 percent of the costs and the states 10 percent. The National Park Service Division of Archeology acted as an adviser in such cases. However, the resources of this archaeological salvage program could not be used when roads other than those in the National

Highway System were involved. Therefore, states had to initiate their own programs. Ultimately, the program adopted by New Mexico became a model used by many other states.

In spite of some active participation in the national and state archaeological salvage programs, few surveys of sites of historical value were available to highway planners, and often the planners never sought such information. There was also insufficient time for reviewing construction plans. Public hearings were held, but there were no provisions for appeal, so many hearings turned into press conferences during which disheartened preservationists were told why a certain property or site could not possibly be saved.

While it did not diminish the scope of highway construction, the 1966 transportation act did commit the federal highway administrator to the national policy for protecting historic places. It also required the Secretary of Transportation to cooperate and consult with the secretaries of the Interior, Housing and Urban Development and Agriculture and with state governments to develop plans that would include measures to maintain or enhance natural beauty. The act further directed the Secretary of Transportation, when necessary, to consider alternate plans that would avoid or minimize harm to the landscape.

A third law passed by the Preservation Congress was the Demonstration Cities and Metropolitan Development Act of 1966 (Public Law 89-754). Signed on November 11, 1966, the act authorized the initiation of the Model Cities program under the U.S. Department of Housing and Urban Development. It also contained congressional versions of the recommendations set forth by the Special Committee on Historic Preservation, declaring "there is a need for timely action to preserve and restore areas, sites and structures of historic or architectural value in order that these remaining evidences of our past history and heritage shall not be lost or destroyed through the expansion and development of the Nation's urban areas."

The significance of this legislation can be appreciated better in light of the relationship existing between preservationists and proponents of urban renewal, which had not always been a harmonious one. The Housing Act of 1949, under which the Urban Renewal Administration was designated as a responsibility of the Housing and Home Finance Agency (the precursor of HUD), was an attempt to meet the severe housing needs of the postwar period. As the nation sought to provide "decent" housing for every American family, slum clearance soon came to mean urban renewal. The most deteriorated areas in many cities were usually the oldest; ironically, they were often the most architecturally and historically significant as well. Thus, urban renewal and historic preservation were frequently working at cross purposes. The latter got the epithet "hysterical preservation," as preservationists were accused of wanting to save everything. On the other hand, proponents of urban renewal, or as some chose to call it, "urban removal," seemed to want to bulldoze everything, giving little consideration to architectural and historical values even when citizens protested.

General public protest against the urban renewal program was not immediate, however. Only after more than 900 projects were approved and the initial steps of the projects, which involved the leveling of vast areas, were implemented did citizens become aware of the threat that the projects posed to older areas of their communities—and only then did they react to the plans. Opponents pointed out that, in addition to the destruction of significant architecture, severe problems would be caused by the uprooting of entire neighborhoods. Preservationists argued that continuity and the quality of the neighborhood had to be preserved for sociological reasons as well as aesthetic ones. This viewpoint was eventually acknowledged by some officials to have validity, but not until many neighborhoods had been destroyed and longtime neighbors separated.

The Housing Act of 1954 authorized redevelopment planning for those areas originally involved, or destined for involvement, in urban renewal projects. The Urban Renewal Administration made urban renewal demonstration grants available to local agencies for such planning. One grant, which supported the 1959 study of the College Hill section of Providence, R.I., resulted in an award-winning study that focused on historic preservation and urban renewal. The project, conducted by the City Planning Commission and the Providence Preservation Society, developed criteria for judging the architectural and historical value of structures and made recommendations for using these criteria in collecting data, evaluating structures and locating structures on maps. Redevelopment techniques were then just evolving and little was known about renewing a historic area or preserving a large number of historic houses. The College Hill study developed a historic area zoning ordinance, a system for rating historic architecture and a technique for integrating areas of historic architecture into proposed redevelopment plans. The study won an American Institute of Architects award and was republished in 1965.

Housing legislation did not directly deal with historic preservation until 1961, when the Housing Act passed that year authorized the Open Space Land Program, enabling cities to preserve unspoiled tracts of green areas for scenic, conservation, recreational or historical purposes. In the first three years of the program, 100,000 acres in 177 communities were saved. In 1965 the act was expanded and the Urban Beautification Program absorbed the Open Space Land Program. A year later, the

Benefit Street in College Hill, Providence, R.I. Before restoration (above) and after restoration (below) by private individuals. (Laurence E. Tilley)

Kennedy-Tower amendment to the 1965 Housing Act, which had created the U.S. Department of Housing and Urban Development, provided funds for relocating endangered historic buildings that were situated within an urban renewal development area. The amendment also authorized money for landscaping and other improvements.

In 1966 housing legislation, while putting no restrictions on federal construction, did strengthen the preservation aspects of earlier programs. For example, it amended the Housing Act of 1954 to make urban renewal demonstration grants available to municipalities and towns of fewer than 50,000 people. Formerly, help had been provided only to larger communities.

More directly affecting preservation efforts, Title VI of the Demonstration Cities and Metropolitan Development Act amended the 1954 law to require "recognition of historic and architectural preservation in urban renewal plans and to authorize preservation activities and planning therefor as eligible project costs." This meant that financing could now include the acquisition and restoration of properties, their relocation inside or outside the project area and "disposition of preserved properties for use in accordance with renewal plans." Title VI also authorized grants-in-aid to local public bodies for expenditures in connection with historic and archaeological preservation.

To the Housing Act of 1961, which authorized the Open Space Land Program, the 1966 law added the Section 709 Program designed specifically for historic preservation. Grants covering up to 50 percent of the cost of a project were made available to state and local public bodies to acquire title or permanent interest in historic properties and to restore and improve them for public use and benefit, whether or not they were located in urban renewal areas. To be eligible for such grants, the properties had to meet criteria comparable to those for inclusion in the National Register.

The 1966 legislation brought the federal government firmly into the preservation field, enabling it to actively initiate and develop broad programs that could have a national impact. The criteria set forth by the government for financial assistance could aid in the effort to raise the standards for preservation to a professional level. Moreover, as the coordinator of related programs on all levels, the federal government could plan programs and adopt policies that would protect the nation's total resources, both natural and cultural. In the development of this legislative breakthrough, the Trust saw the culmination of years of work. It also saw a new beginning and a new challenge.

PART TWO

1966-73

Ghirardelli Square, San Francisco, Calif. An architecturally and financially successful example in the 1960s of adaptive use of a factory in a deteriorated waterfront area as a shopping center. (Lawrence Halprin & Associates)

Mountain Gap School, Leesburg, Va. Part of the Oatlands Historic District, established in 1973 for environmental protection of the area. A property of the National Trust. (Thomas Slade)

CHAPTER FOUR

Toward a Total Environment

Developments in the preservation movement in the years after the 1963 Williamsburg meeting made a reassessment of preservation philosophy and methods necessary. Though the full impact of the 1966 legislation could not be predicted immediately, the passage of the new laws called for basic changes in the movement. Experience in preservation projects had resulted in improved techniques, rendering others obsolete. The growing public consciousness of the national heritage, in terms of natural as well as cultural resources, was increasing the ranks of potential preservationists. Moreover, those who would be directing the new and the expanded federal programs needed a coherent, comprehensive and up-to-date view of the state of preservation in the United States.

Consequently, in March 1967 the National Trust and Colonial Williamsburg sponsored the Williamsburg Workshop II, a follow-up to the 1963 Williamsburg Seminar on Preservation and Restoration, for the purpose of revising the principles and guidelines that the 1963 conferees had approved and that had been published in *Historic Preservation Today*. The 50 leading preservationists who met at the second Williamsburg conference were assigned to work on four panels: Objectives and Scope of the Preservation Movement, chaired by Ronald F. Lee; Survey, Evaluation and Registration, headed by Carl Feiss; Planning for Preservation, led by Charles van Ravenswaay; and Education and Training for Restoration Work, chaired by Walter Muir Whitehill.

The Objectives and Scope panel noted the beginnings of a fundamental change in thinking about preservation: No longer was preservation simply a concern about isolated buildings destined for use as museums. People were now searching for ways to continue the useful lives of old and historic buildings, regarding them as integral parts of the community. This concept reflected the growth of the idea that the environment should be regarded—and protected—in its totality. Moreover, the panelists commented that the concern for this total environment was being shared all over the world.

The panel observed that the leadership of the preservation movement was growing, too. The federal and state governments were now partners in long-range planning and programs. However, the burden of implementation still rested on the private sector. The 1966 legislation had increased the responsibility of those with previous experience in preservation to teach, guide, inspire and encourage new preservation action. For the private sector, the panel defined three specific tasks: to initiate cooperative programs with all levels of government, to make documentation and archives available to the public and to see that private interpretive programs were worthy of emulation and that the roles filled and services offered by various private preservation groups were well defined in order to avoid the duplication of efforts.

For professional organizations in fields related to preservation, such as architecture, law, engineering, planning, history, archaeology and landscape architecture, the panel defined special contributions: to take supportive positions in preservation programs, to see that the highest professional standards were maintained and to initiate preservation training programs. To the Trust, the panel issued a charge to continue the high caliber of its leadership, especially in its program of educating and informing public officials at all levels of government, for it is public officials, said the panel, who make the day-to-day decisions that benefit or hinder preservation efforts.

The three other panels provided "how-to" guidelines for the actual work of preservation. The Planning for Preservation panel emphasized that buildings should not be considered only as isolated structures but rather as living components of neighborhoods. It also reiterated the preservationist credo that a building of contemporary style, if designed in sympathy with surrounding structures, is generally preferable to a reproduction of an older style. Successful preservation and planning could be accomplished, the panel noted, only if undertaken in terms of the total context of each building, the total context including such factors as surrounding buildings, open space, gardens, streets, parking facilities and scenic amenities.

The Survey panel dealt primarily with additions to the National Register and stressed the need for guidelines for surveying and documenting historic buildings. It also stressed the need to develop the use of computers and archival retrieval systems to deal with the vast amount of data that it was anticipated would be collected in the years ahead. The panel especially urged that additions or nominations to the National Register be well publicized so that, in addition to Advisory Council review of federally funded or licensed projects, the force of public opinion would also give some protection to those historic places that were threatened by state funded projects.

From the Education panel came suggestions for fostering public concern and influencing public opinion about preservation. Commending the communications programs of the Trust, it urged the adaptation of such programs at local levels. Significantly, the discussions of the Education panel led to a special study on education and professional training needs, sponsored by the Ford Foundation. (A more detailed discussion on the work and findings of this special committee is included in chapter 7.)

The priorities and directions mapped out at the second Williamsburg meeting were approved by the Trust membership at a special meeting in May 1967 and were published the following year under the title *Historic Preservation Tomorrow*. Gordon Gray ranked the work with the 1966 federal legislation and referred to the new priorities as "guiding lights" for the future of the preservation movement. The guidelines, revised at the Williamsburg workshop, both reflected and influenced new goals being formulated at this time by Trust departments.

In addition to helping implement these new priorities and directions, the Trust was also facing responsibilities and opportunities that extended beyond its former sphere of influence. Because of its position as a national leader of private preservationists, the Trust was designated to serve as the only official statutory representative of private preservation to the Advisory Council on Historic Preservation. This put the Trust in a position to share in the formulation of policy on the federal level. This action was important, for it was anticipated that federal decisions concerning preservation would have a tremendous impact on the field, just as federal decisions on other matters greatly influence other fields. Though the essential work of preservation would continue to be done on the local level, in towns and neighborhoods, policy decisions would come from the top. Preservation victories and defeats now would be viewed in a national context.

The Advisory Council began functioning in March 1967 when 10 citizen members were named by President Lyndon B. Johnson: S.K. Stevens, executive director of the Pennsylvania Historical and Museum Commission, who was named council chairman; former Congressman Albert Rains, president of the Alabama Historical Society and chairman of the Special Committee on Historic Preservation; Harold L. Kennedy, a lawyer and member of the Texas State Historical Society; Lawrence Halprin, San Francisco planner and landscape architect; Mrs. Ernest Ives of Springfield, Ill., leader of a drive to save the Illinois governor's mansion; Russell W. Fridley, president of the American Association for State and Local History and director of the Minnesota Historical Society; Richard D. Daugherty, professor of anthropology, Washington State University; Christopher Tunnard, professor of city planning and chairman of the Department of City Planning, Yale University; Joseph

B. Cummings, chairman of the Georgia State Historical Commission; and John A. May, chief of the Division of Outdoor Recreation and Wildlife, South Carolina Wildlife Resources Department.

Ex-officio members were the secretaries of the Interior, the Treasury, Commerce and Housing and Urban Development; the Attorney General; the administrator of the General Services Administration; and the chairman of the National Trust Board of Trustees.

At its first meeting in July 1967, the council voted to add three ex-officio members whose concerns were vitally linked with preservation: the secretaries of Transportation and Agriculture and the secretary of the Smithsonian Institution. Among other items of organizational business, the council also voted to recommend to Congress and the President that the United States become a member of the International Centre for the Study of the Preservation and the Restoration of Cultural Property, better known then as the Rome Centre.

In August 1967 Robert R. Garvey, Jr., who had been appointed executive secretary of the Advisory Council, was replaced as Trust executive director by Joseph Prendergast, former executive vice president of the National Recreation and Parks Association. At the 1967 annual meeting, the Board of Trustees moved to strengthen the executive leadership of the Trust by naming James Biddle president of the Trust. Biddle, a preservationist and scholar of American history and art, came to the Trust from the Metropolitan Museum of Art in New York City where he had served since 1955, becoming curator of the American Wing in 1963. He had also been treasurer of Olana Preservation, Inc., the organization that saved painter Frederic Edwin Church's residence overlooking the Hudson River; secretary of the Trust's Lyndhurst Council; and an adviser to the White House Fine Arts Committee headed by First Lady Mrs. John F. Kennedy.

In February 1968 the Advisory Council met in regular session in Washington, D.C., to review its first case: a proposed grant from the U.S. Department of Health, Education and Welfare to Georgetown University for the purpose of erecting a tower for its heating and cooling plant. Since the campus lies within the Georgetown Historic District, the council was asked to comment. It began its deliberations by enunciating some basic principles about new construction, which echoed the conclusions of the 1967 Williamsburg conference. Deciding that structures must be considered in their total environment and not as isolated objects, the council declared that any impact made by a new building should improve its surroundings, especially in relation to a landmark, a park or an open space. Effects on traffic and any disturbance of the terrain, hazards involved in any construction projects, were other essential factors the council said it would consider in its rulings. It commented that in general new buildings should be kept together; however, when clustering was impossible, the design of new structures should be harmonious with the surrounding older structures in scale, texture, color and material. Imitation of archaic styles was vigorously discouraged. After consultation with the council, university officials offered to place the tower on another, more secluded, site, which the council found acceptable.

Later in the year, these general principles were refined and made more specific. They were adopted as the council's "criteria for effect."

> A federally financed or licensed undertaking shall be considered to
> have an effect on a National Register listing when any condition
> of the undertaking creates a change in the quality of the historical,
> architectural, archeological or cultural character that qualified
> the property . . . for listing in the National Register.

According to the criteria, an adverse effect was created when conditions "including but not limited to the following" occurred: "destruction or alteration of all or part of a property; isolation from or alteration of its surrounding environment; introduction of visual, audible, or atmospheric elements that are out of character with the property and its setting."

In addition to the work of the Advisory Council, other preservation activities, on both federal and state levels, got under way in 1968. A nationwide series of eight preservation conferences was sponsored by the National Park Service. At these meetings, state liaison officers and Park Service representatives and regional directors presented progress reports and discussed ways of implementing the National Historic Preservation Act. At the Park Service conference in Richmond, Va., Trust representatives joined in discussions with other participants from a wide range of related organizations, including the Society of Architectural Historians, the American Society of Civil Engineers, the American Association for State and Local History, the American Institute of Architects, the Garden Clubs of America, the American Institute of Planners, the Society for American Archaeology and the American Society of Landscape Architects.

For the programs outlined in the National Historic Preservation Act of 1966, Congress had authorized $2 million for fiscal year 1967, with $10 million each year for the following three years—a total funding of $32 million. Since grants provided by the act had to be matched, however, no requests and no appropriations had been made for 1967. In 1968, although the President's budget request for the historic preservation programs of the National Park Service was $2.3 million, Congress appropriated only $770,000. Of this sum the National Trust received

$300,000, which it used for technical assistance, educational programs and maintenance and development of its historic properties.

In the meantime, many states, with the guidance and encouragement of the Trust, took advantage of the historic preservation programs offered by other federal agencies. Shakertown, a historic 19th-century religious community in Pleasant Hill, Ky., was restored with aid from a program administered by the Office of Technical Assistance within the Economic Development Administration, an agency of the U.S. Department of Commerce. The program, authorized by the Public Works and Economic Development Act of 1965, provided assistance to community activities that would create jobs in economically depressed areas. By 1968, 285 new jobs were created in Shakertown, and by 1973 the operating farm, exhibition area and conference center at Pleasant Hill had attracted 233,000 visitors. With a gross income of more than $1 million and a payroll of $520,000, the historic village is virtually a new industry, having taken its community off the list of economically depressed areas.

In 1968 states also took advantage of the historic preservation programs of the U.S. Department of Housing and Urban Development. Under the Open Space Land Program, 15 historic sites, covering more than 4,000 acres, were supported by grants totaling nearly $2.8 million. Ipswich, Mass., received a 1968 urban renewal demonstration grant for a pilot study of the feasibility of using facade easements to protect historic structures. The use of this legal device was determined to be a successful method of protecting the exterior details of a structure from alteration. By 1973 the comprehensive report on the use of facade easements, prepared under the direction of the Ipswich Historical Commission, was in final draft stage, tentatively titled *Something of Value.*

In the fall of 1968, the first grant from the HUD Section 709 Program, which authorized matching grants to local public bodies for the acquisition and restoration of historic properties, was given for the preservation of the Shirley-Eustis House, which is located in a blighted area of Roxbury, Mass. The house, built in 1747, is both architecturally and historically significant. Originally known as Shirley Place, it was among the most formal and imposing Georgian-period houses built in New England. Its builder was William Shirley, who was royal governor of Massachusetts from 1741 to 1756. In 1819, after being used by American forces as a barracks and hospital during the seige of Boston, the house was purchased by Dr. William Eustis, a surgeon in the Revolutionary War. Dr. Eustis also directed the affairs of Massachusetts; he was twice elected governor of the commonwealth.

Submission of the grant application to HUD had been prompted by the Shirley-Eustis Association, a private preservation group that owned the house. Since the HUD program was limited to public agencies, the association formed a three-way partnership with the Massachusetts Historical Commission and the commonwealth of Massachusetts. Through a cooperative effort, funds were raised to match the grant. Although hopes for using the rehabilitated Shirley-Eustis House as a neighborhood center have not yet been realized, the partnership plan provided an example of cooperation for other communities, and many projects were executed under the Section 709 Program.

In contrast, developments at the U.S. Department of Transportation were discouraging. Under section 4(f) of the Transportation Act of 1966 (Public Law 89-670), the Secretary of Transportation could suggest alternatives to transportation plans and projects that endangered places of historical significance, open spaces and wildlife refuges. Preservationists, who were not against highway construction but rather supported careful planning, had counted on this provision to help protect the cultural as well as the natural environment. In July 1968 a proposed amendment to the Federal-Aid Highway Act (H.R. 17134) threatened to greatly reduce this authority.

Though interpretation of the proposed amendment varied, one obvious exclusion from protection was privately owned land, natural areas such as those owned by the Nature Conservancy and the Audubon Society. Other sections of the bill cut back beautification and billboard control programs, as well as adding 1,500 miles to the 41,000 miles of interstate highway system already authorized. The main issue, however, was the question of who had final authority on highway locations, the Secretary of Transportation or state and local officials. Congress was inclined to leave the final decision to local officials, making no provision that feasible alternatives would be considered.

The Trust and other preservationists sounded the alarm across the country, but efforts to block passage of a revised version of the proposed amendment failed. Backed by highway lobbyists, the Federal-Aid Highway Act of 1968 (Public Law 90-495) was passed by Congress in late July. Both as an independent agency and as a member of the Advisory Council, the Trust joined with the National Wildlife Federation, the American Institute of Architects and the Audubon Society to urge President Lyndon B. Johnson to withhold his support. The President believed that the positive features of the bill warranted his signature, but he urged Congress to correct drawbacks in the legislation, such as the withdrawal of billboard control provisions. He also recommended that the protection of parkland be reassured and that the construction of the additional 1,500 miles of highway be preceded by a careful study of long-range transportation needs of the nation. Despite these provisions, editorials around the country decried the victory of "pork

Christmas card from the Conservation Trust of Puerto Rico, 1972, depicts an ancient tradition of children picking grass for the Three Kings—in a modern setting. (Irene and Jack Delano)

barrel" highway lobbies. A *New York Times* editorial on November 21, 1968, stated, "The bureaucrats and contractors have run the highway program too long as their private domain."

Because of the continuing outcry, the cause stayed alive; preservationists and conservationists joined forces to protest the action. Ultimately, the Federal Highway Administration of the U.S. Department of Transportation released new proposed regulations that would insure full public participation in the development of federal highway projects. The new proposals required that two public hearings be held, one before route location decisions had been made, the other prior to highway design approval. It also called upon state agencies to fully consider a wide range of factors—social, economic and environmental—in determining highway location and design. Among matters to be explored at the public hearings would be alternative means of transportation, such as rapid transit. According to the proposal, appeals could be made to the Federal Highway Administration by "any interested person."

During hearings on the proposed regulations, Trust president James Biddle read a few of the 125 letters Trust member organizations had sent in support of the dual hearing system. Stressing the need to preserve the total environment, he called the plan "a way to give the people right-of-way in this domain, which they pay for, own, but do not control."

The governors of all 50 states, however, opposed the appeals procedure, protesting the legal entanglements that would result from imposing federal procedures on extant state highway planning procedures. In the highway regulations filed in January 1969, the Federal Highway Administration solicited suggestions for an alternative appeals system that would not delay "needed highway construction." The proposals concerning alternative means of transportation were deleted on the basis that such considerations should be dealt with earlier in the planning stage. In their final form, the regulations merely required state highway departments to hold public hearings and to consider impact factors. Predictably, on this list of factors, "fast, safe, efficient transportation" was given first priority; the protection of natural and historic landmarks was number 14 on the list.

By 1969 noteworthy progress had been made in the states. Twenty had passed legislation setting up agencies and naming representatives to coordinate their participation in the National Park Service matching grant program; eight others had drafted legislation. In addition, 144 municipalities had created historic districts. New Jersey, Ohio, Rhode Island and Maine had set up historic sites commissions. Maryland, New Mexico, Washington, Tennessee, the Virgin Islands and Virginia had established state registers of historic sites, and Washington had also created a state advisory council, patterned after the national Advisory Council. Other states chose to work through existing agencies or commissions. Together the states could muster nearly $1 million in funds to match the federal grants. However, the total appropriation for the historic preservation programs of the National Park Service in fiscal year 1969 was only $570,000. Funds for grants to the Trust and the states totaled $100,000, with the Trust receiving $17,500.

Of the $32 million authorized for federal preservation programs in 1966, only $1.34 million had been appropriated by 1969. A representative of the National Commission on Urban Renewal Problems, reporting to the Douglas Commission on Housing in the United States, agreed with preservationists that their programs had indeed been "pitifully funded." It was clear that the states would have to develop a collective political force if the funding were to increase.

Despite the cooperative preservation programs made possible by the various HUD grant programs, urban renewal continued to be a serious threat to historic buildings. At the heart of the conflict was the question of whether or not the National Historic Preservation Act of 1966 applied retroactively. Half of all urban renewal projects had been initiated before 1966; thus, if the act were not retroactive, losses would be unavoidable. Preservationists would be forced to stand by, legally powerless, while historic structures were razed.

In 1969 the Grand Rapids, Mich., City Hall, an 1888 Victorian Gothic structure, was scheduled for demolition in an urban renewal plan that had been approved in 1964. In June, however, the building was listed in the National Register of Historic Places. Citizens rallied to find an alternative use or to obtain an amendment to the urban renewal plan. When developers refused to change their plans, the 500 Citizens to Save City Hall requested a stay of demolition. Denied this, they sought an injunction, only to find the court ruling that because they had claimed no injury at the inception of the urban renewal plan, they had no legal standing. By November the structure had been razed. (Although the Michigan decision held that the act was not retroactive, decisions since then involving HUD plans approved before 1966 allow for some degree of federal control, and therefore some input by preservationists.)

One bright spot for preservationists in 1969 was the outcome of a conflict in the New Orleans Vieux Carré Historic District. The decision represented a significant victory for the Advisory Council on Historic Preservation. The need for a roadway parallel to the waterfront had been recognized by city officials in 1927, and through the years various plans had been submitted to the New Orleans city council.

In February 1967 when it was announced that a six-lane expressway would be built, protest was widespread. The Trust membership voted

*City Hall, Grand Rapids, Mich., demolished in an urban renewal project,
November 1969. (John Milhaupt and Mike Dabakey)*

that year at the annual meeting to oppose the plan, and the Italian counterpart of the Trust, Italia Nostra, wrote to the New Orleans city council expressing its concern.

Moreover, because the entire district had been designated a National Historic Landmark in 1965, it thereby came under the review jurisdiction of the Advisory Council, even though the city of New Orleans had elected not to accept the designation certificate. In March 1969, members of the Advisory Council, including Gordon Gray, and James Biddle traveled to New Orleans to meet in special session with preservationists in that city. Among them was Martha Gilmore Robinson, winner of the 1963 Crowninshield Award for her leadership of preservation activities throughout the country, especially in her home state of Louisiana, and abroad in England, Ireland and Italy.

After its New Orleans deliberations, the Advisory Council decided that none of the five highway designs under consideration was acceptable according to its "criteria for effect." Therefore, it recommended to Secretary of Transportation John A. Volpe that the roadway be relocated. The council further suggested the adoption of a depressed design.

After several tense months, preservationists were pleased when, in August, Secretary Volpe announced that he was barring funds for the expressway on the grounds that the Vieux Carré Historic District would be damaged by all five proposals. Instead, he approved a plan whereby a 3.4-mile segment of Interstate 310 would be rerouted to complete a beltway around the city, with 90 percent of the total cost ($90 million) paid by federal funds. Especially encouraging to the council, the Trust and other preservationists were Volpe's remarks at the time of the announced change. He wrote to the chairman of the Advisory Council,

> We appreciate the Council's assistance in the consideration of this extremely complex issue. It is of vital importance that, insofar as feasible, our transportation programs be designed to accomplish their essential public service missions in a manner compatible with the preservation of historic sites and other environmental values. I am highly gratified that in this instance a reasonable compromise could be found which accords fully with the views of the Council.

Although the power of the Advisory Council still lay solely in its moral persuasiveness, Volpe's decision demonstrated the effectiveness of the council, and preservationists everywhere celebrated the victory in New Orleans.

In 1969 the Trust was called on in congressional hearings to offer testimony on two pieces of proposed legislation of importance to preservation: the Tax Reform Bill and a proposal to alter the U.S. Capitol.

United States Capitol, Washington, D.C. West Front. (National Trust)

The Tax Reform Bill contained a gift tax provision that would have drastically altered the tax treatment of those who donate paintings, sculptures and other items (such as furnishings) to museums, libraries and historic preservation organizations. Since 1917 private support of such institutions had been encouraged by allowing donors an income tax deduction equal to the fair market value of the items without also requiring the payment of capital gains tax on any increased value. Under H.R. 13270, however, a donor would have been required to claim a capital gain or to deduct only the amount that was originally paid for the item. Although full deduction still would be permitted on historic houses and securities for their maintenance, the bill made no provision for the contents of such houses. Thus affected, the Trust joined with the College Art Association and the Association of Art Museum Directors in successfully opposing the bill.

The extension of the U.S. Capitol building threatened to become the second scene of the preservationists' nightmare begun in 1955. As early as 1904, Senators and Representatives had commissioned a study of the need for more space in the Capitol, and subsequently built separate office buildings. But no action to expand the Capitol itself was taken until 1955. That year Congress authorized a House-Senate commission headed by Speaker of the House Sam Rayburn to carry out a $10.1

million extension of the East Front of the Capitol to provide additional office space for Senators and Representatives and to repair the overhang of the Capitol dome.

However, for aesthetic and historical reasons, preservationists and others believed the earliest part of the building deserved preservation. William Thornton's design for the Capitol had been approved by George Washington and Thomas Jefferson, and the first President had laid the cornerstone. Completed in 1827, the structure was the work of three architectural geniuses: Thornton, Benjamin Henry Latrobe and Charles Bulfinch. It had served as the background for every inauguration since Andrew Jackson's. When in 1863 a large cast-iron dome designed by Thomas U. Walter replaced the smaller original wooden dome, the West Front could accommodate it, but there was an overhang on the East Front. The effect of the foreshortened base was considered an architectural mistake by some and unique and pleasing by others.

Preservationists rallied to oppose the extension. They were joined by others who opposed spending the approximately $200 per square foot it was estimated the work would cost. *Architectural Forum* magazine reckoned this to be "four times the costliest work space ever erected." In January 1956 a Committee to Preserve the National Capitol was formed, including among its members Trustee Gen. U.S. Grant, III, and then Trust president Richard H. Howland. Other organizations, such as the American Institute of Architects and the Society of Architectural Historians, also opposed the plan, which Frank Lloyd Wright called "profane."

Despite the outcry from private citizens and professional organizations and congressional proposals to block the extension bill or to provide alternatives, the plan was rushed through Congress. Dismantling began in September 1958, and the extension, constructed of marble instead of the original sandstone, was completed by Inauguration Day 1961. The cost was approximately $17 million.

A similar proposal to extend the West Front was defeated in 1966. However, the National Historic Preservation Act passed that same year specifically did not include the White House, the Supreme Court building, the Capitol and related buildings and their surroundings in the new federal historic preservation programs. Thus, the Capitol is subject to further proposals for extension. By law, the fate of the Capitol and its grounds is in the hands of Congress and the Architect of the Capitol. In September 1969 another proposal to extend the West Front came from lawmakers; it was approved by the House of Representatives. Board of Trustees chairman Gordon Gray immediately registered Trust opposition to the proposal with the Senate Appropriations Committee, recommending instead that the sole remaining original portion of the

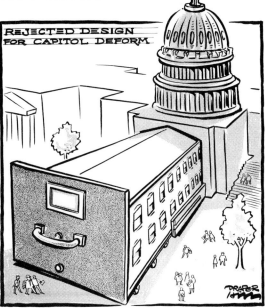

REJECTED DESIGN
FOR CAPITOL DEFORM

"Westward No!"
Cartoon by Draper Hill.
(Preservation News,
February 1971)

facade be restored. Deterioration of the West Front was serious, he admitted, but restoration could solve the problem, as well as preserving the 19th-century west terrace designed by famed landscape architect Frederick Law Olmsted, which would also be lost if the structure were extended.

Gray's testimony and the pressure exerted by now more politically sophisticated preservationists bore fruit. In November the Senate denied funds for an extension, supporting instead a $250,000 National Park Service study on the feasibility of restoring the West Front. The independent study pronounced the West Front restorable for $15 million (as opposed to $60 million for new construction).

Despite this finding, a joint congressional commission in 1972 again approved plans for an 80-foot extension. In doing so, they ignored not only the engineering study but also the fact that the West Front, which they had declared "in danger of collapse," had weathered a major bomb blast in the turbulent spring of 1971. Public outcry against the extension was immediate, and the Senate again voted to deny funds.

In November 1972 a report on masonry consolidation methods, prepared by the Rome Centre at the request of the Architect of the Capitol, was submitted. The result of consultation by international experts, the report recommended injecting cement and epoxy resin into the rubble core to stabilize the West Front walls.

In April 1973, however, the House of Representatives bypassed the study and voted again for the extension. Opposing preservationists pointed out that millions of dollars could be saved by restoring the facade. The American Institute of Architects, which had called for a master plan of the Capitol Hill area so that design alternatives could be considered, proposed the construction of an underground building on the south side of the Capitol. Such a facility would offer at least as much space as the proposed extension, be closer to the floor of the House chamber, cost 25 percent less than extension and preserve the striking visual effect of the dome. Five months after the House action, the Senate voted unanimously against the extension. Instead, Senators authorized the expenditure of $18 million to restore the existing West Front, $15 million to construct underground offices and $300,000 to prepare a master plan for Capitol Hill. This action, it was pointed out, would save $30 million and provide the House of Representatives with three times the additional office space that would have been gained with the extension, at one-seventh the cost per square foot. The problem remains unresolved.

The battle over the extension of the West Front of the Capitol proved that developing "political heft," as one government official had put it, was important in the campaign to save the country's heritage, including both its built and natural resources. Preservationists and conservationists alike were concerned with developing this kind of influence, for the two groups faced similar problems. Until the passage of the 1966 legislation, the preservation of landmarks, similar to the protection of the natural environment, had been largely dependent on the force of public opinion. The Trust, as the national private preservation organization, for many years pointed out the urgent necessity for making common cause with conservationists in order to develop a voice in decision making and to save the total environment from destruction. In one of his first acts as Trust president, James Biddle had flown to Honolulu to testify in hearings concerning highrise development on Diamond Head Crater. The Trust had also helped in attempts to save many natural areas, including Storm King Mountain in New York State and Piscataway Park, a part of the Mount Vernon Overlook on the Maryland shore.

Ironically, the growing concern for the natural environment, to which preservationists had contributed their support, gave rise to a reaction against the built environment. Horror stories of pollution and waste fostered outrage at what man had done to the delicate balance of nature, and some equated all built creations with evil. This kind of thinking, while not extensive, slowed public realization that the "cultural ecology" had to be saved as well. The Trust and the entire preservation community were forced to double their efforts, constantly reiterating the message, People do more than survive—they create.

Diamond Head Crater, Waikiki, Hawaii. Threatened with highrise development in 1968. (National Trust)

As a member of the Advisory Council, the Trust was able to participate in the design of the National Environmental Policy Act, passed by Congress in late 1969. On the first day of 1970, President Richard Nixon signed the bill into law, declaring it a national policy to encourage productive and enjoyable harmony between citizens and their environment. The act established within the Office of the President a Council on Environmental Quality, charged to study the condition of the nation's environment, to develop new environmental programs and policies, to coordinate all previously established federal environmental efforts and to advise the President on solutions to major environmental problems. In addition, the council was given the responsibility for seeing that all federal activities took environmental considerations into account.

To insure that federal decision making was based as much on environmental values as on economic and technological considerations, the law required each federal agency to prepare a detailed environmental impact statement to be made public in advance of any activity that would significantly affect the quality of the environment. Moreover, it required that in preparing each statement the federal agency planning to implement the activity would consult with any other agency (state and local, as well as federal) having jurisdiction by law over the area to be affected or having special expertise in the field involved. Included in the areas of possible impact were historic and archaeological sites, and the Advisory Council on Historic Preservation was designated as one of two agencies to receive and comment on such statements.

In 1969 the National Historic Preservation Act of 1966 came before Congress for funding reauthorization. Throughout January and February 1970, Gordon Gray and James Biddle testified in behalf of the Trust at public hearings of the appropriate House subcommittees, in support of the reauthorization and of the National Park Service appropriation. They asked Congress to "sustain the momentum" of the current historic preservation efforts. They were joined this time by representatives from states actively supporting preservation, including the state liaison officers, who organized as a group in 1967.

As the bill was first introduced, only $11 million would have been available over a six-year funding period. Therefore, amendments were made to reestablish the pattern of funding set forth in the original 1966 legislation. Under the amended bill, historic preservation programs would be funded for three years; $7 million would be authorized for the first year (1971), $10 million for the second and $15 million the third, for a total of $32 million. Thus, it was possible that the President's 1971 budget request of $6.95 million for historic preservation programs of the U.S. Department of the Interior would be covered. Past experience, however, made full funding seem doubtful. By this time, only $2.99 million—or less than one-tenth of the original $32 million authorized under the 1966 act—had been appropriated.

However, the new funding authorization, with its attendant provisions for an increase in the size of the Advisory Council and continued membership for the United States in the Rome Centre, was passed by Congress and signed into law in May 1970. For fiscal year 1971, the House approved appropriations for Interior Department preservation programs in the amount of $6.81 million. By the time the appropriations were approved by the Senate in August, the amount had been reduced further. Still, $5.9 million was available to the Trust and the states, the largest appropriation yet received for historic preservation.

The significance of United States membership in the Rome Centre lay in the educational benefits of such an international affiliation and in the cooperative ventures it made possible. To implement participation in the centre and to coordinate future activities, a standing committee was appointed by the Advisory Council. The committee consisted of 18 delegates from preservation and related fields and three ex-officio members—the director of the National Park Service, the chairman of the Trust Board of Trustees and the secretary of the Smithsonian Institution, who was named committee chairman. In its initial meeting on February 3, 1971, the standing committee recommended sending a United States delegation to the 6th General Assembly of the Rome Centre in April of that year. The Advisory Council agreed and a delegation was formed. It included the chief of the Office of Archeology and Historic Preservation, National Park Service; the chairman of the American Group, International Institute for Conservation of Historic and Artistic Works; representatives of Congress; and Mrs. W. Randolph Burgess, former National Trust Trustee and member of the United States Commission for UNESCO.

The idea that preservation was an international concern was further reflected by President Nixon's Special Message to Congress Proposing the 1971 Environmental Program, delivered in February. In the message, he proposed the creation of a World Heritage Trust by which international protection could be provided for the cultural heritage of all nations. The plan called for the establishment of an inventory of the resources in each country and the passage of appropriate protective legislation. The legislation would respect the sovereignty of each country, yet it would protect the common heritage. A convention to establish the World Heritage Trust was included as one of the proposals presented at the United Nations Conference on the Human Environment in Stockholm the following year, and the convention was passed by the delegates. A World Heritage Committee was then set up to review and aid endangered international sites and to establish a fund for this work. (The convention entered its ratification period in early 1973, and in December 1973 the United States was the first nation to ratify it.)

The President's environmental quality message also focused attention on the need for a national land use policy, so that haphazard development, which had produced suburban sprawl and center-city blight, might be avoided in the future by careful planning. Preservation was listed in the message as a major environmental factor in land use decisions, with historic preservation districts regarded as "areas of critical environmental concern." Several other specific proposals also were addressed to saving historic structures: Among them was the creation of tax incentives to encourage the restoration of historic buildings. Also suggested was a change in the policy affecting the transfer of surplus federal historic landmarks to state and local governments, allowing the properties to be used for revenue-producing purposes and leased to private developers for adaptive uses. Formerly, the structures could be maintained only for museums and other public purposes, such as education, health or recreation. In addition, the President called for a "Legacy of Parks," the expansion of park areas and open spaces under programs of the U.S. Department of Housing and Urban Development and the National Park Service.

Although contingent on the introduction of specific legislation in Congress, such proposals gave preservationists reason to anticipate a major development, for the President had stated, "I am taking action to insure that no Federally-owned property is demolished until its historic significance has first been reviewed." On May 13, 1971, the hopes of preservationists for such a mandate were rewarded. Executive Order 11593, officially titled The Protection and Enhancement of the Cultural Environment, made historic preservation an explicit mission of every federal agency by calling on each agency to locate, inventory and nominate to the National Register all federal properties of historical value administered by the agency. This was to be done by July 1, 1973. It was estimated that the executive order would affect approximately 2,000 unrecorded properties, many of them at military installations, in addition to thousands of archaeological sites. Agencies were warned that in the interim they should not inadvertently transfer, sell, demolish or alter any property of possible historical significance.

To properly implement the executive order, agency heads were to work in cooperation with the Secretary of the Interior, the Advisory Council and state historic preservation officers. Each agency was required to make records of any properties that were to be altered or demolished and to maintain all properties of possible historical significance at professional standards, submitting annual maintenance plans to the Secretary of the Interior beginning in January 1972. The long-range importance of the executive order was obvious: It called for a formal recognition of historic preservation as a national priority and afforded essentially the same protection to not-yet-listed federal properties as the National Historic Preservation Act of 1966 afforded to structures and sites in the National Register. As a result of the President's action, all federal agencies were now officially directed to view problems and make decisions in light of preservation considerations. The order also strengthened the review powers of the Advisory Council over both federal and nonfederal plans affecting federal historic properties.

While progress continued on the federal level, a major preservation conflict was developing in Chicago. The situation renewed preservationists' realization that preservation battles would not cease. The conflict arose in February 1970, when the Chicago Commission on Historical and Architectural Landmarks was notified that highrise developers were planning to demolish the Stock Exchange Building. The exchange

Main streets in American small towns are areas of critical environmental concern. This Madison, Ind., main street, with the Jefferson County Court- house in the background, is part of the Madison Historic District. The Down- town Restoration Committee, comprising Historic Madison, Inc., local merchants and the chamber of commerce, is studying methods of developing more sympathetic design of signage within the district. (Mark Chester)

was one of the first modern skyscrapers and was designed by Dankmar Adler and Louis Sullivan, leading architects of the Chicago school of architecture. After nearly 80 years as an office building, it was still in good condition and had a high occupancy rate. In contrast to the 43-story building that was proposed, the 13 floors of the Stock Exchange left a potential 27 stories of money-making space unused. The commission had recommended that the building be designated a landmark under the new city preservation ordinance, thereby protecting it from demolition or alteration. This provision, with its design control restrictions and tax burdens, made the owners of the Stock Exchange unwilling to accept such a designation.

By August 1970 the original developers sold their interest in the Stock Exchange, and preservation of the building continued to be doubtful, for the new owners planned to erect a $45 million office building on the site. When the Committee on Cultural and Economic Development, a part of the Chicago City Council, was asked to consider the designation of the building as a landmark, a move opposed by the owners of the exchange, the committee decided that Chicago could not "afford" another landmark. The committee placed the cost of rehabilitation at a formidable $16 million. The preservationists' suggestion that development rights might be transferred was dismissed as pure conjecture.

At this time, although the feasibility of using the transfer of development rights as a means to protect landmarks had yet to be fully evaluated, the concept had been in use in New York City for more than five years. (The New York City program permits owners of historic buildings, which do not usually reach the maximum height allowance for an area, to sell the unused development rights on their property to owners of adjacent lots. An adjacent lot is defined as one that is contiguous to or across a street or intersection from a landmark lot; it may also be one of a series of lots that connect with the landmark, provided that all of these lots are in single ownership. A lot owner may then use the development rights to erect on the property a structure that is taller than the height the city normally would allow for a building on that property. The additional height permitted is based on how much of the unused development rights the owner of the adjacent lot has acquired.) Basically, the transfer of development rights program is designed to balance the economic burden of preserving a historic structure in an area where more extensive development is permitted with the additional income expected from a new structure that has been permitted to exceed certain zoning limitations. Preservationists were hopeful that such a plan could be adapted for use in Chicago.

In September the Chicago City Council voted to deny landmark status to the Stock Exchange. One dissenting member, however, filed a minority report, charging that the council had misinterpreted the city preservation ordinance, that it had not thoroughly studied rehabilitation costs and that it had failed to investigate the transfer of development rights proposal adequately. Within a month, the Chicago Chapter of the American Institute of Architects mobilized to help save the building, and the Art Institute of Chicago sponsored a special exhibit featuring the Stock Exchange.

By July 1971 support in the Illinois legislature was strong for enacting legislation that would have made it possible for Chicago to use the transfer method, and the state congressional delegation requested comment on the matter from the Advisory Council on Historic Preservation. Despite the fact that the jurisdiction of the Advisory Council is federal in scope, the council agreed to comment on the grounds that, as a final major work of influential architects and as an example of a uniquely American architectural form, the Stock Exchange was of national significance. While landmark designation was being restudied by the Chicago City Council, the Advisory Council formed a special task force, including Trust representatives, to explore ways and means of continuing the Stock Exchange's use. Upon completion of the task force study, the Advisory Council recommended that the building be maintained for its original purpose—office space—and that plans for its preservation include restrictive easements to protect such design features as the facade, the Exchange Room and ornamentation designs in the lobby and corridor. Offering to assist the special committee appointed by Chicago Mayor Richard J. Daley to study methods of preserving and reusing the building, the Advisory Council further suggested that a thorough economic feasibility study be conducted to analyze possible variations of zoning laws and other ways of making the Stock Exchange economically attractive to developers.

Meanwhile, preservationists, working against time and the owners' application for a permit to demolish, persuaded a Chicago development firm to investigate reuse of the Stock Exchange. The firm agreed in late summer to conduct its own study to find means of restoring and redeveloping the building. Preservationists, cheered by this turn of events, waited. However, when the report was completed, the company found the cost of restoration to be beyond its means. Again, it appeared that the desire to maintain beautiful, even productive, buildings was in futile competition with tax systems penalizing less-than-maximum use and was outweighed by the tremendous financial potential that could be realized only through maximum development of the site.

Although in late August the Illinois legislature amended the state zoning enabling acts, allowing Chicago to use the transfer method to save the building, the city council steadfastly refused to designate the

Removal of cornice before demolition of Stock Exchange, Chicago, Ill., March 1972. (Richard Nickel)

Stock Exchange a landmark, and on October 1, 1971, a permit to demolish the building was granted. Efforts by two private groups, the Chicago Chapter of the American Institute of Architects and the Landmarks Preservation Council, to compel the council to protect the Stock Exchange by complying with its duty to give the building landmark status had failed. The Landmarks Preservation Council had even submitted a cooperative city, state and federal plan for restoration and had managed to raise $200,000 of an estimated initial capital of $1 million for restoration. Demolition finally began in late October. Preservationists took little consolation in the fact that some of the ornamental details on the building were saved. The Advisory Council, commended by preservationists for its willingness to become involved in a preservation matter outside its stated realm of responsibility, had been unable to find a solution to help save the Stock Exchange Building.

Out of the battle, however, came a much clearer picture of the economic dimensions of the landmarks dilemma and a technique, development rights transfer, which was advanced by John J. Costonis, professor of law at the University of Illinois. A grant from the U.S. Department of Housing and Urban Development to the National Trust enabled Costonis to further expand on the applicability of the transfer method in a book, *Space Adrift: Saving Urban Landmarks through the Chicago Plan*. Another outgrowth of the Stock Exchange battle was the proposal for a National Cultural Park by Secretary of the Interior Rogers C. B. Morton. The report, "The Chicago School of Architecture," issued in 1973, proposed federal acquisition of unused development rights of buildings in the Chicago Loop area to facilitate joint federal, municipal and private preservation and interpretation of Chicago's architectural landmarks.

In May 1972 the Advisory Council was asked by the federal Domestic Council for its views on a plan being proposed by the Administration—revenue sharing. Basically, revenue sharing was explained as a method to put fiscal resources (that is, revenue derived from the federal income tax) and the responsibility for their expenditure at a level of government the Administration considered more directly responsible to the people, state and local governments. The plan was in two parts: general revenue sharing and special revenue sharing. Under general revenue sharing, state and local governments would determine how funds were to be spent. In contrast, special revenue sharing funds were to be used for certain purposes designated by the federal government. According to the Administration, special revenue sharing was being proposed in an effort to reduce the complicated management and duplicate efforts involved in administering approximately 150 federal grant programs. Instead of applying for these federal grants, states and local communities would use their special revenue sharing monies to fund various programs in six broad areas of national concern: law enforcement, manpower training, urban development, rural development, transportation and education. These special revenue sharing funds would be distributed by appropriate federal agencies, which would also monitor, but not control, their expenditure.

In commenting on the Administration proposal, many agencies, organizations and individuals noted a major drawback: Policies adopted by states and local communities to expedite progress in one area might well jeopardize gains made in others. The Advisory Council, in its investigation of revenue sharing, recognized the possible adverse impact of the new plan on historic preservation. Working closely with the Trust and the departments of Transportation, Justice and Housing and Urban Development, the Advisory Council prepared an issue paper expressing concern that the protection of historic places from potentially harmful federal or federally assisted projects might be jeopardized by court interpretations. It was feared that the courts might rule that projects financed by revenue sharing funds were outside the strictures covering federally assisted projects.

Preservationists were especially concerned about the elimination of federal grants for historic preservation as proposed under special revenue sharing legislation, for HUD historic preservation program grants had become a major source of funds for preservation projects. Between fiscal year 1968 and fiscal year 1971, 33 states, the District of Columbia and Puerto Rico had initiated 75 projects with HUD historic preservation program grants totaling $4.3 million. These grants had aided in preserving a variety of structures—an adobe school in Arizona; buildings in Sacramento, Calif., dating from the gold mining days; the first synagogue (1876) built in Washington, D.C.; and the Iolani Palace State Monument in Honolulu. For fiscal year 1972, almost $3 million had been granted. To insure that federal funds would continue to be available, preservationists focused their attention on the special revenue sharing legislation dealing with urban development. By early 1972, at the urging of the Trust, the Advisory Council and others, historic preservation was included as one of the 15 activities eligible for funding under the proposed special revenue sharing funds to be distributed by HUD.

In October 1972, the State and Local Fiscal Assistance Act, establishing general revenue sharing, was passed by Congress, and just as preservationists had anticipated, the act failed to stipulate whether or not projects financed by general revenue sharing monies were subject to the criteria and review procedures set up in section 106 of the National Historic Preservation Act of 1966 and in section 102 of the National

Iolani Palace, Honolulu, Hawaii. State-owned landmark restored by Friends of Iolani Palace based on initial research by the Junior League of Honolulu with the aid of grants from the state and the U.S. Department of Housing and Urban Development. (E. Blaine Cliver)

Environmental Policy Act. In January 1973, there was more distressing news for preservationists. That month, in anticipation of the passage of special revenue sharing legislation, all funds for the HUD historic preservation program were frozen; it was possible that it might be 12 to 18 months before the new legislation could be implemented.

Overall, preservationists were apprehensive about revenue sharing. Congress, too, was skeptical and expressed concern that if the review policies that had been attached to federal grants were removed, corruption in some state and local governments would lead to "misshapen priorities." Although lawmakers did eventually approve general revenue sharing, special revenue sharing legislation was never passed. (Later, however, legislation designed to consolidate many federal grant programs was approved. Of special interest to preservationists was the Housing and Community Development Act of 1974. Under the new law, which became effective January 1, 1975, federal money from former categorical grant programs of the U.S. Department of Housing and Urban Development—urban renewal; open space, including urban beautification and historic preservation; model cities; rehabilitation loans; public facility loans; neighborhood facilities; sewer and water grants and neighborhood development programs—is pooled into one block grant for each community. The funds are then spent according to local officials' estimates of their communities' needs, which are determined by regulations that include the process of public hearings.)

Theoretically, the revenue sharing plan could mean an increase in funding for historic preservation programs within a community. In Seattle, Wash., for example, a city sensitive to and active in historic preservation concerns, the $8.1 million general revenue sharing apportionment was used in a model way to support preservation. The city council under Mayor Wes Uhlman's leadership voted to establish a historic preservation revolving fund, to create a housing rehabilitation trust fund, to develop an Indian Cultural Center and to open an Asian Cultural and Community Center. The city also planned to open an Office of Historic Preservation to distribute funds to the two historic districts in the city and to the community as a whole. But preservationists in other towns despaired over past local decision making and its detrimental effects on preservation.

While revenue sharing, which caused preservationists much concern, was being initiated, one major preservation conflict, the San Francisco Mint, ended in victory and another victory, over the Old Post Office in St. Louis, appeared to be developing. The preservation of the mint and the post office had been a controversial topic for many years. At the Trust 1962 annual meeting in San Francisco, preservationists gathered at the mint and, after seeing the effects of neglect on the historic structure, voted to work to save it. Designated a National Historic Landmark, the Classical Revival building was built in 1874; it was designed by Alfred B. Mullett, who was also the architect of the State, War and Navy Building (now called the Old Executive Office Building), which flanks the White House. The San Francisco Mint was once a major mint in the United States and was the chief federal depository for gold and silver produced in the West during the 19th-century mineral boom. Though it had survived the 1906 earthquake and fire, it was not surviving 30 years of neglect.

In 1970 San Francisco State College proposed to demolish the building and construct new educational facilities on the site. Since the U.S. Department of Health, Education and Welfare had obtained the mint in 1969 for conveyance for educational purposes when the General Services Administration declared it surplus, Health, Education and Welfare

U.S. Mint, San Francisco, Calif. Unharmed after 1906 earthquake (above).
(Bureau of the Mint) Visited by preservationists during 1962 National Trust
annual meeting (below). (Reprinted by permission of Chronicle
Publishing Co.)

Secretary Robert H. Finch appointed a committee to study the proposal. The committee determined that rehabilitation of the building was not economically feasible and that demolition should be allowed. The Advisory Council disagreed with the committee assessment that rehabilitation would be too costly, assuring the college that preservation and educational needs could be reconciled. However, the college plan was withdrawn, and the building was returned to the General Services Administration in 1971. Suggestions for use of the mint as a federal court building or as a western branch of the Smithsonian Institution came to nothing.

Not until March 1972 was preservation of the mint assured. In that month the General Services Administration transferred the building to the U.S. Treasury Department to be remodeled for use by the Numismatic Service Division of the Bureau of the Mint. The restoration plan, initiated by Mary Brooks, director of the mint, called for the restoration of the exterior over a four to five-year period and the establishment of a museum in the front rooms of the building where mineral discovery and silver mining in California would be interpreted. The cost of restoration ($4 to $5 million) was expected to be absorbed quickly, because the income to the Bureau of the Mint from numismatists is sizable.

Government action following recommendations of the Advisory Council may eventually help to preserve the Old Post Office in St. Louis, also designed by Mullett. The U.S. General Services Administration had earlier approved a plan to turn the post office into a commercial center containing a hotel, restaurants and shops, but there was no legislation to allow a transfer to a commercial developer. At the urging of the President in the 1971 environmental quality message to Congress, however, the General Services Administration had drafted legislation that would amend the Surplus Property Act of 1949 to allow this transaction. The new law, signed on August 4, 1972, made possible the preservation by a revenue-producing use of a nationally significant historic structure, providing an example for the use of other surplus properties in the nation.

The year 1972 was marked by progress in funding also. The first project funds authorized by the National Historic Preservation Act of 1966 were awarded by the U.S. Department of the Interior. Totaling $2.3 million, grants could be used to cover the costs of acquiring historic sites and actual costs incurred in preserving such sites; formerly, grants had been used only for statewide surveys and planning. Additional congressional appropriations for historic preservation programs of the Interior Department in fiscal year 1972 totaled $5.03 million, almost equaling the department request for $5.9 million. Of that total, the Trust received $1.3 million.

Old Post Office, St. Louis, Mo. Federal legislation in 1972 made
possible the adaptation of this and other surplus federal structures for
revenue-producing use. (Library of Congress)

Viewed from the federal and state levels, the preservation story from 1966 to 1973 was one of both victories and defeats, stalemates and compromises. It was, nevertheless, a success story. The growth of a concept is difficult to measure, for no idea develops in a vacuum. However, the basic premise of the preservation philosophy—that the human race has an obligation to protect the resources it has inherited—gained unprecedented popular acceptance during that period. In promoting public awareness of this responsibility, the National Trust, as a member of the Advisory Council, as a national representative of preservation in Congress and as the leader and coordinator of private preservation efforts, made a significant contribution.

Citizens of Morristown, N.J., picket against the routing of Interstate Highway 287 near the Ford Mansion, Morristown National Historic Park, N.J., 1965. (Neal Boenzi/ NYT Pictures)

Representatives of landmarks commissions meet in Cleveland City Council chamber during 1973 Trust annual meeting in Cleveland, Ohio. (Carleton Knight, III)

CHAPTER FIVE

Preservation
Is People

The acceptance by the federal government of new responsibilities in behalf of historic preservation marked a turning point for the preservation movement. The federal legislation passed in 1966 gave an added impetus to ongoing preservation activities and ushered in new programs to supplement the effectiveness of previous efforts. Moreover, the involvement of the federal government helped to broadcast the voice of preservation to a nationwide audience. The contributions of the National Trust toward formulating this new federal awareness and in assisting in the development of state programs were crucial, but Trust work with private endeavors was even more so.

Recognizing that its underlying strength was in its membership and its alliances, the Trust worked hard to develop and increase both. Its efforts were rewarded: Individual membership more than tripled during the first half of the 1960s—from 2,700 individual members in 1960 to more than 8,500 in 1966. The number of organizational members doubled—from almost 350 to more than 650, representing a constituency of several hundred thousand preservationists. Alliances with both private groups and government agencies were also cultivated. In addition to cooperation with its traditional private allies, such as the American Institute of Architects, the American Association for State and Local History and the American Association of Museums, the Trust since its inception had maintained a strong cooperative relationship with the National Park Service. Through its membership on the Advisory Council on Historic Preservation, the Trust also hoped to strengthen its ties with other government agencies.

The growth of Trust programs, however, was limited by two factors. The first was finances. As a private, nonprofit organization, the Trust had an operating budget that was based primarily on membership dues, contributions and endowments. While funds from these sources were adequate for current Trust programs, the budget did not allow for significant expansion. Under Public Law 89–665, the Trust was eligible for federal funding, but even when authorizations and appropriations were forthcoming, the Trust could receive funds only in amounts it was able to match equally. Fund-raising activities would therefore continue to demand a major commitment of time and energy.

The second factor was related to the legal status of the Trust and accompanying limitations on its activities. Because it is a charitable, non-profit organization, the Trust is limited in the expenditure of organizational time and money in influencing legislation. However, the Trust can sound the alarm: It can agitate, initiate, teach, guide, inspire, support and point the way. Therefore, Trust leaders realized that if the Trust hoped to continue to influence policy making for the benefit of preservation, the Trust would have to convince citizens of the value of preservation, inform them of impending problems and spur them to action. To insure the continuation of the preservation movement, the Trust determined to broaden the base of its public support by continuing to recruit new members of all ages and planning a publicity program to make its services and needs more widely known. One way Trust leaders believed these goals could be accomplished was through Trust publications. They reasoned that after the public knew about the work of the Trust, Americans would lend their support to the preservation cause by becoming Trust members.

Under the staff reorganization in 1966, the Publications Office, directed by Terry B. Morton, became a part of the Department of Program. The main responsibility of the Publications Office was the production of the two Trust periodicals, *Historic Preservation* and *Preservation News*. The publications staff also devoted considerable time to support work, aiding in the publication of increasing amounts of material initiated by other Trust departments and by other professionals in the preservation field.

In 1967 the format of the monthly *Preservation News* was changed to that of an eight-page tabloid newspaper. The old newsletter format was inadequate; more space was needed to increase reports on the burgeoning developments in the preservation world. In addition, the new and often complex federal legislation and programs demanded interpretation and guidance for preservation efforts at the local level.

According to its newly adopted editorial policy, the newspaper "signaled one attempt to stimulate new and fresh approaches to an appreciation of America's past." Using its space for longer news items, *Preservation News* would give main coverage to national activity and the projects of member organizations, reporting on Trust programs only secondarily, for the *raison d'être* of the Trust lay in inspiring others to carry out most of the preservation work. By providing recognition of worthwhile endeavors of its member organizations, the Trust hoped to stimulate similar undertakings by other groups. Perhaps the most impor-

Preservation News *and* Historic Preservation, *the National Trust monthly newspaper and quarterly magazine, in 1970 format. (National Trust)*

tant purpose of *Preservation News,* however, was to help unite preservationists into a dynamic, sophisticated force on a nationwide basis.

The new *Preservation News,* supplemented by special features in *Historic Preservation,* rapidly began to fulfill its primary purpose. At no time was this more critical than in late 1966 and early 1967, when, in order to obtain federal aid and qualify for participation in the new federal programs, the states were required to establish historic preservation offices. An editorial in the November-December 1966 issue of *Historic Preservation* warned: "Now is no time for our members and member organizations to sit down and assume that federal programs will carry on their work. To accomplish the programs as set out in the laws, everyone must muster more activity and dedication than ever before."

Preservation News followed immediately with specific instructions in an article entitled "New Federal Laws to Help Your Project: How to Implement Recent Legislation." It suggested that Trust members obtain copies of the new laws from their Senators or Representatives and give them to state and local leaders, taking the initiative to see that officials became familiar with all provisions of the laws. Preservationists were also urged to enlist the aid of state legal officers to determine whether or not their states had enabling legislation for the new programs. If there were none, the article noted, preservationists should find out what was necessary to have such legislation introduced and should take appropriate action before the state legislatures reconvened in January. Members were also encouraged to work with state and local historical societies and local chapters of the American Institute of Architects and the American Institute of Planners to inform all those concerned—from urban planners to state highway officials—of legislative details. An interpretation of the new laws was made available by the Trust in an eight-page brochure entitled *The Preservation Congress.*

The November-December 1966 issue of *Historic Preservation* also printed abstracts of speeches and comments from the Trust 1966 annual meeting. These included addresses from a representative of the U.S. Department of Housing and Urban Development, the director of the National Park Service and the administrators of the U.S. General Services Administration and the Bureau of Public Roads (now the Federal Highway Administration). In early 1968, the magazine carried speeches of government officials who had given progress reports at the 1967 annual meeting.

During 1967 *Preservation News* covered a variety of preservation stories and printed editorials decrying well-meaning architectural reproductions and supporting good contemporary design, urging the appreciation of regional architecture and protesting that in national studies of housing and urban planning, little attention was paid to historic preservation. Also included were descriptions of Trust programs.

For its work in informing and spurring Trust members and other preservationists to action, the 1967 volume of *Preservation News* was honored by a unanimous resolution of the Historic Resources Committee of the American Institute of Architects.

Preservation News provides the cause of preservation in the United States with a tool of inestimable value. The paper's editorial freshness and well-written, well-illustrated news has brought the preservation movement in this country to a new level of maturity in step with urgencies and opportunities created in the 89th Congress.

During the next two years, the paper continued to expand its coverage and to add new features. Starting in 1968, the work of editorial cartoonist Draper Hill was carried regularly to underscore the preservation message in the news. A column by Trust president James Biddle, begun in March 1968, kept readers aware of Trust activities and plans for the future.

In 1969, to keep readers up to date on important ongoing stories, the paper added an In Brief section, a bimonthly column on preservation legislation, a column featuring state preservation activities, descriptions of new preservation films, notable quotes and, for fun, a crossword puzzle based on general historic preservation topics and current news stories.

More sections were added to *Preservation News* in 1971. Activities held at Trust properties were reported with member organization activities in a calendar of events; the newspaper also regularly carried notices of items for sale at Trust headquarters and properties, listings of job opportunities in the preservation field and classified advertisements of historic properties for sale.

Two issues each year were devoted to annual meeting topics and review, and a third regular issue, Government and Preservation, was introduced in May 1969. This issue described federal preservation programs, listed grant recipients, assessed the work of the leaders of the three federal agencies that most affected preservation—the departments of Transportation, Housing and Urban Development and the Interior—and examined and explained the implications of changes in administrative policy. Letters from the directors of many groups with interests in preservation, including the National Park Service, the American Association for State and Local History and the Historic Resources Committee of the American Institute of Architects, praised the issue. A special election-year section in 1972 presented the preservation views of eight presidential candidates, including Sens. Henry M. Jackson, Hubert H. Humphrey, Edmund S. Muskie and George McGovern. An offer of extra copies at a bulk rate to the membership prompted orders for 3,000 newspapers.

Preservation News has often been cited by *New York Times* architectural critic Ada Louise Huxtable. Calling the newspaper "an excellent publication," she wrote in a July 27, 1969, column, "I am beginning to think that if this brisk and intelligent paper were compulsory reading for administrators, editors and that amorphous group called 'community leaders' everywhere, there might be a sudden blossoming of civilized thought and action in the nation."

Historic Preservation, the Trust quarterly magazine, complemented *Preservation News*. The magazine carried articles on such preservation-related subjects as federal grant recipients, historical interiors, preservation in various European countries, the problems of tourism in historic areas, the work of famous architects, building crafts and interpretive techniques at a variety of historic sites.

In 1967 two issues of the magazine were combined into a single issue devoted to Decatur House, the new Trust headquarters, presenting essays about its occupants, historical context, architecture and furnishings and other articles concerning its restoration and interpretation. A second double issue, on Belle Grove, appeared as the July-December 1968 magazine. For the third combined issue devoted to a property (April-December 1969), this one on the Pope-Leighey House, the Trust gathered information from oral history sessions, conducting interviews of the people most closely involved with the house.

Members of the properties staff, in cooperation with the publications staff, held oral history sessions at the house. Those interviewed included Mrs. Robert A. Leighey, who had returned to her home after missionary service in Japan, and Loren B. Pope, the original owner of the house. *Historic Preservation* readers were given a thorough account of this Trust property, from its conceptualization by Wright, the architectural genius, and his client to its rescue from destruction.

The recommitment of the Trust to broaden its membership prompted the redesign of *Historic Preservation* in 1972. While it retained its scholarly flavor, the magazine, now with a number of color photographs, widened its general public appeal, not only in format but also in content. Continuing a theme highlighted at the 1970 annual meeting, "Preservation for the People," *Historic Preservation* featured articles on preservation activities in inner-city neighborhoods and rural communities and stories on the work of youth groups and organizations of many ethnic backgrounds. Articles covered the spectrum of American cultures

Oral history sessions on history and preservation of the Pope-Leighey House provided material for special issue of Historic Preservation *(April-September 1969). (Jack E. Boucher)*

Historic Preservation *in format adopted 1972. (John J-G. Blumenson)*

—from the culture of Appalachia to the black urban experience to the traditions of Alaskan Indians. The magazine used its color photographs to full advantage to illustrate the diversity of America's heritage. Other articles focused on the effects of preservation on wildlife, crafts that flourished during the Depression, bridges and other engineering landmarks, even the underground riches of subway art. Book reviews and a Letters to the Editor section were added to the redesigned magazine.

A philosophy relating to the broadening Trust programs was expressed in a *Historic Preservation* editorial, "Preservation Is People," which appeared in the October-December 1972 issue.

> Historic preservation is people. Although preservation should be for the people and by the people—as has been stressed in National Trust programs and publications—preservation, more importantly, is people. It is not just the cataloguing of historic landmarks; preservation means action, and it is realized by the people involved: old people, middle-aged people, young people; rich people, poor people; black people, red, brown, yellow and white people; one person, a few people, many; volunteers, professionals; patrons and voters; interpreters, appreciators; joiners and activists. . . . If it should evolve that preservation is *not* people, it will be a symptom that our movement has faded and passed. It will mean that America is progressing all the more rapidly and all the more without regard to past and future. Even the present will be shallow. . . . We continue to seek a national Utopia, the dream of America since its founding. Preservation people are contributing much; through historic landmarks we defend the roots, foundations and settings that betoken America's progress toward its ideal. Upon these roots the nation builds.

So effective was the new format of *Historic Preservation* that in the summer of 1973 it won several awards in local and national design competitions. The Art Directors Club of Metropolitan Washington awarded a silver medal to the magazine for its first year's issues, and the designer of *Historic Preservation*, Tom Engeman, also received an award for his photographic coverage of the Brandywine River Valley in the January-March 1972 issue. The Educational Press Association of America honored *Historic Preservation* with three prizes for its overall excellence, specifically citing the design work of Engeman and the "Preservation Is People" editorial by Terry B. Morton.

Historic Preservation was also included in the Talking Books series, a program through which books and magazines are recorded for the blind and physically handicapped. Produced by the American Foundation for the Blind in New York City and the American Printing House

Watercolor illustration by Paul Salmon for Historic Preservation (*April-June 1972*).

for the Blind in Louisville, Ky., records and tape cassettes are made available as a free service from the Library of Congress.

Supplementing *Preservation News* and *Historic Preservation* were other resources that the Trust used to publicize the endeavors of preservation-related programs. These included not only technical publications and other printed materials but also exhibits, tours, awards, public service television and radio announcements, special celebrations and a host of other activities and tangible reminders designed to promote preservation.

In 1968 a retrospective exhibit cosponsored by the Trust and the Library of Congress featured 35 years of work by the Historic American Buildings Survey. The HABS collection already encompassed 30,000 measured drawings, 40,000 photographs and 10,000 pages of written data on 13,000 significant American buildings. The exhibit, "Preservation through Documentation," highlighted the progress that had been made in survey technology. One of the most valuable of the techniques encouraged by HABS was architectural photogrammetry, a system of photographing elaborate or remote details (such as church spires) on stereographic glass plates. The technique makes it possible, even years later, to convert the plates into accurate scale drawings by using plotting machines similar to those used in producing contour maps. Such improved data-gathering methods further illustrated the need for sophisticated archival retrieval systems, which had been called for in the revised principles and guidelines issued after the 1967 Williamsburg meeting.

In addition to maintaining its invaluable collection of data, HABS had given on-site preservation experience to hundreds of young people. Since 1951 the National Park Service had executed much of the HABS summer field work with architectural students; there had been 85 teams with students, many of whom went on to pursue careers in preservation. The prototype of HABS had also inspired the American Society of Civil Engineers to form a Committee on the History and Heritage of American Civil Engineering in 1964. Cooperating informally with the Smithsonian Institution, the committee began designating National Civil Engineering Landmarks, and in 1969 the committee joined with the Library of Congress and the National Park Service to establish the Historic American Engineering Record as a National Park Service program similar to HABS but concentrating on such engineering structures as factories, canals, tunnels, railways, powerhouses and airports. By 1974 HAER had collected approximately 400 measured drawings and 2,100 photographs documenting more than 300 structures.

In another joint effort, the Trust combined forces with conservationists to promote the activities of Earth Day, April 22, 1970. Initiated by Sen. Gaylord Nelson (D-Wis.) and Rep. Paul N. McCloskey, Jr. (R-

Calif.), Earth Day was marked by environmental teach-ins and other programs designed to make the public aware of the environmental crisis. The Publications Department sponsored Trust participation in Earth Day 1970 and Earth Week 1971-72, planning programs and encouraging Trust members in the Washington, D.C., area to join in local activities. For Earth Day 1970, two seminars on "Our Polluted Cityscape" were cosponsored by the Trust and the George Washington University Department of Urban and Regional Planning. At the seminars, held in Decatur House, professionals and government officials working on environmental problems discussed the cityscape and students from St. Alban's School for Boys in Washington heard lectures. Afterward, bus tours to representative areas of the city gave students a chance to see the visual pollution behind the "official" capital.

The preservationist belief was summed up by Trust president James Biddle in a statement later published in *Preservation News:* "To disfigure our country by destroying its landmarks, by paving it over from one end to the other, by bad planning and poor design is pollution of our environment no less than strewing trash across the countryside, emptying industrial wastes and raw sewage into our waterways or firing noxious gases into the atmosphere."

At Belle Grove, a week of activities celebrated Virginia Improved Environment Week, also held in April 1970. Among the activities was a Plant-Out, in which plant-bearing visitors were admitted free of charge, and Clean Valley Day, on which Girl Scout troops collected discarded cans in the area. Visual pollution was also illustrated in a traveling exhibit entitled "Reason for Concern," designed and sent across the country under the auspices of the Public Affairs Department.

In 1971 Earth Day became Earth Week and, as yet having no Preservation Week, the Trust continued its participation; staff members joined with lecturers from the Washington Ecology Center Speakers Bureau to discuss preservation and the environment at District of Columbia schools. Meanwhile, a group of Washington preservationists held a demonstration in front of the Old Post Office, then threatened by federal proposals. The effort, led by Trust members Alison Owings and Terry B. Morton, resulted in the formation of a local action group, Don't Tear It Down, which worked with other groups for the eventual rescue of the structure.

As a part of Earth Week 1972, the Trust made a direct contribution to preservation in the District of Columbia by conducting a community forum in cooperation with the Latrobe Chapter of the Society of Architectural Historians. The preservation conference included speeches and panel discussions covering preservation accomplishments and proposals in the federal city. In "The Citizens Speak," a panel of concerned

During Earth Week 1971, preservationists demonstrated in front of the Old Post Office, Washington, D.C. (John J-G. Blumenson) For Earth Week 1972 a rally was held to save Franklin School, Washington, D.C. (Sabin Robbins)

Washingtonians was invited to air its views on projects in and around the District. Controversial highway plans and highrise development that threatened the historic waterfront area of Georgetown were subjects of vigorous discussion. Prime topics were the Three Sisters Bridge, proposed to span the Potomac River, and an $86 million tunnel designed to go under the Lincoln Memorial and to pass within 750 feet of the Washington Monument. The conference proceedings were published by the Trust.

Besides its public information services, the publications staff performed a variety of additional support functions. In 1971 the Publications Office was reorganized as a full department under the direction of Terry B. Morton, and staff members were added to handle the expanding publications program initiated by Trust departments. They worked on such projects as the directory, *National Trust Member Organizations and Their Historic Properties,* which contained the names and properties of Trust member organizations and listed the Board of Advisors members and the state historic preservation officers; materials for Trust annual meetings and regional conferences; technical leaflets and fact sheets for distribution to the public; and the Trust annual report.

The Publications Department also was responsible for the production of material relating to Trust properties. New informational leaflets to be distributed at the properties were designed in 1972 and were selected to be shown by the Art Directors Club of Metropolitan Washington at its annual exhibit in the capital city. A series of silkscreened property posters, the first two featuring Lyndhurst and Chesterwood, was also begun.

Trust reprint and discount book services, which made various publications available on order to the membership through the publications list, expanded predictably after the mid-60s, and in 1971 a major event was the opening of the Preservation Bookstore at Trust headquarters in the Decatur House complex, under the direction and management of the Historic Properties Department. The formal opening was celebrated with an autograph party for author Constance M. Greiff and Trust president James Biddle, who contributed the foreword to her book *Lost America: From the Atlantic to the Mississippi.* As its opening exhibit, the bookstore featured a photographic display of Daniel Chester French's works in the capital area. In addition to Trust publications and those of its member organizations, the bookstore carried basic and unusual books on preservation, posters, postcards and gift items, all of which are listed regularly in the *Preservation Bookstore Catalogue.*

During 1971-72 the Publications Department administered three grants on behalf of the Trust. A $500 grant was given to Charles B. Hosmer, Jr., for research on the second volume of his history of the pres-

Opening of National Trust Preservation Bookstore, 1971. (National Trust)

ervation movement. A $2,000 grant was awarded to the Chicago Chapter Foundation of the American Institute of Architects to help finance a study of development rights transfer methods by John J. Costonis, professor of law at the University of Illinois, and Jared Shlaes. Costonis also directed a project on the nationwide applicability of the transfer method under a $75,355 urban renewal demonstration study and publications grant awarded to the Trust by the U.S. Department of Housing and Urban Development. The report, entitled *Space Adrift: Saving Urban Landmarks through the Chicago Plan*, was published for the Trust by the University of Illinois Press in 1974. Other special projects included the production of the *Directory for Bicentennial Planners* and work on a book of walking tours of Washington, D.C., to be sold at the National Visitor Center, scheduled to open in 1976. In 1973 the Publications Department announced an expanded advisory service to help local preservation groups improve or economize their publications programs.

The Public Affairs Department, established in 1966, was in charge of developing publicity to make the Trust better known, to encourage historic preservation activity through special recognition of those who made significant contributions to the movement, and, generally, to

John J. Costonis, author of Space Adrift: Saving Urban Landmarks through the Chicago Plan, *autographs his book after 1974 Awards Luncheon, observed by William J. Murtagh, keeper of the National Register (left), and Ernest A. Connally, associate director for professional services, National Park Service (right). (Carleton Knight, III)*

spread the preservation message. J. William Bethea was the first director of the department. Two years later, he resigned and Frederick Haupt, III, became director of the Public Affairs Department.

One of the responsibilities of the new department was to further develop and oversee the Trust awards program. To honor superlative achievement, the Trust in 1960 had established the Louise du Pont Crowninshield Award, which had come to be regarded as the highest award in the field of historic preservation. To encourage public participation in preservation, the Trust steadily expanded its awards program, beginning with a series of special citations in 1966 to honor some of those responsible for the great strides made in historic preservation legislation. The Trust presented certificates of recognition to Reps. Wayne N. Aspinall, John B. Saylor, William B. Widnall, Albert Rains and Roy A. Taylor and Sens. Alan Bible, Henry M. Jackson, Thomas H. Kuchel and Edmund S. Muskie.

*Frances R. Edmunds, director of Historic Charleston Foundation, Charleston,
S.C., accepts 1971 Crowninshield Award from James Biddle, Trust president
(left), and Gordon Gray, chairman of the Board of Trustees (right), at the
National Trust annual meeting in San Diego, Calif. (John J-G. Blumenson)*

Resolutions were presented to Helen Duprey Bullock, Hiroshi
Daifuku, Carl Feiss, Robert R. Garvey, Jr.; John J. Gunther; George B.
Hartzog, Jr.; Patrick Healy; Laurance G. Henderson; Philip H. Hoff;
Casey Ireland; Lawson B. Knott, Jr.; Ronald F. Lee; Gillis Long; Walter
I. Pozen; William A. Schmidt; William L. Slayton; Raymond R. Tucker;
and Rex M. Whitton.

Letters of appreciation were sent to Sen. Everett McKinley Dirksen,
Richard H. Howland, Sidney Hyman, Dorn C. McGrath, Frederick D.
Nichols, Christopher Tunnard, Stewart L. Udall, Joseph Watterson,
Robert C. Weaver, Walter Muir Whitehill, Albert B. Wolfe and George
Zabriskie.

In 1968 special recognition was given to Mrs. Lyndon B. Johnson,
who as First Lady espoused historic preservation as a part of her

beautification work. Besides serving as honorary chairman of the American Landmarks Celebration in 1964, she had supported the work of the Special Committee on Historic Preservation, contributing the foreword to its report *With Heritage So Rich*. In addition to focusing attention on the critical need to save the nation's cultural heritage and its natural resources, Mrs. Johnson made many aware of the consequences of urban decay. Organizing the Committee for a More Beautiful Capital in 1965, she led prominent Washingtonians on Broken Window tours, reminding them of the slums that blighted their city. Through her influence, more than $2 million was donated for establishing parks and playgrounds in the capital, and thereby providing employment for youth and opportunities for small business firms.

In a Discover America tour in 1968, she traveled more than 140,000 miles from the Big Sur to Maine, publicizing the nation's natural and cultural heritage. During part of the tour, which dealt with America's beginnings on the Hudson River, she came to Lyndhurst, the Trust property at Tarrytown, N.Y., where in keeping with the theme of that part of the tour, the Trust assembled an exhibit of paintings in the romantic landscape tradition of the Hudson River School, the first American style of painting. In a special ceremony, Trust president James Biddle presented Mrs. Johnson with an honorary membership in the Trust, citing her valuable contributions to preservation. (All living First Ladies have been extended honorary membership in the Trust and all have accepted.)

In the spring of 1971, the Trust held its first Awards Luncheon. In ceremonies at the National Gallery of Art, awards for achievement in historic preservation were presented by First Lady Mrs. Richard Nixon. The awards, designed by Arthur King of New York City, are made of American rock crystal mounted in silver on wooden bases, symbolizing the natural and built environments. Recipients of the first awards were Ada Louise Huxtable, preservationist and architectural critic of the *New York Times*, and Nancy Carson Shirk and Nancy Dixon Schultz of the U.S. Department of Housing and Urban Development. Citations were awarded to James L. Cogar, president of Shakertown, Pleasant Hill, Ky.; Lydia Chichester Laird, New Castle, Del.; the Society for the Preservation of Weeksville and Bedford-Stuyvesant History, Brooklyn, N.Y.; and the Foundation for Historic Christ Church, Inc., Irvington, Va.

Award winners in 1972 were artist-photographer Samuel Chamberlain, for his 35 years of outstanding photography and etchings of American architecture, and Sen. William S. James of the Maryland General Assembly, for his support of state preservation legislation. Citations went to the Pittsburgh History & Landmarks Foundation, for its work in preserving inner-city neighborhoods; the Citizens to Preserve Over-

Mrs. Richard Nixon presents citation to representatives from Society for the Preservation of Weeksville and Bedford-Stuyvesant History, Brooklyn, N.Y., at first National Trust Awards Luncheon, held at the National Gallery of Art, spring 1971. (National Trust)

ton Park, for its long battle to save the Memphis, Tenn., city park from bisection by an expressway; and the Old Santa Fe Association of New Mexico, for saving the Spanish Colonial architecture in the community.

In 1973 awards went to Virginia Daiker of the Library of Congress; A. Edwin Kendrew, restoration architect of Colonial Williamsburg; and George McCue, arts editor of the *St. Louis Post-Dispatch*. Citations were given to the Bishop Hill Heritage Association, Bishop Hill, Ill.; Mrs. Malcolm G. Chace, Jr., Providence, R.I.; Pearl Chase of Santa Barbara, Calif.; and Mrs. Lawrence K. Miller, Hancock, Mass., for outstanding preservation work in their communities.

Also that year, in an attempt to involve young people in preservation projects, the Trust joined with *American Girl*, the official magazine of the Girl Scouts of America, in developing the "Give Yesterday a Tomorrow" competition. The two winning groups were honored at the Awards Luncheon: The Cadette Girl Scout Troop #365 of Hillside, N.J., was honored for refurbishing a train depot and the Junior Meadowbrook Guild of Rochester, Minn., won an award for restoring and staffing Knole Cottage, a child's playhouse.

The first Trust student journalism award was given in 1973. It went to Mark Latus, a student from Milwaukee, Wis., for his essay on preservation and the energy crisis. The award was established when Alice

Winchester, winner of the 1972 Crowninshield Award, returned her award stipend to the Publications Department, which used the funds to establish an annual writing competition for students.

Awards were but one facet of the public affairs program of the Trust, however. A variety of means were used to convey to the public the tangible and intangible benefits of preservation. In 1971, for example, a poster was designed to mark the opening of an exhibit of President John F. Kennedy's model ships at Decatur House. On the poster, featuring a sketch of scrimshaw like that in the President's collection, artist Corita Kent added Kennedy's words: "I look forward to an America which will not be afraid of grace and beauty, which will preserve the great old American houses and parks of our national past, and which will build handsome and balanced cities for our future. . . . And I look forward to an America which commands respect throughout the world not only for its strength, but for its civilization as well."

The 1970 conflict in Chicago over preservation of the Stock Exchange was a clear example of the age-old clash between measurable monetary values and intangible aesthetic and historical values. It had been an important part of the mission of the Trust to inculcate in the public mind a full appreciation of structures, not simply an awareness of their revenue-producing possibilities. It had made some progress. As Ada Louise Huxtable wrote in the *New York Times* in a June 1968 column, "Culture Is As Culture Does,"

> The trend toward preservation is significant, not only because it
> is saving and restoring some superior buildings that are testimonial
> to the creative achievements of other times but because it is bucking
> the conventional wisdom of the conventional power structure . . .
> the wisdom that "you don't keep old buildings; they are obsolete.
> Anything new is better than anything old and anything bigger
> is better than anything small and if a few cultural values are lost
> along the way it is not too large a price to pay."

The Trust realized that if concern for America's cultural heritage did not begin to equal the appreciation of dollars and cents, the preservation movement would always be a defensive one.

The voice of preservation was perhaps weakest when it spoke about buildings of the 19th and 20th centuries. The Trust found that appreciation of 17th and 18th-century structures was easier to foster than appreciation of 19th or 20th-century architecture, which, because it was more common, did not engender the same respect. To increase appreciation of the more recent past, the Metropolitan Museum of Art and the New York chapter of the American Institute of Architects sponsored "19th Century America," a show of architecture, painting, sculpture and decorative arts assembled to celebrate the founding of the Metro-politan in 1870. A main feature of the show was an exhibit, cosponsored by the Trust, on "The Rise of an American Architecture, 1815-1915."

The exhibit explored many facets of 19th-century architecture—commercial buildings, small homes for middle-class families, parks and squares. Trust president James Biddle described the diversity of the exhibit, "from the romanticism of Benjamin Henry Latrobe through the bourgeois-commercial of Sullivan to the aristocratic and searching design of Frank Lloyd Wright." As a shocking climax to the architectural exhibit, the Trust helped assemble film footage of the destruction of landmark structures.

From this film, the Trust produced a 60-second television spot announcement entitled *Your Heritage*, and the spot was distributed to 300 television stations. Combining films of a wrecking ball demolishing historic buildings and the sound of a tolling bell, the film made a dramatic plea for preservation to a wide audience.

The effectiveness of the advertisement was confirmed in 1972 when viewers of a Chicago television station selected *Your Heritage* from among 80 commercials telecast during prime time as the winner of the Gold Hugo award, the top prize of the Annual Chicago International Film Festival. In the United States Television Commercials Festival, it also won a first prize for editing and a merit award for creative excellence.

In 1973 a series of public service advertisements on historic preservation was designed for magazines and other publications. Ten advertisements were printed on large reproduction sheets and mailed to 1,000 publications, ranging from such respected journals as *American Scholar* to widely read regional magazines such as *Yankee*. By midyear more than 50 advertisements had appeared in many periodicals, including *Time, House Beautiful* and *Antiques*. It was estimated that the advertisements represented $75,000 in free publicity and accounted for the addition of approximately 50 new members a month.

Another public affairs effort reached the mass audience in a different way. In August 1971 four historic preservation commemorative stamps were issued by the U.S. Postal Service. Featured subjects on the stamps were San Xavier del Bac Mission (1700), near Tucson, Ariz., the *Charles W. Morgan*, a wooden whaler (1841), moored at Mystic Seaport, Conn.; San Francisco's cable cars (1873); and Decatur House (1819). These stamps were historic preservation reminders on more than 130 million pieces of mail, and because a Trust property was chosen as one of the historic landmarks to be honored, the Trust received $3,900 in royalties from the sale of first-day covers by a private firm.

The Trust succeeded in establishing a National Historic Preservation

Public service announcements distributed by the National Trust in 1973.

Week in 1973. A resolution introduced by Sen. Henry M. Jackson was adopted by both houses of Congress, and a presidential proclamation urged community celebrations during the week of May 6–12. The Public Affairs Department of the Trust developed an idea kit, which was used by more than 80 member organizations in 34 states and Guam to plan more than 200 events. Seminars, exhibits, heritage fairs, antique car parades, walking tours, bus tours and bike tours (one led by a state governor) marked the occasion, as did six gubernatorial and mayoral proclamations. Trust president James Biddle's appearance on the NBC television "Today" show prompted many inquiries about the Trust.

Programs for the American Bicentennial also offered opportunities to promote preservation efforts. The American Revolution Bicentennial Commission, formed in 1970 and since reorganized as the American Revolution Bicentennial Administration, set 1970–87 as the Bicentennial Era, with 1976 as the focal year. The official title of the celebration was selected, Festival of Freedom—U.S.A. 200, and plans were made for programs under three principal themes. These were Heritage '76, focusing on the past; Festival U.S.A., centering on the present; and Horizons '76, concentrating on America's future. Trust president James Biddle was named chairman of the Heritage '76 program. He and his special assistant, Helen B. Byrd, who joined the Trust staff in 1971, fostered Bicentennial programs through the Trust: a Bicentennial Kit, which is a guide for community programs, and the Heritage Meeting House proposal to set up state environmental study centers in 55 properties threatened by demolition though listed in the National Register. This proposal is still being considered by Congress. As a further goal for the Bicentennial, the Trust pledged to contact all owners of National Historic Landmarks to offer whatever advisory assistance is necessary for the preservation of these structures.

Other public affairs programs initiated in the 1966–73 period were designed to publicize the Trust and its services in order to recruit members. Using the most visible resources of the Trust—its historic properties—radio and television spot announcements, newspaper articles and magazine advertisements were prepared to appeal to a mass audience. As a follow-up to *Your Heritage*, another public service film was made, this one about the Woodrow Wilson House. Burgess Meredith's narration of the film was adapted for use as a radio announcement, and in 1969 a two-month advertising campaign was begun to raise attendance at the property. Bus posters and tear-off cards announced "Woodrow Wilson House Wants You" and Washington, D.C., cabdrivers were encouraged to tell their tourist customers about the Woodrow Wilson House and invite them there for free iced tea. Attendance tripled.

*Delta Queen at Tiptonville, Tenn., landing during May 1971 cruise.
(Sabin Robbins)*

Another film, entitled *Past and Progress*, featuring all the Trust properties also brought satisfying results.

In 1970 the Trust launched a new project designed to raise funds
while also making the properties more widely known and used. The Department of Public Affairs mailed out 10,000 copies of *Historic Settings*,
an illustrated booklet announcing that Trust properties were available
for rent for use as advertising and commercial photography backdrops.
Booklets were sent to advertising agencies, public relations firms and
professional photographers. By extending rental opportunities to include
commercial organizations (the properties had always been available to
nonprofit groups), the program within a year had attracted more than
100 groups, for functions ranging from a women's club tea at the
Woodrow Wilson House to the filming of a vampire movie, *Dark
Shadows*, at Lyndhurst.

Membership recruitment and fund raising were also aided by the
expansion of the Trust domestic tour program. Tours had been regularly
scheduled as the finale to each year's annual meeting, but in 1970 the
Trust was presented with an opportunity to expand its tour program
and at the same time pursue its mission. This expansion grew out of
Trust attempts to save the *Delta Queen*, the last steam-powered river-

boat still making overnight trips in the continental United States. Under fire provisions of the 1966 Safety at Sea Law, the wooden *Delta Queen* had been condemned, and it was to cease operation by November 1970. Early that year, two groups of voyagers went on cruises from New Orleans to Memphis and back to publicize the plight of the *Delta Queen*. In March Trust members sent telegrams to the President and government leaders, urging that the riverboat be granted a permanent exemption from what it termed "unreasonable and inapplicable" regulations.

Though the House declined to grant the exemption, the Senate approved a rider to grant the riverboat three more years of life. During the spring 1971 Trust charter cruise in celebration of the reprieve, the *Delta Queen* raced with her sister paddlewheeler, the *Belle of Louisville*, up the Ohio River, to the accompaniment of bands and cheering crowds. Even though the *Queen* was beaten to the finish line, it was a happy occasion, for the paddlewheeler could continue to ply the rivers—at least until 1973. However, when the extension of the exemption came to an end, the *Queen* again faced a congressional decision. Once more the Trust, joining with Rep. Leonor K. Sullivan (D-Mo.), who introduced H.R. 5649 proposing extended exemption, rallied public opinion and succeeded in saving the *Delta Queen* for another five years.

In 1971 the Trust began a year-round tour program offering members a variety of tours abroad. Through this travel service, U.S. preservationists were given a chance to view preservation activities around the world and to establish stronger relations with foreign preservation organizations. Accompanied by Trust president James Biddle, 27 members took the first tour, which was cosponsored by the English National Trust. They traveled through the English countryside, stopping to view a number of historic country residences. In the fall, another group of preservationists visited French chateaux in a tour designed to aid Friends for the Restoration of the Chateaux of Hautefort, an organization supporting international preservation legislation. Costs of the tours included a tax-deductible contribution to the Trust. Subsequent trips have been made to Scotland and Venice, and tours of the ancient castles of Ireland and the Baroque castles of southern Germany have been sponsored.

A long-time goal of the Trust had been to establish a National Historic Preservation Fund to make low-interest loans available to communities to be used to establish local revolving funds for the acquisition and development of historic properties. This technique was already being successfully used in Savannah, Ga., Charleston, S.C., and Annapolis, Md. To raise initial funds toward the goal of $10 million, the Trust hosted a Preservation Ball at Lyndhurst in September 1970. The gala,

Holyrood Abbey, Scotland. Visited during National Trust tour of Scotland, 1973. (National Trust)

Luncheon at Evergreen Plantation, Edgard, La. Part of Trust fund-raising gala in New Orleans, La., April 1972, for the National Historic Preservation Fund. (Sabin Robbins)

which featured a banquet and a fireworks display for more than 300 guests, raised more than $25,000. A second gala, held in New Orleans in April 1972, added more than $17,000 to the fund.

The Trust continued to carry on membership recruitment through direct-mail campaigns. From 1966, when individual membership stood at approximately 8,500, membership grew to almost 14,000 in 1968, with the number of member organizations increasing from 613 to 758. It was gratifying to Trust leaders that the largest single source of new members was old members, who provided more than 17,000 names of potential members. With dues, contributions and the first of its government funds, the Trust looked optimistically at the future and pursued its aggressive membership renewal program.

In 1968 annual letters containing copies of newspaper articles on Trust activities produced an unusually high renewal rate of 83.9 percent, fund-raising programs netted $338,769, an increase of $73,545 over the previous year, and the Trust received a $500,000 gift from the Rockefeller Brothers Fund. In 1969 the Trust also began a bequest program, sending letters and a brochure entitled "A Future for the Past," which described testamentary methods of giving money or property to the Trust, to all members and 1,000 bank trust officers. As a result, 1970 was a banner year for the Trust. Membership reached 23,670, and the renewal rate rose to 87.3 percent. Fund-raising efforts were successful and several large donations were made.

In 1971 the Department of Plans and Development was established to handle the growing responsibilities of membership recruitment and fund raising; it was headed by interim director Frederick Haupt, III, who was also serving as director of the Public Affairs Department at that time, until a permanent director could be found for Plans and Development. Mark N. Beach, then director of planning and development for the National Cathedral in Washington, D.C., was employed by the Trust in 1972 to fill the position. With a staff to promote membership and raise funds, the Trust experienced even greater growth. A test-mailing program was begun, and the most effective appeals were used in the direct-mail campaign. New bequest brochures were prepared and recruiting techniques were improved. Consequently, by June 1973 Trust membership exceeded 40,000, and bequests and contributions were the largest in the history of the Trust.

Although statistics are useful as a measure of growth, they do not reflect what Trust leaders believed was the most significant aspect of the growth of the Trust: the variety of people who heard the message and joined the preservation movement. The Trust membership in 1973 covered a wide range of interests and professions: garden clubs, historical societies, planning commissions, corporations, genealogical societies, Junior League chapters, museum associations, architectural groups, interior designers, black history societies, real estate companies, special-interest groups (Victoriana, covered bridges, early American glass, brownstone architecture, cast-iron buildings, antique automobiles), law firms, civic beautification groups, libraries, historic property associations, construction companies, art schools, public and private high schools, publishing firms, printing companies, film workshops, art galleries, veterans organizations, conservation societies, Planned Parenthood and many more.

Fireworks at Lyndhurst, Tarrytown, N.Y., highlighted September 1970 Preservation Ball sponsored by the National Trust. (National Trust)

CHAPTER SIX

Living Landmarks

As he announced goals for the National Trust property program at the 1966 Philadelphia meeting, Gordon Gray reiterated the need to recognize the economic facts of life. Quoting from the catalogue prepared for an exhibit, "New Life for Landmarks," then circulating under the auspices of the American Federation of Arts, he said,

> The best hope of saving our cities' landmarks is to find new uses
> for them. . . . We have no patience with simply embalming a building
> that is dead. The job is only worth doing if it creates a more in-
> teresting environment than the one that is there now. We come
> not to bury these buildings, but to bring them back alive. . . . As the
> cities of Europe prove, it is the surest way of preserving the
> grace and continuity of urban living.

If preservationists were going to be able to save buildings, they would indeed have to "bring them back alive," by finding new uses for many of them, especially in urban areas. The average city simply could not bear the tax burden of an underused building. If historic structures were to be preserved, they would have to be made financially desirable, as well as socially and aesthetically beneficial. Thus, if a building could not be rehabilitated and used for the purpose for which it was built, an adaptive use was one of the most practical courses available. The Trust was already encouraging the preservation of structures by this method through advice in individual cases and by the example of the dual use of Decatur House as a historic house museum and as Trust headquarters.

In 1966 the Trust also renewed its pledge to make its own properties models of preservation, administration and interpretation. It was determined to make these properties landmarks in the fullest sense of the word by developing them into active community centers. The properties program, however, was the most expensive of the Trust programs: Maintenance and repair costs always exceeded Trust financial resources. Even though federal assistance was anticipated, financial pressure would continue to require the imaginative use of present resources.

As a national leader in ownership of historic properties, the Trust also saw an obligation to acquire a greater variety of properties, in terms of geography, historical associations and building types and uses. At this time, six of the nine Trust properties were located within the Virginia–metropolitan Washington, D.C., area. Similarly, the collection contained only residences; no working places, such as laboratories; no commercial buildings or churches. It also failed to include properties associated with science, Americans of minority ethnic backgrounds, the lives and works of artists and the American worker.

The Trust was encouraged by the federal programs established by the 1966 legislation. Not until 1970, however, did funds allotted under the Historic Preservation Act of 1966 substantially offset the costs of carrying on the properties program. Under the direction of curator John N. Pearce, the properties staff continued to work with what resources it had, the major focus of its activities in 1967–68 being educational programs and special events for the community, designed to attract visitors and revenue.

The school tour program that had been developed at Woodlawn during 1966 was expanded during the 1967–68 school year, and other Washington, D.C., area properties became the scene of a variety of educational activities. At the Woodrow Wilson House, for example, seminars in period furniture were held for groups of home economics students from nearby high schools. Students who visited Woodlawn, the early 19th-century plantation house owned by the Trust, were now exposed not to one, but to two life-styles, as the Woodlawn tour was revised to include a visit to the 20th-century Pope-Leighey House. In this "What Is A House?" program, junior and senior high school students compared the architecture, restoration techniques and use of the two properties.

In the summer of 1968, the Trust became a cosponsor with the Social Studies Department of Virginia and the Fairfax County School of a six-week course for high school seniors, funded by a grant from the U.S. Department of Health, Education and Welfare. In the course, The Community—Past and Present, 100 students spent three weeks at Woodlawn Plantation studying 19th-century plantation life and three weeks in Reston, Va., a new town in Fairfax County, studying life in a 20th-century planned community. Students compared the two settings in terms of social order, transportation systems, leisure-time activities, economic conditions and community arts.

In addition to programs for school groups, the Woodlawn staff developed a Museum Guides program for Girl Scouts in the neighboring community, and needlework classes for the public were offered at the plantation. Other Trust properties in Virginia likewise developed and

Participants in Woodlawn Conference for Historic Preservation Associates, 1973, tour University of Virginia, Charlottesville, Va. (John J-G. Blumenson)

offered programs. The carriage house at Oatlands was adapted for meeting use, and in 1968 the Trust began using it by conducting a seminar for training hostesses and guides. At Belle Grove, opened to the public in July 1967, seminars on museum occupations and career opportunities in architecture were held for high school students. Docent training was also provided for volunteer guides. For the general public, the property became a community center where lectures, seminars and exhibits focused on local history, traditional farm crafts and folk art.

Throughout 1966, the properties staff carried on the continuing task of cataloguing the contents of the Trust historic houses, conducting research on historic objects and original materials and then preparing master plans for restoration, interpretation and use based on results of the studies. Findings were shared with preservationists through publications. For example, such information was used to prepare two of the previously mentioned special double issues of *Historic Preservation*, one on Decatur House and the other on Belle Grove.

For all of the programs conducted at the properties, the Trust depended heavily on the time and talents of volunteers. The restoration of Decatur House, for example, was made possible by funds raised by the Decatur House Naval Committee under the chairmanship of Adm. Jerauld Wright, USN (Ret.). The committee also arranged for pieces of original Decatur furniture to be lent to the Trust for a six-month-long exhibit. Members of the Washington, D.C., chapter of the American Institute of Interior Designers acted as consultants on the exhibit. At Oatlands, the Oatlands Equestrian Center Committee raised funds for the construction of a pony ring and a point-to-point course and served as an advisory body to plan the numerous equestrian events held at the property. At Belle Grove, students served as volunteer docents, and local garden clubs aided in both fund raising and actual restoration work at the Woodrow Wilson House, Lyndhurst and Woodlawn.

Foremost among the volunteers were members of the Trust property councils. They served in many ways, helping to plan yearly events, giving advice and consultation to property staffs and developing good public relations with the neighboring community of each property. Through the Trust assistant for properties, Pierre G.T. Beauregard, the councils helped keep the headquarters staff in touch with outlying properties.

In 1969, the Trust again reorganized its staff in order to function more efficiently and effectively. As a result, the Properties Office, which had been under the Department of Program, became a full department with a new name—the Department of Historic Properties. The new department continued its previous, successful community use and educational programs at the properties and a variety of new programs were launched that year.

At Oatlands, in addition to equestrian events sponsored in the fall, the first Loudoun County Day was held, featuring horsemanship, crafts, local exhibits and high school bands. The event, which became an annual celebration, drew a large portion of the county population. Conversations at Oatlands, a series of informal evening seminars with prominent national leaders and such scholars as British historian Sir Kenneth Clark, was also well attended by the Leesburg, Va., community, as well as by residents of metropolitan Washington, D.C.

Similarly, Westchester County Day was initiated at Lyndhurst, and the Westchester Symphony began giving summertime outdoor concerts sponsored by the Trust and the Westchester Conservatory of Music. In the fall of 1969, a special concert drew 4,500 people to the estate. One of a series of shows arranged by the Hudson River Sloop Association to raise money to combat pollution in its home waters, the concert featured singers Pete Seeger and Arlo Guthrie who arrived for their performance on board the sloop *Clearwater.*

Other programs focused on the historical eras related to Trust properties. At Woodlawn a special Independence Day celebration in 1969 (held on July 2, the date John Adams had suggested for the observance) drew 300 visitors, who paid an admission charge of $17.76. They were entertained by the First Maryland Regiment and Fife and Drum Corps

First Loudoun County Day, 1969, at Oatlands, Leesburg, Va. (Allen)

and dined on authentic colonial food and drink, including stone fence (a beverage made of applejack and cider), cheddar biscuits and Brunswick stew.

Exhibits at the Woodrow Wilson House were designed to make the character of the President and his part in history come alive for the visitor. Displays commemorated such events as the signing of the Treaty of Versailles, the anniversaries of Polish and Czechoslovakian independence and Wilson's trips to promote the League of Nations. Exhibits included photographs, documents, private letters, even Wilson's wombat

Visitors watch cooper demonstrate barrel-making at Farm Craft Days, held annually at Belle Grove, Middletown, Va. (John J-G. Blumenson)

coat and his silk tophat. In a special radio broadcast on February 4 from the President's home on S Street, journalist Arthur Krock reminisced about the days of Wilson's presidency.

At Belle Grove, exhibits and lectures focused on the architecture and farming history of the Shenandoah Valley. A Summer on the Farm program was begun in 1969 and attracted thousands of visitors to see farming crafts much as they were in the 19th century. Farm Craft Days featured such skills as sheepshearing, basketweaving, wood carving, horseshoeing, cobbling, leatherwork, spinning, weaving and music-making by groups from the surrounding region.

At Decatur House, receptions were held by and for the White House staff, members of Congress, representatives of foreign governments, North Atlantic Treaty Organization foreign ministers, Cabinet members and members of the Advisory Council on Historic Preservation. One of the most innovative programs at Decatur House actually took place across the street at Lafayette Park. While the National Park Service carried out landscaping in the park, historically referred to as the President's Park, a gray fence was erected around the area to screen the operations from the neighborhood. To put the fence to good use the Trust invited students from 13 District of Columbia high schools to a Paint-In. After an orientation session at Decatur House, during which the students learned the history of the square from old prints, documents and contemporary histories of early community life in the capital, 175 students and 21 professional painters went to work with donated paint, creating a 2,400-foot mural in eight hours. When completed, the fence provided a panorama of the "Painted Past of President's Park." Views of Decatur House and its occupants were interspersed with pictures of neighboring buildings, such as the Dolley Madison House, St. John's Church, the White House and the Treasury Building, and portraits of Indians, patriots and First Ladies. Among the onlookers was Tricia Nixon, who invited the painters to the White House for refreshments when the work was completed. Later, the Capital Ballet Company, inspired by the fence project, danced its interpretation of the city's history in the park, and Wednesday evening tours of the fence provided as unique an experience for visitors as painting it had been for the artists. As a result of the activity, the Publications Office produced a technical leaflet entitled "Paint Your Own Fence" for use by preservation groups.

To help meet maintenance costs at the historic properties, fund-raising events and programs were continued. At Lyndhurst, wine-tasting parties and an annual Bon Marché antiques auction provided supplementary funds for that property, and a men's boutique during the Christmas season helped to raise funds for Decatur House. At the Woodrow Wil-

Paint-In at Lafayette Park, 1969, across the street from Decatur House, Trust headquarters, Washington, D.C. (M. Susan Miller for the National Trust)

son House, an annual book sale was initiated. The Trust also began offering for sale at its properties and headquarters such gift items as neckties, scarves and glasses decorated with the Trust emblem.

One of the major parts of the year's work concerned the acquisition and preparation for public view of the 10th Trust property, Chesterwood, in Stockbridge, Mass. The studio of sculptor Daniel Chester French, both a National Historic Landmark and a Massachusetts Historic Landmark, brought to the Trust collection a new dimension. Designed by Henry Bacon, the architect of the Lincoln Memorial, which features one of French's most famous works, the *Seated Lincoln*, the studio has two especially noteworthy construction features: the large 22-foot double doors, which were constructed to accommodate the first

Chesterwood, Stockbridge, Mass. Visitors examine Daniel Chester French's tools in the sculptor's studio. A property of the National Trust. (Paul Rocheleau)

statue that French executed in his new studio—an equestrian figure of George Washington holding a raised sword, now on the place d'Iéna in Paris—and a modeling table on railroad tracks that enabled French to wheel his sculpture outdoors and to study the effects of natural light. Included in the gift from the Daniel Chester French Foundation, formed by French's daughter, Margaret French Cresson, were many museum items, such as French's models, tools and sculpture. This was the largest single accession of museum items to the Trust collection. The foundation also donated a nature trail and 75 acres of land in the Berkshire Hills. The following year two gifts of land further protected and enhanced the property. Mrs. Stewart C. Woodworth donated the Meadowlark Studio to the Trust, along with 5 acres of land, and William M.

Judd gave 5½ acres, extending the estate to its original boundary, the Housatonic River.

Oatlands also received additional protection in 1969 when Mr. and Mrs. David E. Finley and Mrs. Eustis Emmet gave scenic easements on 237 acres of surrounding land to the commonwealth of Virginia under the Virginia Open Space Land Act of 1966. This legal device defined the scenic and natural values of the area that could not be altered without the consent of the easement holder.

In 1970, the Trust was able to expand its program of restoration projects under Ralph G. Schwarz, who became interim director of the Department of Properties after the resignation of John N. Pearce. With the help of the Decatur House Naval Committee, the first floor of Decatur House was furnished with objects and furniture from the Decatur era (c.1819), and the second floor was filled with the Beales' own furniture, reflecting the period of their occupancy, 1872-1956. Archaeological research and renovation continued in the Decatur House garden, made possible by funds from the Morris and Gwendolyn Cafritz Foundation of Washington, D.C., and the Colonial Dames of America. Floodlights were added around the property. In 1970 office space for the growing Trust staff was made available by the U.S. General Services Administration in two new buildings directly south of Decatur House.

At Lyndhurst one of the greenhouses and a work shed were rehabilitated for use as a laboratory by groups studying horticulture under the auspices of Community Education Services of Westchester County. Trees and shrubs were planted, and landscaping was done by a professional horticulturist whose services were obtained with a grant from the New York Council on the Arts and donations from several community garden clubs. At the 1970 International Flower Show in New York City, the Lyndhurst exhibit, "Neighborly Pride," won a first prize. The Lyndhurst rose garden, designed and planted by the Hudson River Garden Club, also received a citation.

Repairs and restoration went on at The Shadows, Chesterwood, Belle Grove, the Woodrow Wilson House and Woodlawn. At Oatlands the roof of the mansion was replaced, power and telephone lines were placed underground and the formal boxwood gardens restored. At Woodlawn gifts from Albert H. Small and the National Audubon Society enabled the Trust to create two nature trails, one featuring wild flowers and the other, birds and plant life. Gardening work was also done at the Woodrow Wilson House.

The newly refurbished Trust houses and grounds were put to good use as the sites of special activities and events. In conjunction with the Metropolitan Museum of Art centennial exhibit, featuring 19th-century art and architecture, a seminar in 19th-century landscape architecture

Annual Needlework Exhibit at Woodlawn Plantation, Mount Vernon, Va.,
1968. Nellie Custis Lewis harp and needlepoint firescreen in background.
(National Trust)

was held at Lyndhurst. Classes in this subject and in 19th-century decorative arts were held for the community during the summer. The New Iberia, La., Sugar Cane Festival used The Shadows as its theme, reproducing the facade of the bayou town house on the stage of the local auditorium. Later, at the annual parade one of the floats was dedicated to the Trust.

At some of the Washington, D.C., area properties, there were exhibits and special experiences awaiting visitors. A display of antique toys was on view at Decatur House, and a new Touch and Try program was begun at Woodlawn Plantation in an attempt to lower the "velvet-rope barrier" that many visitors feel in historic house museums. In one room adults were encouraged to pick up and examine some of the historic artifacts. Children were invited to walk on stilts, roll hoops and bowl on the lawn as the Lewis children had done. Inside they could play with an old-fashioned dollhouse, do needlework, assemble wooden block puzzles or even play a mandolin or violin.

To increase visitation, promotional leaflets were produced in 1970 and distributed by tourist-service organizations in communities near Trust properties.

In 1971, after the National Historic Preservation Act of 1966 and its grant programs were reauthorized by Congress, $411,291 of the Trust allotment of $1.04 million was used for maintenance and administration of Trust properties. Repairs were made to the roof of the Lyndhurst mansion, public restrooms were added to accommodate visitors, two historic cottages were restored and work continued on the grounds and the main greenhouse. Some funds were also used to restore the summer house at The Shadows. Upon completion of the work, the summer house was dedicated to the late Richard Koch, who had donated time and talent to the restoration of the mansion and funds for the restoration of the summer house. At the Woodrow Wilson House, the kitchen was restored to reflect the early 1920s, the period of the Wilson occupancy.

Belle Grove continued to be used as a community center, its programs focusing on traditional 19th-century folk arts and farm crafts. An ecology tour of the Cedar Creek area was added to the program. Part of the restored studio at Chesterwood was used by guests to try sculpting with plastelene. At Lyndhurst gifts from Mrs. Lee Simon and the Geigy Chemical Corporation allowed the initiation of an annual summer Performing Arts Series.

The year 1972 marked a turning point in the Trust property program. In July the Historic Properties Department gained the services of a full-time director, James C. Massey, who had been chief of the Historic American Buildings Survey since 1966. Also, the department stepped up its programs; $545,000 was designated for support of Trust properties and programs of the Historic Properties Department. The technical assistance offered to preservationists was expanded through conferences, professional consultations by the properties staff and publications. Increased research and documentation led to more accurate preservation and property interpretation programs that reflected a historical continuum rather than a limited period in the history of the property. For example, work began at Woodlawn Plantation to revise the interpretation to show the history of those who lived there after the Lewises, including a group of Quakers, an eminent anthropologist, a playwright and a U.S. Senator.

In addition to revising and expanding programs, the Historic Properties Department reviewed the operating budgets of the properties, developed plans to make administration of the properties more uniform and began an investigation of new less-than-fee methods of acquiring, preserving and protecting historic resources.

Although finances were limited, much was accomplished by the Historic Properties Department in 1972. Representative of the research done by the increased Trust professional staff was the extensive work carried out at Oatlands. There, the architectural historian studied land records, family papers, photographs and drawings. The historical architect employed mortar and paint analyses and X-ray photography to discover the composition and color of original paints for future restoration work. Archaeological studies were also undertaken to determine the original structure of the main house and the outbuildings and to ascertain the layout of the Carter and Eustis gardens. Oral history sessions were conducted to supplement the documentary evidence. Measured drawings and photographs of the house, its grounds, outbuildings and the surrounding area were produced as part of the continuing cooperative program with the Historic American Buildings Survey for recording Trust properties.

Maintenance work at the properties also progressed. With an anonymous donation of $10,000, work on the main greenhouse at Lyndhurst was resumed, a security system installed, two work sheds converted to living spaces for Lyndhurst staff and landscaping continued. Maintenance at Chesterwood and Belle Grove was aided by students in the Neighborhood Youth Corps, a work-training program established by the Equal Opportunity Act of 1965.

Students not only assisted in maintaining these two Trust properties, they also met for study at one. In the summer of 1972, the first work-study seminar in historic archaeology for college students began at Belle Grove, conducted by the Department of Historic Properties. The participants, who lived on the property for six weeks, carried out excavation under professional direction. In addition, they attended daily

Architectural student Maryann Thomas executes interior cross section of Cliveden, Germantown, Pa., as part of Historic American Buildings Survey summer project, 1972. (Jack E. Boucher for HABS)

College students participate in archaeological research at Belle Grove, Middletown, Va., as part of work-study seminar in historic archaeology begun in 1972. (George Smith)

classes at Lord Fairfax Community College in Middletown, Va. Courses included methods of excavation, site and artifact interpretation, mapping, laboratory techniques and documentation. The students received 10 quarter-hours of academic credit for their work.

Other educational activities were held at the properties, too. The Field Services Department planned and arranged for a technical conference on museum conservation methods to be held at Chesterwood. At Oatlands a follow-up seminar focused on the experiences and knowledge gained by participants in a county planning workshop held in England in January and sponsored by the Oatlands council. Discussions centered on solving problems of population expansion and open space needs. A conference for a number of owners of National Historic Landmarks in Virginia was held at Decatur House. Ways to bequeath such property were discussed, as were the questions of how to implement land use planning and how to undertake the donation of easements to preserve properties and to provide financial benefits to owners under existing laws.

A program of technical assistance to preservationists was developed by the Properties Department in 1973, such services previously having been provided by the Field Services Department. In addition to lecturing at a number of universities and professional association meetings, the Properties Department staff at Trust headquarters advised preservation groups on restoration, curatorial programs, interpretation and management of their properties through field trips throughout the country. The staff also did research and wrote articles on Trust properties for *Historic Preservation* and professional journals. For general assistance, pamphlets such as "Documented Reproduction Fabrics and Wallpapers" were produced. This was a catalogue of quality reproductions and names of their manufacturers. It was assembled to aid restoration committees with limited resources and those at a distance from large commercial centers.

In the fall of 1973, the Trust cosponsored a symposium on measured drawings to commemorate the 40th anniversary of the Historic American Buildings Survey. During the preceding years, HABS summer teams had produced measured drawings of six Trust properties, beginning with Lyndhurst in 1971. These were published and made available in the Preservation Bookstore in time for the conference.

In conjunction with the Publications Department, the Historic Properties Department published the first of a series of major technical publications undertaken in cooperation with Columbia University. The first title in the series on early American building was *Introduction to Early American Masonry: Stone, Brick, Mortar and Plaster* by Harley J. McKee, emeritus professor of architecture at Syracuse University.

By 1973 publications available from the Preservation Bookstore had grown from a collection of 270 titles to approximately 620 titles, including books and monographs from commercial publishing companies, regional presses and member organizations, as well as Trust publications. In addition to serving as a resource center to staff members, the bookstore provided a valuable service to members, with 90 percent of its business being done by mail order.

The Historic Properties Department also initiated programs to improve communications between headquarters and the staffs at Trust properties. A Joint Properties Committee was established and met regularly to review overall Trust policies and programs concerning properties. A newsletter, *Properties*, was begun in 1972. The newsletter covered property events, headquarters news items, new programs and personnel changes. It was sent to all Historic Properties Department employees, to members of each property council, to all Trust departments and to the Board of Trustees members. Instead of a single staff member serving as the Trust representative to all property council meetings, a number of staff members were assigned as liaison with specific councils.

In the spring of 1973, a regular schedule of seminars for Trust property administrators was resumed at Decatur House. Policies concerning tours, admissions, the work of guides, reporting procedures and other

Cliveden, Philadelphia, Pa. Opening day ceremonies, October 1972. A property of the National Trust. (Raymond Shepherd)

administrative matters were reviewed. For the administrators' use, the professional staff prepared checklists for the maintenance of structures, objects and furnishings. Administrators also received a maintenance manual for the property gardens. In addition, a grounds crew and a maintenance carpenter were hired to care for the properties and gardens in the metropolitan Washington, D.C., area. More than 40 capital improvement projects were completed during the year.

Also in 1973 the first phase of a major Trust goal was accomplished with the establishment of the Restoration Workshop at Lyndhurst. With a simple beginning to a major new program, two apprentices aided a master carpenter appointed as chief of the workshop in carrying out repairs while they learned the special carpentry skills required to become restoration craftsmen. This program was seen as the prototype for other programs geared to answering the need for craftsmen. During the summer, the same principle of on-the-job training was used in the summer intern program, which employed students in horticulture and landscape architecture to work at the Trust properties under the supervision of the staff horticulturist.

An important development during this period was the use of new methods by the Trust to acquire, preserve and protect historic properties. In February 1972, the Trust was able to acquire its oldest and one of its most historic properties, Cliveden, in Germantown, Pa., a Palladian mansion, built in 1763–67 by master carpenter Jacob Knor. The estate and an endowment and major American Chippendale, Sheraton and Hepplewhite furnishings, which include some of the most important Philadelphia furniture in existence, were offered to the Trust by the Chew family, the sixth-generation descendants of its original owner, Benjamin Chew.

The historic house and its owner had witnessed turbulent times during the American Revolution. Chew, who had been chief justice of the province of Pennsylvania, was a loyal colonist, but because he had been appointed to his position by the British, Congress was suspicious of his political allegiance and ordered him arrested and sent to prison. While Chew was confined, his home, Cliveden, was occupied by British soldiers, who on October 4, 1777, turned away George Washington and his troops in the Battle of Germantown. When released from prison, Chew returned to find Cliveden, which ironically was named after the English estate where King George III spent his childhood, "an absolute wreck." With his position uncertain and his house in ruins, Chew decided to sell Cliveden and live elsewhere. After the Revolution, however, it became clear that Chew neither conspired with nor supported the British, and in 1791, he was asked to serve as president of the High Court of Errors and Appeals for the commonwealth of Pennsylvania. In 1797,

Cooper-Molera Adobe, Monterey, Calif. A property of the National Trust. (Joshua Freiwald)

he was able to repurchase Cliveden and upon his death passed the estate on to his heirs.

After its acquisition by the Trust, Cliveden was thoroughly document-ed by the Historic American Buildings Survey. Plans were developed to use the National Historic Landmark for special Trust events relating to 18th-century life and, appropriately, as a focal point for some Trust Bicentennial programs.

Also in 1972, a bequest by Frances M. Molera of San Francisco gave the Trust an opportunity to accept property on a new basis. The property was the Cooper-Molera Adobe, a series of one and two-story structures on two acres of land across the street from Casa Amesti in Monterey, Calif. Construction of the house was started in 1829 by Juan Batista Rogers Cooper, an English-born Massachusetts sea captain who went to California during the Mexican-American War period and occupied the house until 1850. To insure the maintenance of Cooper-Molera, one of the oldest, largest and most important groupings of historic buildings in Monterey, the Trust leased the property for a 30-year period to the California Department of Parks and Recreation, which under Trust supervision is to initiate restoration and interpretation of the house. It will be a part of the Monterey State Historic Park.

The Trust pioneered still another method of acquisition in 1973. With

Wainwright Building, St. Louis, Mo. The first urban commercial property for which the National Trust purchased an option. (Piaget for the Historic American Building Survey)

the Historic Charleston Foundation, the Trust entered into a joint lease agreement with an option to purchase Drayton Hall, perhaps the most important Georgian mansion in the South. Drayton Hall (c.1738) was one of numerous plantation houses on the Ashley River in the Carolina Low Country above Charleston. It was used as a smallpox hospital during the Civil War and thus was one of three mansions to survive Gen. William Sherman's infamous March to the Sea. In the 1910s the area became a center for phosphate mining. The joint lease-purchase agreement on the property, entered into for two years between the Historic Charleston Foundation and the Trust, covered the mansion and 633 acres of surrounding woods and marsh. The lease gave the two groups time to develop a feasible approach to preservation of the property, which was theatened by sale and development, and to undertake a fund-raising effort for purchase of the property.

In December 1973, the Trust tried to solve a serious preservation problem: the saving of a major urban structure. With the National Heritage Corporation, the Trust acquired an option to purchase the Wainwright Building in St. Louis, perhaps the most important early skyscraper in the world. Designed by Dankmar Adler and Louis Sullivan in 1890, the 10-story structure was one of the first modern office

*Drayton Hall, Charleston, S.C., in the 1930s. A property of the National Trust.
(Frances Benjamin Johnston, Library of Congress)*

buildings. As the first tall building to utilize a steel frame, the Wainwright Building set a pattern for future skyscraper development. The option provided protection for the National Historic Landmark while the Trust and the National Heritage Corporation sought means to rehabilitate and restore it as a modern office building. The result of these efforts came in February 1974 when Missouri Gov. Christopher S. Bond announced that the state would preserve the Wainwright Building and rehabilitate it for state office space.

The news was warmly welcomed by Trust leaders, for it not only marked the first time that the Trust as an organization had become so directly involved in the preservation of a major urban landmark, but it also proved that obstacles encountered in trying to save large historic buildings in downtown areas could be overcome.

As the Trust began to use the acquisition of less-than-fee interests to save historic properties, it also began to utilize other legal techniques for protecting the properties and their surroundings from encroachment by adjacent development or from physical alteration. As the Criteria for Effect drawn up by the Advisory Council on Historic Preservation had pointed out, a historic structure could not be regarded simply as an isolated structure. The visitor's experience at the site, as well as the physical endurance of the structure, depended on the protection of the site and structure from various kinds of pollution—including visual pollution. The Trust had warned its members against the dangers of encroachment for many years and demonstrated its concern by protecting its own properties: Considerable planning had gone into the relocation of the Pope-Leighey House at Woodlawn Plantation to make sure that the house and the mansion would retain scenic integrity.

Recognizing these problems, the Executive Committee of the Board of Trustees in December 1972 approved a policy to allow the Trust to accept historic and scenic easements on an ad hoc basis. The committee stipulated, among other things, that the specific features protected under the easement be clearly indicated, that the property be accessible for Trust inspection and repair and that annual reports be filed outlining any material changes under consideration.

In the spring of 1973, the Trust accepted its first exterior (or facade) easement. The easement was on the Haas-Lilienthal House in San Francisco, Calif., a Victorian residence built in 1886 and long regarded as one of the major architectural landmarks in the city. The owners had donated the house to a new preservation organization, the Foundation for San Francisco's Architectural Heritage, and gave the Trust a remainder interest that insured the preservation of the house by transferring it to the Trust should the foundation cease to function, allowing time to find another suitable use for the building. Later, in the fall of the year, the Trust accepted an exterior easement on the 18th-century Reynolds Tavern in Annapolis, Md., donated by the Public Library Association of Annapolis and Anne Arundel County.

At Oatlands, in addition to protecting the property through the easements donated to the commonwealth of Virginia, the Trust undertook a broad program of environmental protection. A picturesque 19th-century one-room schoolhouse, Mountain Gap School, and its surrounding land were transferred to the Trust from Washington and Lee University through the generosity of Wilbur C. Hall. The nearby Oatlands Mill site and two scenic easements west of Oatlands were also given to the Trust by Mr. and Mrs. David E. Finley and Mrs. Eustis Emmet. With other donated acreage, a total of 918 acres came under environmental protection, and in 1973 the Oatlands Historic District was added to the National Register. The nomination noted that "the expansion of the district permits presentation of a visually integrated ensemble to the public . . . and will assist in the maintenance of this historic landscape."

In an effort to similarly protect the environment of Belle Grove, the Trust accepted in 1973 half interest in 124 acres bordering Cedar Creek. The land, including part of the Cedar Creek Battlefield, a National Historic Landmark, includes some of the most scenic areas along Cedar Creek, with high cliffs, caves and unusual plant life.

In 1973 negotiations also began for the donation of Mount Harmon Plantation at World's End, an 18th-century estate on the Eastern Shore of Maryland near Earleville in Cecil County. This important tobacco plantation on the Sassafras River was owned by Mrs. Harry Clark Boden, IV. Although it will be owned by the Trust, the estate, designated a National Trust Historic House, will not be operated as a museum but rather will be maintained as a residence.

Throughout its history, the Trust has been the recipient of many more offers of property than it could accept. In 1973, as part of a coordinated new properties program, it became an active adviser and catalyst in the transfer of properties to assure their preservation. Through consultation, conferences and advertising in *Preservation News*, the Trust aided building owners who wished to dispose of their property to find uses and purchasers who would protect and preserve that property. In a program area that suffers from inevitable financial limitations the Trust made many valuable contributions to the preservation movement. During fiscal year 1973, the Trust was involved in the preservation of more than 40 historic sites and structures, and this program was growing rapidly at the close of the year. The Trust had moved from a property ownership program limited to house museums to a broader advisory program aiding in the protection and preservation of major, often threatened, buildings as a demonstration for local and regional groups.

*James Marston Fitch and students at Columbia University School of
Architecture. (National Trust)*

CHAPTER SEVEN

A Truly National Trust

Through its communications programs, the National Trust alerted citizens to the need to preserve the national heritage and gathered support for the continuation of its own work. Through its property program, the Trust sought to inspire others to use a variety of techniques of acquisition, interpretation and restoration. Through educational and advisory programs, the Trust supplied the basic "how-to's" of preservation. Realizing from the outset that alone it could never accomplish all that had to be done, the Trust attempted instead to make its services and its broad mission truly national by encouraging others, throughout the United States, to form their own preservation organizations. The task was not only to teach the average person how to plan for preservation but also to provide for the instruction of craftsmen and professionals so that the actual work of preservation and restoration could be carried out.

The 1963 Williamsburg Seminar on Preservation and Restoration had focused on a sorely neglected area: the need to create technical courses in preservation and restoration at colleges and universities. As the need to preserve was realized, the call for people to do the work was overwhelming. In 1964 James Marston Fitch of the Columbia University School of Architecture started the first graduate course in the preservation of historic architecture, and within three years two other universities, Cornell and the University of Virginia, established graduate degree programs in preservation-related studies. The establishment of these programs in turn created a demand for financial support programs to insure their continuation.

Shortly before the second Williamsburg preservation conference in 1967, when the 1963 principles and guidelines were revised, the Trust received a $23,000 grant from the Ford Foundation for a special study of preservation education and training. Walter Muir Whitehill, chairman of the Education panel at Williamsburg, was selected to head this special study. Also serving on the special study committee were Francis L. Berkeley, Jr., assistant to the president of the University of Virginia, who was vice chairman of the committee; John Peterson Elder, dean of the Harvard Graduate School of Arts and Sciences; Leonard Carmichael, vice president for research and exploration of the National Geographic Society and former secretary of the Smithsonian Institution; Ronald F. Lee, special assistant to the director of the National Park Service; Charles van Ravenswaay, director of the Henry Francis du Pont Wintherthur Museum; J.O. Brew, director of the Peabody Museum of Archaeology and Ethnology at Harvard University; and Ralph G. Schwarz, director of operations, Ford Foundation. William G. Wing, a journalist formerly with the *New York Herald-Tribune*, handled the necessary staff work as the committee pursued its five-month-long national investigation, meeting in New York City, Wilmington, Del., and Washington, D.C.

A summary of the committee report was incorporated into the Williamsburg conference report, *Historic Preservation Tomorrow*, which set forth the revised principles and guidelines adopted at the conference. Entitled "Education and Training for Restoration Work," the committee report dealt with the creation of programs for professionals and for volunteers, such as the use of public relations and community education programs to reach the public and create a climate for preservation.

In assembling the special Ford Foundation–sponsored report, known also as the Whitehill report, the committee declared itself concerned "solely with the problem of the people who are so urgently needed to carry out the physical aspects of preservation and restoration." Ironically, the growing enthusiasm for preservation lessened the difficulty of raising funds for projects, but a more complex problem was finding craftsmen to implement them.

In the building trade, the skills of traditional carpentry and masonry were no longer being passed on, because projects did not require such workmanship. The National Park Service Mission 66 program of the previous decade had sparked a brief renaissance in these skills, but generally, the rapid changes in building design, techniques and materials (such as prefabricated parts) had made rare the ability to repair or reproduce details in old buildings. The National Park Service and Colonial Williamsburg by necessity had trained their own staffs in these crafts.

Most modern architects, too, were ill-equipped to deal with restoration projects. According to the report, architecture school curricula for the most part evidenced little interest in the grammar of historic styles and in draftsmanship. Education in these disciplines and training in restoration architecture would have to be increased in U.S. schools. The committee recommended that these goals be pursued initially at schools where broad environmental concerns already characterized the curricula —such as Cornell, Columbia and the University of Virginia. A con-

*Walter Muir Whitehill (left) chairing committee for Ford Foundation–
sponsored study, 1968. (National Trust)*

comitant need was for textbooks, reference books, study specimens and
case histories of both successes and failures.

Specifically, the report said, needs included finding artisans interested
in traditional work in wood, metal and masonry; architects, planners
and landscape architects who could carry out a restoration; and others
who could maintain the completed work. Apprenticeship programs were
needed to generate training, certification standards had to be established and the path from training to employment had to be opened
through rosters of craftsmen and referral systems.

To encourage a growth of the professional spirit in preservation and
to control the standards for future training and practice in the field, the
Whitehill committee looked to the Trust to supply national leadership,
suggesting a variety of specific goals. It urged that the Trust seek
foundation grants for the establishment of a support system for formal
educational programs. It also called on the Trust to set up mechanisms
for gathering information concerning all types of preservation education in the United States and to initiate joint efforts between the government and the private sector to provide careers in the preservation
field. Finally, the committee charged the Trust to make sure that tradi-

Cast plaster medallion in entrance hall of Oatlands, Leesburg, Va., illustrates early building crafts that preservationists seek to perpetuate. (Allen)

tional building crafts were perpetuated, that standards of work were set and maintained and that the public was educated to an appreciation of these skills. The Whitehill report was made public in the fall of 1968.

During this period, the Trust membership and training services staff expanded current educational programs. From the audiovisual collection, the American Landmarks Illustrated Program, a series of slide talks for national distribution, was created; the programs were used by 120 groups in the first year. A list of films pertaining to historic preservation, the environment, urban planning and other preservation-related subjects was also prepared and distributed to the membership. Included on the list was the first Trust film, *How Will We Know It's Us?*, produced by the Membership and Training Services Department with an urban renewal demonstration grant awarded to the Trust by the U.S. Department of Housing and Urban Development in 1967.

The film showed how HUD urban renewal programs could be used to preserve and revitalize city areas. It featured projects in New Haven, Conn., San Francisco and Monterey, Calif., Providence, R.I., and Galena, Ill. Supplementary sequences were filmed in Denver, Colo., Philadelphia, Pa., New York City and Tarrytown, N.Y. The theme of the film was taken from John Steinbeck's *The Grapes of Wrath*, in which a woman uprooted by the Depression gathers her few possessions for the trip West, asking "How will we know it's us without our past?" In 1968 *How Will We Know It's Us?* won two documentary awards in a competition sponsored by the National Visual Education Association and in the Columbus, Ohio, Film Festival. In its first six months of public availability, it was seen by an estimated 3.2 million television viewers; between 1968 and 1973 it reached an estimated 22 million people.

The Woodlawn Seminar for Historic Museum Associates, designed for the professional and volunteer staffs of historic house museums, and the Williamsburg Seminar for Historic Administrators continued, giving invaluable experience to those who planned careers in the historic preservation field. In 1968 the membership and training services staff also began to administer an annual scholarship for Trust staff members, enabling them to attend the summer course sponsored by the English National Trust at Attingham Park in Shropshire. Established in 1948, the course provided technical instruction as well as field trips to the numerous English National Trust historic house properties.

In addition to the education of graduate students and professionals, the Trust had from its beginning sought to actively involve young people in preservation. The first of several Trust seminars on professional opportunities in preservation-related fields was held in November 1966 for high school students planning college majors in history. In 1967 another seminar featured the professional opportunities in historical museum work. Trust president James Biddle saw education as a priority program, and in his lectures and through his column in *Preservation News*, he solicited supplementary donations to the Walden Fund to enable the Trust to establish summer fellowships for undergraduates.

In 1968 private gifts and a portion of the federal assistance allotted to the Trust made it possible for six undergraduate interns to spend the summer at Trust headquarters, gaining on-the-job training and learning firsthand about the work of various Trust departments, including community education programs, advisory services and membership recruitment techniques.

A gift of $50,000 from the Edward John Noble Foundation enabled the Trust to sponsor seven regional preservation conferences in 1967-68. They were held in Columbus, Tenn., Houston and Austin, Tex., Oakland, Calif., Newark, N.J., Jackson, Tenn., and Annapolis, Md.

The annual meeting and preservation conferences, as national forums, continued to reflect nationwide concerns. In the first two years of the "decade of decision," 1966–67, panel discussions and workshops at Philadelphia and St. Louis featured government officials and professional preservationists speaking on the topic of their respective responsibilities in preservation. In Savannah, Ga., in 1968 the Trust annual meeting theme, "Preservation and the Total Environment," reflected the growing public awareness that cultural as well as natural resources should be saved. At that meeting, in addition to the regular features of member organization exhibits, a preservation film festival and technical consultation sessions which matched experts one-to-one with information seekers, working breakfasts were held for the first time since 1957.

In 1969 the Trust headquarters staff was again reorganized and the Membership and Training Services Office became the Education and Training Services Office, a part of the Department of Programs and Services. At the same time, its functions were more clearly defined. Educational programs were also aided by the creation of a formal Field Services Office. Although its major program would be advising on the local level, the Field Services Office would also produce technical materials, encourage research, help in securing funds for technical conferences and aid in building up alliances between the Trust and other preservation-related agencies. This freed the education and training services staff to expand regular programs: developing educational programs for the general public; coordinating the annual meetings and regional conferences; maintaining the Trust archives, library and visual aids collection; assisting researchers; and supervising the work of summer interns.

In 1969 and 1970 grants from the National Endowment for the

Humanities made possible the establishment of six additional fellow-ships for the Williamsburg Seminar, enabling 24 persons to attend. The stipend of each participant was increased from $450 to $500 for the six-week term. A 1968 survey found that 49 percent of the Williamsburg fellows were working at historical agencies and 32 percent were teaching. At the 1970 Woodlawn Seminar, 14 historical museum associates came from 13 states, reflecting the wide influence of the program.

The NEH grants also allowed the Trust to award its first two research fellowships in 1970. Open to students of history, architecture, architectural history, archaeology, city planning, American civilization and cultural and environmental studies, each research fellowship provided $7,000 for a year of Trust-supervised work. The completed studies, "Adaptive Use of Historic Structures, A Series of Case Studies" by Myra F. Harrison and "The Feasibility of Tax Credits as Incentives for Historic Preservation" by Louis S. Wall, were reproduced and made available in the Trust library in 1972.

During 1969-70 regional preservation conferences were cosponsored in Boston, Mass., Chattanooga, Tenn., Round Top, Tex., Annapolis, Md., Alfred, N.Y., and Grand Rapids, Mich., where citizens were rallying to win other urban renewal battles after their City Hall defeat. The 1969 annual meeting and preservation conference in Denver, Colo., focused on the relation of preservation to the business community. Arnold Gingrich, editor of *Esquire* magazine and originator of the magazine's Business in the Arts awards, was the keynote speaker. In Charleston, S.C., in 1970 preservationists considered the question, What is preservation doing for the inner city? A "town meeting" forum gave preservationists an opportunity to discuss nationwide problems. Panel sessions on preservation law and a discussion comparing the efficacy of easements and zoning laws were other features of the national meeting, which attracted more than 1,600 members.

The Trust library and archives continued to grow as a resource center for staff members, and provisions were made for its use by outside researchers. Planning also began for the establishment of an inter-library loan policy among the Trust, the Library of Congress and the District of Columbia Public Library. In a three-year period, Trust archivist Patricia E. Williams supervised cataloguing of more than 3,300 books, pamphlets and periodicals and developed and updated a card catalogue and indexing system. Besides books relating to the technical aspects of preservation, the library included works on related disciplines, including archaeology, architecture, city planning, political science and technology.

In 1971, the Education and Training Services Office became the Department of Education, continuing under the direction of Glenn E.

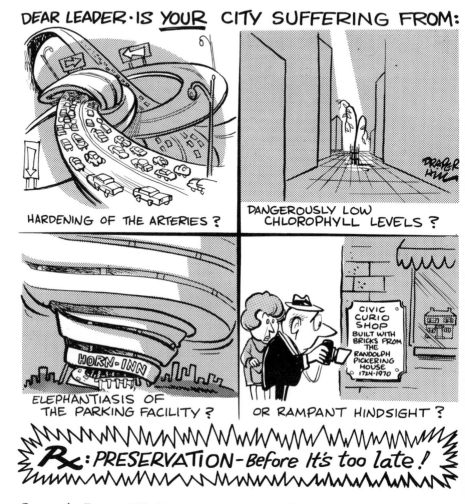

Cartoon by Draper Hill. (*Preservation News, April 1971*)

Thompson. During that year, the Education Department expanded the content of training courses, both at regional conferences and at the annual meeting.

Regional conferences were held in New Orleans, La., and Memphis, Tenn. The name of the Woodlawn Seminar was changed to the Woodlawn Seminar for Historic Preservation Associates to more accurately reflect the training offered there. At the 1971 annual meeting in San Diego, Calif., a new area of discussion was opened with a panel discussion "Preservation for the People." This session concentrated on the attitudes toward historic preservation held by ethnic minorities; another session focused on young people. Consultation sessions with technicians and preservation experts continued as before.

In November 1971 the Education Department implemented the first phase of programs designed in response to the Whitehill report by coordinating the Trust-sponsored Conference on Training for the Building Crafts. Participants at the conference addressed themselves to three problems: finding craftsmen interested in acquiring skills for historic preservation work; training and, if necessary, retraining such craftsmen; and finding resources among the institutions represented by the participants to alleviate the shortage of skilled craftsmen. (Among the organizations represented were the Association for Preservation Technology, which was formed in 1968 to address itself to the same problems; the American Institute of Interior Designers; the National Park Service; and the National Society of Interior Designers.)

A major concern was how to create a climate that might attract young people into restoration craft work. It was suggested that the two biggest obstacles were economic and social: In the United States, craftsmen are generally not well paid, nor is their work particularly highly regarded by the general public. Public appreciation, it was decided, must be fostered before the ranks of restoration craftsmen could begin to fill. Methods discussed for revitalizing the arts required for restoration included establishing a central council to coordinate training for the building crafts, setting up an expanded apprenticeship system, building regional training centers like those operated by the National Park Service, reprinting historical publications on crafts, compiling a roster of qualified craftsmen available to do restoration work and recognizing craftsmanship with special awards. The Education Department took over ongoing plans for an institute for historic preservation and restoration to be established when funds were available.

In the meantime, the Education Department coordinated Trust participation as the U.S. representative in two significant international educational programs. The first, the European Traveling Summer School for Restorationists, was directed by 1965 Crowninshield Award-winner Charles E. Peterson. This program, funded by grants from the National Endowment for the Arts and the National Endowment for the Humanities, gave 18 U.S. and Canadian students and young professionals an opportunity to see preservation work firsthand in England, France, Belgium and the Netherlands.

The Trust was also responsible for the first program sponsored by the United States as a member of the Rome Centre. The Department of Field Services and the Education Department coordinated the North

Participants in North American International Regional Conference on Preservation and Conservation observe archaeological excavations at Williamsburg, Va., September 1972. (John J-G. Blumenson)

American International Regional Conference on Preservation and Conservation, held in September 1972 in Williamsburg and Philadelphia. The program brought together 160 professionals for discussions on the theme that there is "only one world" for both conservation and preservation. Made possible by grants from the Rome Centre, the National Trust, the National Endowment for the Humanities, Colonial Williamsburg, the National Park Service and the Pennsylvania Historical and Museum Commission, the conference featured more than 50 panel members, speakers and commentators from North America and Europe, who dealt with such subjects as occupations in preservation, the role of organizations in the preservation movement, materials and techniques, maintenance standards and education. Plans were made for the publication of the conference proceedings.

In another special program cosponsored in 1972 by the Trust and the National Association of Counties, a study of English planning was made available to 36 officials from Loudoun and Fauquier counties in Virginia. In England, where the public good is placed before an individual's right to develop land, the county officials studied public policies, administration procedures and planning tools and techniques, including tax structures and land use legislation.

To aid in the placement of craftsmen and other preservation professionals, the Education Department began production in 1972 of a bulletin listing job opportunities in the preservation field. Its title, *Work*, reflected the emphasis on recruiting craftsmen, historians, architects, administrators and others (including young professionals and artisans) into the preservation field for careers; preservation had too long been regarded as an avocation, and the need for vocational training and placement had been documented by the Whitehill report. Through 1973 *Work* was made available bimonthly by subscription to all member organizations, universities and colleges and individuals. Later it was incorporated as a regular section of *Preservation News* because the Trust believed it could provide a greater service by publishing job opportunities on a monthly basis.

In 1972 the Education Department gained the services of its first full-time visual aids coordinator since 1967. More than 2,800 slides were added to the Trust collection, and a viewing machine was purchased for use by staff and researchers. The preservation film list was also updated and added to the Bicentennial Kit being distributed by the Trust. Three lectures were added to the American Landmarks Illustrated Program series. Throughout the year, some 80 researchers used the library and archives for their work.

Regional conferences were held during 1972 in New Orleans, La., the District of Columbia and Portland, Maine. The Washington, D.C., annual meeting was planned around an appropriate theme for a presidential election year: "Preservation and the American Political System." Panel discussions and workshops covered such topics as the politics of preservation; problems of inner-city preservation as it relates to the urban population; the economic effects of establishing historic districts; new preservation fields, such as industrial architecture and engineering history; and the use of restrictive covenants for historic preservation. At this meeting Helen Duprey Bullock, resigning after 24 years of service to the Trust, was honored with a special ceremony.

In 1973 the Trust internship program was expanded to include 12 college students working for 10 weeks at Trust headquarters and historic properties. Three students in horticulture and landscape architecture worked at Woodlawn Plantation, and at headquarters six students were assigned to the departments of Properties, Publications and Education. In addition, three students on a Historic American Buildings Survey team worked at Oatlands.

Regional conferences in 1973 were held in Santa Fe, N.M., and St. Paul, Minn., and a semester-long preservation seminar was cosponsored by the Trust and Old Sturbridge Village in Sturbridge, Mass. The 1973 annual meeting in Cleveland, Ohio, with the theme "Preservation in Your Town," reflected the range of services the Trust was able to provide. Recognizing the fact that most preservation action is accomplished on the local level, workshops and discussions were planed to help local groups organize and utilize their community resources. Experts in various fields chaired sessions, explaining to participants how to carry on business procedures in preservation groups, develop educational activities on a community level, produce publications on a limited budget, establish good public relations and generate publicity, raise funds and apply for grants, use and preserve historic house museums and prepare and fund Bicentennial projects. These presentations, including some case studies, were to be published as a handbook in 1974 to provide further help to local groups.

The Trust had actively sought ways to begin providing support for professional training in preservation since 1971 when it sponsored the Conference on Training in the Building Crafts. In the interim, an ad hoc committee made up of leading preservationists from all parts of the country had investigated the possibilities of implementing some of the forthcoming suggestions. In January 1973 the Trust began a study of the ways and means of developing a preservation institute. The study was under the direction of Richard W. Haupt, former director of the Cincinnati Historical Society. In July, following the resignation of Glenn E. Thompson, Haupt joined the Trust staff as director of the Education Department. Planning began for the implementation of programs to fill the needs revealed by his study.

By the end of 1973 programs were under way to build closer relations with universities and training institutions that offer courses in preservation and related fields and with professional associations and to make their educational programs and career opportunities in preservation more widely known.

The establishment in January 1969 of the Field Services Office in the Department of Programs and Services was the fulfillment of a long-time Trust goal. For 22 years the Trust had provided a myriad of services to preservation groups of all levels of expertise throughout the country. Despite the lack of money and personnel, the gargantuan efforts of the small staff made the service program one of the main features of the Trust. During the early 60s, outgoing correspondence sometimes averaged 1,000 letters a month. Yet this was a "putting out fires" approach.

In goals set forth in 1966 for the "decade of decision," three main programs were concerned with services to local groups: to provide organizations with professional consultation and with qualified staff to permit scholarly evaluative surveys so that the states could take advantage of the federal preservation matching grants programs; to make field services available wherever needed for actual preservation work, sending teams of architects, architectural historians, landscape designers, publications and public relations experts and fund raisers to assist local groups; and to provide loans and challenge grants to save significant properties in emergency situations.

Predictably, requests for service proliferated after the passage of the 1966 National Historic Preservation Act as states began to develop master plans for preservation and to apply for federal aid. Senior editor and historian Helen Duprey Bullock, in charge of consultation and correspondence, worked with the Trust Board of Advisors, government representatives, including state liaison officers, and representatives of the American Institute of Architects and the American Society of Civil Engineers to keep in constant touch with all areas of the country. All Trust departments responded to requests, by mail, by telephone, through research at headquarters and through field trips and lectures.

But the number of requests for assistance necessitated a separate and complete program. In 1968 a $500,000 grant from the Rockefeller Brothers Fund made it possible for the Trust to establish a staff devoted exclusively to providing professional assistance to preservation organizations and government programs on a nationwide basis. To direct the program of the Field Services Office, the Trust obtained the services of Russell V. Keune, former assistant keeper of the National Register of Historic Places and a 1964 fellow of the Williamsburg Seminar for Historic Administrators.

In February 1969 the Board of Trustees Advisory Committee on Field Services met to endorse some primary goals: to establish personal contact and maintain liaison with Washington-based representatives of national professional organizations and federal agencies concerned with historic preservation; to organize and implement a consultant service grant program; to prepare and publish a guide to federal service programs and grants available to the states; and to develop an advisory program to assist groups in preparing and submitting applications for federal grants-in-aid.

With the assistance of the Advisory Council on Historic Preservation, the Field Services Office began work on the federal guide, using a survey of federal agencies relating to historic preservation undertaken by the Legislative Reference Service of the Library of Congress. The study was designed to reflect changes in federal policy since the passage of the 1966 legislation, such as the new U.S. Department of Transportation regulations. The directory, *A Guide to Federal Programs: Programs and Activities Related to Historic Preservation*, which describes more than 200 programs, was scheduled for publication in 1974.

In January 1970 an $8,000 grant from the National Endowment for the Humanities also made it possible for work to begin on a companion volume: *A Guide to State Programs*, designed for use by local groups.

The Lafayette Square Restoration Committee, St. Louis, Mo., received a National Historic Preservation Fund loan in 1973 to help restore these town-houses. (Ken J. MacSwan, St. Louis Post-Dispatch)

This manual was published by the Trust in 1972. The guide was based on information gathered from state liaison officers by the field services staff. The first step in the process was the compilation of information presented at National Park Service–sponsored nationwide conferences of 1967 and 1968; later the field services staff sent questionnaires and survey forms to all state liaison officers asking them to update the information. Designed to answer a critical need to provide such information to local groups, the manual contained comprehensive details of state preservation legislation and programs, and it listed all state preservation officials. Editing and production for both guides were supplied by the Department of Publications.

In its first year, inquiries to the field services staff reflected a variety of needs and were handled by letter, telephone, personal consultation and staff field trips. Plans began for the development of a corps of outside consultants in such preservation-related fields as city planning, architecture, redevelopment, law, archaeology and historical research. Preliminary work also began on programs to teach preservation groups how to conduct architectural surveys of their communities and how to organize and finance preservation efforts. The staff also initiated a column on state historic preservation programs for *Preservation News* and produced *Historic Preservation and the Tourist Industry* for distribution as part of the Trust technical leaflet series.

In January 1970 the Field Services Office launched another valuable program by giving its first consultant service grants, a total of $20,400 in aid to 24 communities. Typical of the matching grants was a $600 grant to Sistersville, W.Va., to enable townspeople to conduct a survey of their historic oil boomtown on which to base an application for federal funding. Specifically designed to enable preservationists to obtain expert help in some technical phase of preservation work rather than to fund entire projects or acquisitions of property, the matching consultant service grants have been used by preservationists to obtain a variety of services. For example, a grant to a St. Louis, Mo., citizens group helped pay for a feasibility study on the rehabilitation of the Old Post Office. Others have financed consultant services in museology (French Cable Museum in Orleans, Mass.), surveying (Old West Side, Ann Arbor, Mich.) and economics (Pioneer Square Historic District, Seattle, Wash.). Since the inception of the program, 167 grants ranging from $200 to $2,000 and totaling more than $100,000 have been awarded. The first four of a series of case studies arising from work done under a grant have been published: *Fisher Hall, Miami University, Oxford, Ohio: Its Preservation Potential; The Park-McCullough House, North Bennington, Vermont: A Program of Use; Water Street Study, Chillicothe, Ohio: Suggestions for Rehabilitation* and *West Virginia Independence Hall, Wheeling, West Virginia: A Master Plan for Restoration and Use.*

In May 1970 the Field Services Office coordinated the first regional workshop for Trust Board of Advisors members, in Chicago. The workshop was designed to establish liaison among advisors, National Park Service personnel and the state liaison officers in each state. Made possible by the Edward John Noble Foundation grant, the pilot project brought together private, professional, state and federal historic preservation program representatives from Illinois, Indiana, Iowa, Kentucky, Michigan, Minnesota, Missouri, Ohio and Wisconsin. A second workshop was held in Santa Fe, N.M., in December 1970 for the benefit of representatives from Arizona, Colorado, New Mexico, Oklahoma, Texas and Utah. From 1970–73 the state liaison officers (organized as the National Conference of State Historic Preservation Officers) met in conjunction with the Trust annual meeting, enabling the Board of Advisors to plan and develop programs in cooperation with the states.

In 1971 two private gifts totaling $10,000 made it possible for the Board of Advisors to expand its activities. Communications among advisors were strengthened by the initiation of a bimonthly newsletter in 1972. The advisors also began receiving copies of all substantive Trust correspondence pertinent to their areas and annual field reports, which are published and distributed by the Trust.

Since its beginning the Trust had rendered legal aid to preservationists. The nucleus of its legal archives was a collection of local, state and federal preservation law, updated in 1962 and again in 1969. Information on legislation had been prepared over the years under the auspices of the Trust, including publication of Jacob H. Morrison's book *Historic Preservation Law*. In 1970 the Trust was called upon to become even more directly involved by entering two legal battles: Overton Park in Memphis, Tenn., threatened by highway construction, and a historic area in Lexington, Ky., scheduled for demolition in an urban renewal project.

The Overton Park case was similar to the situation in the Vieux Carré, in New Orleans, La. A design for a six-lane federally aided expressway bisecting the mid-city park had been approved in 1947. However, when public hearings were held in 1957, protest resulted in the formation of an activist group, Citizens to Preserve Overton Park. At that time, the mayor and several city commissioners supported the citizens group. In 1968, however, the city council approved the original location. In 1969, even though the final design was not yet approved, the state highway department began to purchase rights-of-way.

When Secretary of Transportation John A. Volpe also approved the route, the Citizens to Preserve Overton Park challenged the decision in court. The suit alleged that the public hearing procedures of the 1968 Federal-Aid Highway Act had not been followed and that neither Secretary Volpe nor his predecessor, Alan S. Boyd, had sought "prudent and feasible alternatives" as directed by the Transportation Act of 1966. The citizens requested a preliminary injunction to halt construction, but in March the federal district judge ruled against the plaintiffs. When an appeal was also rejected, a Trust consultant service grant enabled the organization to hire a transportation planner to study the effects the expressway would have on the park.

Memphis preservationists appealed to the Supreme Court in 1970 and the Trust provided a second consultant service grant for obtaining expert testimony. In this instance the Court reversed the decision of the district court, ordering it to review the earlier decision and to require personal testimony about formal findings concerning the location of the highway. Secretary Volpe vetoed the expressway location in January 1972 on environmental grounds. However, because the state retained the option of using state rather than federal funds to construct the road to circumvent federal restrictions, the Overton Park fight continues.

The Trust knew from bitter experience that laws were effective only if followed in good faith. In the field of historic preservation, the

M. MARCEL MARCEAU, A DISTINGUISHED VISITOR IN TOWN, HAS GRACIOUSLY VOLUNTEERED A PROGRESS REPORT ON I-40 THROUGH OVERTON PARK...

Cartoon by Draper Hill. (The Commercial Appeal, *Memphis, Tenn.,* *February 1, 1975*)

passage of protective legislation evoked restrained rejoicing, for a building could still be destroyed "by mistake" (as was the Curry House in Santa Fe, N.M., razed in 1968 while its nomination to the National Register was being approved) or altered beyond repair while interpretation and applicability were argued in the courts.

The Lexington, Ky., urban renewal conflict started in early 1967 when the Blue Grass Trust, a long-time Trust member organization, began a fight to save 14 historic buildings in the West High Street Historic District. Ignoring these efforts, the Lexington Renewal Authority in December 1969 razed seven of the buildings. Enraged citizens responded by forming the South Hill Neighborhood Association and filed suit against Secretary of Housing and Urban Development George Romney, challenging the right of urban renewal programs to destroy property listed in the National Register.

By April 1970, after setbacks on the district court level, the case reached the Supreme Court, the preservationists having filed for a writ of certiorari. Whether or not preservationists and owners of National Historic Landmarks had legal standing to complain of violations of section 106 of the National Historic Preservation Act, which protects landmarks from federally aided projects, was a pertinent question in the appeal. Another question was similar to the one posed in Grand Rapids, Mich.: Do provisions of the National Historic Preservation Act apply to properties that have been added to the National Register subsequent to the initial approval of a project by a federal agency? In support of the petition, the Trust filed an amicus curiae brief on the grounds that the decision of the lower court could threaten the effectiveness of federal preservation legislation and thereby the entire progress of the preservation movement.

To the dismay of preservationists, the Supreme Court declined to review the case, thereby upholding the decision of the lower court.

In view of the legal complexities involved in historic preservation, the Trust featured in the July 1970 issue of *Preservation News* an article by Robert E. Stipe, professor of public law and government at the University of North Carolina, entitled "Preservation Lawyers—Unite!" Pointing out that all other professionals in the preservation field (such as architects, planners and historians) had developed communications networks through newsletters, Stipe urged lawyers interested in historic preservation to do likewise. In addition, he listed other critical needs, including an annotated bibliography of published materials on the legal aspects of preservation, indexed, kept up to date and available at a low price; a published collection of legal documents and forms pertaining to private preservation problems; and the dissemination of legal information through an advisory body of preservation lawyers. Other steps he recommended included commissioning specific research and publishing material on new preservation techniques, investigating the efficacy of amicus curiae briefs (such as had been filed by the Trust), keeping new court decisions in front of lawyers by means of a loose-leaf reporter, publishing case histories, generating more activity in legislative drafting and urging universities to start courses in historic preservation law.

Preservationists realized that the discouraging developments in court called for more than conservative, defensive moves. By mid-1970 a special Trustee Advisory Committee on Historic Preservation Law was formed, and the Trust scheduled the first national conference on legal techniques in historic preservation to be held in May of the following year. The conference drew more than 80 lawyers and 60 observers to Washington for two days of lectures and discussions. Topics included the response of federal and state legislation to historic preservation; zoning and historic districts; the standing of preservation issues before the courts; implications of tax policies on historic preservation; and the use of easements and the transfer of development rights concept to protect historic property. Selected papers from the conference were published in the fall 1971 symposium issue of *Law and Contemporary*

Problems, a publication of the Duke University Law School, Durham, N.C., and others were included in *Legal Techniques in Historic Preservation,* published by the Trust in 1972.

As his part of the proceedings, Trust president James Biddle outlined the growing involvement of the Trust in the legal areas of historic preservation and announced the scheduled addition of an attorney to the field services staff to direct a formal program of legal information service.

The Field Services Office became a full department in July 1971. The same date marked the opening of the first Trust regional field services office, in San Francisco. The Trust had sought for years to become more national by establishing a permanent advisory staff west of the Mississippi River. Too often it had had to counter the charge of eastern provincialism by pointing out that one of its first properties was Casa Amesti, that annual meetings had been held in the West (in San Francisco, San Antonio and Denver) and that its membership drives, its consultation services and its grants reached all the way to the Pacific. The establishment of the western field office was made possible by a grant of $60,000 over three years from the San Francisco Foundation, itself a recipient of residual funds from the estate of Mrs. Henry P. Russell, a Trustee from 1952-66 and first chairman of the Casa Amesti Council. Through the work of local Trust members and a gift from Mrs. John A. McCone, a member of the Board of Trustees, office space was obtained from the California Historical Society, a Trust member organization. In 1972 the western field services office was moved to Jackson Square, San Francisco's first historic district.

The primary function of the field office staff during the first six months was to meet with a maximum number of member organizations in the 13 western states and to establish personal contact with state historic preservation officers and the state preservation coordinators of the American Institute of Architects to assess the needs of the area. John L. Frisbee, III, director of the western field services office, on the way to his territory, conferred with preservationists in Topeka, Kans., Denver, Colo., Cheyenne, Wyo., Salt Lake City, Utah, and Carson City, Nev. A report of the first full year of activity by the field office staff, *Preservation in the West,* was published by the Trust in April 1973.

Other 1971 activities of the Field Services Department involved supplying assistance to both novice and professional preservationists. A consultant service clinic was held in April for the benefit of organizations in the Cincinnati area. At this conference, each local group could meet for 1½-hour question-and-answer sessions with a panel of experts who gave advice on particular preservation problems. In May the field services staff coordinated the first of a series of conferences focusing on

Jackson Square Historic District, San Francisco, Calif., includes the former Columbia Bank, now a radio station office. Western Regional Office of the National Trust is nearby. (Carleton Knight, III)

the preservation programs of the U.S. Department of Housing and Urban Development. Preservationists came to Washington, D.C., and met with HUD representatives to learn how to apply for grants. Two follow-up conferences were held the next year. The field services staff also provided assistance through such publications as a pamphlet entitled "Careers in Historic Preservation," which was issued in 1971.

Research began in 1971 for the assembly of a consultant reference file to provide local groups with access to professionals in historic preservation. Until that time, there had been no central reference source of qualified firms or individuals. By 1972 the file listed more than 200 professionals in such areas as architecture, landscape architecture, archaeology, construction engineering, historical research, museum operation and interpretation, crafts, interior design, furnishing, planning and real estate, law, economics, finance and administration, journalism, photography and public relations.

A special Trust advisory committee had begun fund-raising plans in 1970 for a National Historic Preservation Fund, by which the Trust could aid local groups in acquiring properties. Primarily a revolving fund, the principal of the fund would be used to make both matching and nonmatching grants; loans would be interest bearing but would allow deferred repayment. In addition to the consultant service grants, the fund loans would also supply matching grants (limited to $3,000) for consultant services in evaluating properties being considered for purchase. A guaranty fund to be used only in special circumstances would guarantee such obligations as second mortgages and notes on local commercial loans used to establish revolving funds.

Raising funds for a revolving fund had advantages over soliciting donations to an endowment: Since the money would be in continuous use, donors could see tangible results. The revolving fund idea was also desirable as "a quick way to gain political stature" by making a contribution to the community real estate market by buying, restoring, selling or renting and buying again.

By the end of 1971, the fund, under the direction of Ralph G. Schwarz, totaled more than $300,000. The first loan, for $10,000, was awarded to Harrisville, N.H., a mill town threatened when its woolen mills declared bankruptcy and closed. Harrisville used the money to organize Historic Harrisville and to begin programs for preservation of the town. By the end of the year, the woolen mills were back in use by a company producing water cooling systems, and a small part of the mill was once again being used to process wool in the form of hand yarns. The loan also aided in the establishment of a historic district and the drafting of restrictive covenants on older buildings.

In 1972 the National Historic Preservation Fund came under the supervision of the Field Services Department. The Lafayette Square Restoration Committee in St. Louis, Mo., a representative recipient, was loaned $25,000 in June 1973 to aid in establishing a revolving fund. The revolving fund is used for the purchase, renovation and resale of historic properties in the Lafayette Square Historic District and has stimulated local private loans and municipal revenue sharing funds.

At the request of the Council on Environmental Quality, the Advisory Council on Historic Preservation began in 1972 to develop guidelines to assist state governments in drafting historic preservation legislation. The Field Services Department assisted the council with research on the project. In the summer of 1972, the *Suggested Guidelines for State Historic Preservation* were adopted by the Council of State Governments, which published and distributed copies to state legislators throughout the nation. The Advisory Council printed copies for distribution to individuals, local governments and professional organizations.

The field services staff also prepared a Trust position paper on federal tax policies that was used by the Advisory Council in 1972 to draft the proposed Environmental Protection Tax Act. The proposal was designed to encourage historic preservation by giving tax credits for rehabilitation and restoration and for charitable donations of partial interest in land, such as scenic easements, for conservation purposes. President Richard Nixon proposed the legislation to Congress in 1973, and appropriate bills were introduced in both houses.

In addition to assisting in these projects, the Field Services Department gave on-site and written comments concerning proposed historic district ordinances and enabling legislation. With the help of a summer intern, the legal archives were indexed and cross-referenced for use in the department's growing information and advisory services. Two more amicus curiae briefs were also prepared. One brief was entered in the case of *Penn Central, et al.* vs. *The Landmarks Preservation Commission of New York City*, in which the plaintiffs charged that the city landmarks law violated both the New York State and the United States constitutions.

The second brief concerned the protection of the natural and the built environments. In 1970 the commonwealth of Virginia had announced plans to build a 1,200-acre prison facility in Green Springs, a historic rural area in which three properties listed in the National Register were located. The project was to be financed by a grant from the Law Enforcement Assistance Administration of the U.S. Department of Justice. However, a citizens group, the Green Springs Association, filed suit in federal court, charging that construction of the prison without due consideration for its effect on the surrounding historic area would violate the protective procedures outlined in both the National Historic Preservation Act and the National Environmental Policy Act. The group sought a permanent injunction to prevent the appropriation of funds. The Trust filed an amicus curiae brief, and Russell V. Keune, director of the Field Services Department, testified in the first hearings.

In January 1971 the court ruled that the plaintiffs did indeed have standing under the federal acts to demand a review of such action. However, the court failed to grant the injunction on the grounds that the Law Enforcement Assistance Administration was under no duty to comply with the two environmental protection statutes, because of a conflicting duty under the statute governing LEAA grants. The conflict, then, pitted the right of the state to select a construction site against the right of the plaintiffs to seek to prevent an adverse environmental impact.

By further court orders, the Virginia State Department of Welfare

Cartoon by Draper Hill. (Preservation News, *November 1972*)

and Institutions was compelled to file an environmental impact statement; however, its 200-page report claimed that the prison would have
no adverse impact on the historic rural area. The LEAA, in turn filing
a report, likewise reported that no adverse environmental effects would
result. The Green Springs Association, suspicious of the legitimacy of
the studies, again went to court to force the release of substantiating
material—specifically, a report by the National Clearinghouse for Crim-
inal Justice Planning and Architecture, a group from the University of
Illinois that had served as a consultant on the LEAA study. When on

Technical workshop, What To Do Before the Conservator Is Hired, at Chesterwood Studio, Stockbridge, Mass., May 1972. (Paul Rocheleau)

court orders the study was released, its findings were discovered to have been negative on prison construction. The LEAA claimed that these findings were "not an objective analysis."

In the face of this dispute, Virginia Gov. A. Linwood Holton, Jr., announced in 1972 that the prison would be moved elsewhere if the Green Springs residents would donate scenic easements on their property to the state, insuring preservation of the area as a historic district. Ironically, the owners had offered such easements two years earlier when the conflict began, only to be turned down by the state.

In 1973, however, Governor Holton announced that the prison would be built after all. At his request, the Virginia Historic Landmarks Commission had prepared an opinion on the preservation of the area. Despite the fact that the land owners had given easements on more than 6,500 acres to the state, action that the commission commended as "a remark-able, unprecedented achievement," it also declared that the land covered was like a checkerboard, and thus, full preservation could not be assured. Meanwhile, the whole area, including more than 10,000 acres and 33 structures, was nominated to the National Register, making it one of the largest rural historic districts in the United States. Although the state did begin construction of the prison in the fall of 1973, pres-ervationists hoped that the area would be declared a National Historic Landmark and that the Virginia general election would bring a change in the state administration. It was further hoped that the new leaders would be willing to reconsider the decision to establish the prison in the Green Springs area. (In 1974, Gov. Mills E. Godwin reversed his predecessor and announced that the prison would not be located in Green Springs.)

In 1972 the Field Services Department also coordinated Trust partici-pation in a number of special studies and programs. To provide museum services, the department dealt with questions concerning operation, interpretation, conservation and administration procedures and began to compile an annotated bibliography of articles on historic museums. With the Education Department, the Field Services Department directed a two-day technical workshop in May 1972 at Chesterwood on What To Do Before the Conservator Is Hired, which attracted 60 participants from the New England states.

Field services staff members were also called upon to review the manuscript of a guide prepared with a $21,000 grant from the U.S. Department of Transportation. The guide, which focused on methods of including historic preservation factors in transportation systems design, was scheduled for release in 1974 under the title *Techniques for Incorporating Historic Preservation Objectives into the Highway Plan-ning Process.*

In 1973 the Trust supported, through congressional testimony by Gordon Gray and James Biddle, the Museum Services Act, proposed in both houses of Congress. The bill was designed to supply $40 million in brick-and-mortar matching grants to American Association of Museums–accredited museums through the U.S. Department of Health, Education and Welfare, much as National Register properties are aided by Interior Department grants authorized under the National Historic Preservation Act of 1966. At the time, federal funding of museums through the Smithsonian Institution and the National Endowment for the Arts was available only for programs, not for facilities. The bill also proposed the establishment of an Institute for the Improvement of Museum Services. With plans of its own for establishing mechanisms to train professionals in preservation, the Trust saw that in concert with museums much could be done for the entire historic preservation movement. Speaking before a congressional subcommittee in support of the bill, Trust president James Biddle emphasized that museums "fill an important need for both their local communities and the traveling American and foreign public." This legislation is still being considered by Congress.

In March 1973 the Field Services Department directed the first regional historic preservation law conference in Mobile, Ala. The Southeast Preservation Law Conference, cosponsored by the Trust and the Mobile Historic Development Commission , was attended by approximately 100 lawyers, planners and local public officials from five states. In response to a record number of requests for information following this conference, the staff prepared fact sheets on various aspects of preservation law, including one that compared existing historic preservation ordinances. Staff members also began producing summaries of litigation, state historic preservation tax statutes and historic preservation tax bills pending before Congress.

In the summers of 1972 and 1973, the Field Services and Education departments coordinated and planned summer architectural preservation courses for the Preservation Institute: Nantucket, a program conducted by the University of Florida, which in the fall of 1970 began its own graduate-level program in preservation. The courses sponsored by the institute on Nantucket Island, Mass., were designed for students and for professionals involved in preservation. In the summer-long program, course participants updated guides to the area and proposed designs for the downtown district. The increasing tourism gave them an opportunity to study firsthand the effects such an influx of visitors can have on land use policies and plans for development.

Other conferences were designed to provide technical assistance to professionals in specialized fields. In October 1973 at the Trust annual meeting in Cleveland, Ohio, the Field Services Department held a conference for representatives of landmarks commissions. In November a conference was held in Madison, Wis., for the technical staffs of the state historic preservation officers. Technical assistance was given to other professional groups through the Consultant Service Grant Program.

With a $32,000 grant from the National Endowment for the Arts, the Field Services Department undertook a definitive analysis of a representative sample of historic districts under the NEA City Edges Program, the second in a series of NEA programs on urban design and planning. The goal of the study was to identify and describe those elements—built and natural—that form the edges of historic districts and to delineate what effect these edges have on the historic districts themselves and on the surrounding areas. Under the City Edges Program, the National

Endowment for the Arts gave a total of $1,119,724 to 12 other preservation-related projects.

By the end of 1972 the director of the western field services office had visited 200 organizations, including groups in Alaska and Hawaii. In addition, members of the Board of Advisors and the Board of Trustees from western states had traveled a total of 75,000 miles, meeting with and advising local preservation groups. Two-day experimental visits were made to Eureka and Yreka, Calif., for meetings with representatives of the news media, city and county officials, business executives and citizens. Trust representatives encouraged them to include historic preservation in the long-range development plans for their cities. In 1973 a major program was the further development of regional workshops and preservation clinics, held in cosponsorship with state and local organizations. In March another consultant service clinic, similar to one conducted in Cincinnati, was held in Los Angeles. A third consultant service clinic was held in Salt Lake City for preservationists from Utah, Colorado and Idaho. A two-day Arizona preservation workshop took place in April, cosponsored by the Trust, the Arizona State Parks Board, the Arizona Historical Society and the Arizona State Museum. Workshops were also held in Eureka, and in Sitka and Talkeetna, Alaska. Partially because of these services, membership in the West grew markedly, increasing 35 percent during 1973.

Encouraged by the success of the field services office in the West, in May 1973 the Trust established a field services office in Chicago to provide service to 11 midwestern states. Mary C. Means, formerly on the staff of the National Register, joined the Trust as director of the office. She began extensive traveling to each of the states, making appearances on radio and television and presenting testimony before landmarks commissions. Appropriately, the midwestern field office is located in a portion of the Glessner House, designed by H.H. Richardson and one of the first officially designated landmarks in Chicago. The planning for the restoration of the Glessner House had been assisted by a 1970 Trust consultant service grant.

Because of requests for a field services office in the New England area, the Historic Properties Department in 1972 began an experimental program, with the administrator of Chesterwood making field visits throughout the region. In 1973, at the invitation of the Society for the Preservation of New England Antiquities, discussions began for the future joint establishment of a field office in New England. These plans for expansion are typical of the Trust's determination to provide more and better assistance to all of the nation's preservationists by being closer to the day-to-day problems on the preservation scene.

Cartoon by Draper Hill. (Preservation News, *April 1970*)

Throughout the years and in all its activities, the Trust has pledged itself to preserve the quality of life and the tangible evidence of the foundations on which America is built. It has dedicated its efforts to making citizens aware of the riches, both natural and cultural, around them. The Trust is determined to continue these tasks, confident that the nation will see the practicality and value of historic preservation. Now, during the Bicentennial era, the Trust hopes that millions of Americans will begin to see, to appreciate and to defend this heritage, for it is only on a foundation of understanding and respect for the past that a better future will be built.

Appendixes

Some material in these appendixes was published in David E. Finley's *History of the National Trust for Historic Preservation*, *1947–1963* (Washington, D.C.: National Trust, 1965). Whenever appropriate, information has been updated through 1973.

APPENDIX 1

CERTIFICATE OF INCORPORATION OF THE NATIONAL COUNCIL FOR HISTORIC SITES AND BUILDINGS, 1947

OFFICE OF THE RECORDER OF DEEDS
DISTRICT OF COLUMBIA
OPO 680562

RECORDER OF DEEDS
WASHINGTON

District of Columbia
SEAL

THIS IS TO CERTIFY that the pages attached hereto constitute a full, true, and complete copy of

A Certificate of Incorporation of National Council of Historic Sites and Buildings, dated on the 11th day of June A.D. 1947 and recorded on the 23rd day of June A.D. 1947 at 9:17 A.M.

as the same appears of record in this office.

Recorder of Deeds
SEAL
District of Columbia

IN TESTIMONY WHEREOF,
I have hereunto set my hand and caused the seal of this office to be affirmed, this the 23rd day of
June   A.D. 1947

Marshall L. Shepard,
Recorder of Deeds, D. C.

By (Signed) Eleanore Lee Degue
Deputy Recorder of Deeds

U. S. Government Printing Office 16—44255-1

No. 30815 Recorded June 23, 1947
at 9:17 A.M.

CERTIFICATE OF INCORPORATION

We, the undersigned, all citizens of the United States, and a majority citizens and residents of of the District of Columbia, desiring to associate ourselves as a corporation pursuant to the provisions of Title 29 of Chapter 6 of the District of Columbia Code (1940) do hereby certify as follows:

First. The name or title by which this corporation shall be known in law shall be

NATIONAL COUNCIL FOR HISTORIC SITES AND BUILDINGS

Second. The term for which it is organized shall be perpetual.

Third. The particular business and objects of said corporation shall be educational and scientific, and to further the preservation and interpretation, for the public benefit, of sites and buildings situated in the United States and its possessions and significant for American history and culture.

Fourth. The number of its trustees, directors, or managers for the first year of its existence shall be ten.

In Testimony Whereof, we have this 11th day of June 1947, hereunto set our hands and seal.

U. S. Grant 3rd	(Seal)
George McAneny	(Seal)
David E. Finley	(Seal)
Guy Stanton Ford	(Seal)
Waldo G. Leland	(Seal)

District of Columbia, ss

I, Charles B. Walstrom, a Notary Public in and for the District of Columbia, do hereby certify that U. S. Grant, 3rd, George McAneny, David E. Finley, Guy Stanton Ford, and Waldo G. Leland parties to a certain Certificate of Incorporation bearing date on the 11th day of June 1947, and hereto annexed, personally appeared before me in said District, the said U. S. Grant, 3rd, George McAneny, David E. Finley, Guy Stanton Ford, and Waldo G. Leland being personally well known to me as the persons who executed the said Certificate of Incorporation, and severally acknowledged the same to be their act and deed.

Given under my hand and seal this 11th day of June 1947.
(Notarial Seal)

Charles B. Walstrom
Notary Public

My Commission Expires
April 30, 1951.

REPORT OF THE COMMITTEE ON ORGANIZATION
OF THE NATIONAL TRUST, 1948*

I.

THE NEED FOR HISTORICAL PRESERVATION

"If America forgets where she came from, if the people lose sight of what brought them along, if she listens to the deniers and mockers, then will rot and dissolution begin."
—Carl Sandburg, *Remembrance Rock*

Soil can be conserved, forests replanted, substitutes found for exhausted mineral resources, but once destroyed, our historical sites and structures are forever lost to the nation. They are the tangible reminders of our past; they are priceless treasures of the national wealth; and they are irreplaceable, for although copies can be made, they never have the meaning of the originals. We are spendthrifts indeed if we sit idly by, allowing the obliteration for all time of these monuments to our national democratic heritage. We are worse than spendthrifts if we disregard the educational opportunities for the strengthening of our democratic foundations which these sites and buildings exemplify.

II.

THE NEED FOR AN
AMERICAN NATIONAL TRUST

National instrumentalities exist for the preservation or conservation of our na-

---

* The report was presented November 4, 1948, by H. Alexander Smith, Jr., committee chairman. Members of the committee were George McAneny, A.E. Demaray and Huntington Cairns; Ronald F. Lee and Frederick L. Rath, Jr., were ex-officio members of the committee.

tional wealth in a number of important fields. Our lands are protected by the Office of Land Utilization, the Bureau of Land Management, the Bureau of Reclamation, the Agricultural Research Administration, and the Soil Conservation Service; our sub-surface resources by the Bureau of Mines; our fauna by the Fish and Wildlife Service; our forests by the Forest Service; and phases of our culture by the Commission of Fine Arts, the National Capital Park and Planning Commission, Smithsonian Institution, the National Gallery of Art, the Library of Congress, and the National Archives.

To the National Park Service is given the task of conserving not only our scenic and scientific treasures but also our historic heritage. The need for preserving and interpreting the great monuments of history, architecture, and archaeology in the United States and its possessions, however, exceeds the available or anticipated resources for these purposes of the National Park Service or any other Governmental agency.

The rapid spread of urbanization and industrialization, the sharp impact of population increases on older communities, the changing preferences in domestic living, the march of new public and private construction—all these and other causes have combined to place an increasing number of significant American landmarks in critical jeopardy. Unless broader support, new benefits, and new funds from non-governmental sources are provided, the next few decades will almost certainly witness the irreplaceable loss of further portions of our rapidly diminishing historical heritage. While the National Park Service will continue to do all in its power as a Federal agency to meet these problems, its activities must be complemented by outside endeavor on a national scale if the heritage of this generation is to be passed on unimpaired.

An American National Trust can mobilize resources and secure benefits not available to the National Park Service, and frequently not available to local agencies, and therefore can materially further the preservation and interpretation of historic sites and buildings in the United States. With some few very important exceptions, experience demonstrates that private persons are disinclined to give or devise property or to make substantial voluntary contributions of funds to the Federal Government. They are equally unlikely to enter into trusteeship arrangements or restrictive covenants with such a Federal agency. It is anticipated, however, that a quasi-public body having all the scope and dignity of a National Trust will be more favorably looked upon as a recipient of gifts. The proposed national body can therefore be expected to enlist healthy voluntary support and participation throughout the country in a way that no Federal agency or any State or local organization can possibly do.

Some critical preservation problems are inherently beyond the power of the National Park Service to meet. Unexpected emergencies inevitably arise in the preservation of historic sites and buildings which require immediate action long before any Governmental body could secure the necessary authority and funds. Some of the most urgent preservation problems fall exactly into this category. A National Trust, properly supported and financed to act, could meet emergencies which no existing organization in this country is now prepared to meet. It appears also to be true that the type of preservation arrangement which involves continued occupancy of the property by the owner or former owner can be more effectively consummated and maintained by a quasi-public body than by an agency of the Federal Government. There is likely to be more flexibility in such arrangements possible to the National Trust than to the National Park Service. It is

in just this field of flexible arrangements for continued occupancy of historic property that the English National Trust appears to have made some of its most important contributions to preservation. These contributions were presumably impossible for the British Governmental preservation organization, the Office of Works, to accomplish, and would be equally impossible for the National Park Service.

Beyond all these considerations, there remains the great intangible value of the sentiments, ideas, and public opinion brought together, mobilized, and embodied in the National Trust. The preservation of the physical body of our historic sites and buildings is only a part of the task. To interpret and perpetuate the best in our historical traditions in association with the great places of the nation calls for the participation of persons outside of any Governmental organization. Many of these persons are already members of regional, State, and local bodies attempting the work on a limited scale, but there is needed the coordination of an effective non-Governmental national organization. The National Trust will not only preserve property, but it will also contribute to the perpetuation of the historical fabric of our national life in a way that only the mobilized participation of all interested societies and individual citizens can do.

III.

FOREIGN PRECEDENTS

1. *Official Agencies.* Thomas J. Schneider, in a *Report to the Secretary of the Interior on the Preservation of Historic Sites and Buildings* (1935), remarked "that practically every nation, excepting the United States, with any substantial background of history has long before this interested itself in preserving the best and most significant products of man's handiwork." Beginning with Italy in the 15th century he traced national interest in preservation in Great Britain, France, Belgium, Germany, Poland, Sweden, Canada, Mexico, and Japan. In all these countries there are official agencies for historical preservation.

2. *Quasi-Public Agencies.* In several of the countries there are non-profit organizations to assist in preservation. Included are:

a. Belgium. Friends of the Royal Commission of Sites and Monuments acquires, administers, and maintains monuments, buildings, and sites classified by the Royal Commission.

b. France. The Institute of France not only cooperates with and advises the official Beaux-Arts but it owns a number of monuments donated or willed to it. The French Archaeological Society and the Touring Club of France are also active in phases of preservation.

c. Sweden. The "Nordiska Museet" features an open-air musum, *Skansen,* where buildings from various parts of Sweden typify different sectional characteristics and periods of historic development.

d. Scotland. The National Trust for Scotland is the counterpart of the English National Trust and has actively engaged in preservation work since 1931.

e. England. Both the Society for the Protection of Ancient Buildings and the National Trust for Places of Historic Interest or Natural Beauty engage in preservation. The latter is the more active and its operation serves as an illuminating illustration for the proposed National Trust in this country.

IV.

AMERICAN PRECEDENTS

The National Park Service is the only counterpart in this country to the official national agencies abroad, but, as previously indicated, this agency itself recognizes that it cannot alone do the whole job. And there is no American counterpart to the quasi-public foreign agencies, although there are State and regional organizations that were formed in order to carry on localized historical preservation work. Many of the most important of these bodies, fortunately, are already represented in the National Council for Historic Sites and Buildings and will collaborate in the setting up of a National Trust.

States and municipalities officially have interested themselves in recent years in historic matters and a number of them have been active in preservation and restoration undertakings. Many historic houses have been acquired and preserved or restored by the States and cities and are maintained for the benefit of the public. This work continues to go forward and Pennsylvania and Ohio, for example, have acquired significant new properties in the last three years. Vermont has recently established an Historic Sites Commission and in 1945, Missouri incorporated into its new Constitution a section providing for preservation of places of historic or archaeologic interest.

Legal precedents for the establishment of the proposed National Trust may be found in the charters of quasi-public agencies in other fields. All of these institutions were founded by Congressional charter in the years indicated: Smithsonian Institution (1846), National Academy of Sciences (1863), American Historical Association (1889), American Red Cross (1905), and the National Gallery of Art (1937), chartered as a bureau of the Smithsonian Institution. So, while we are entering upon unchartered fields in proposing an American National Trust, we are not without worthy precedents to guide us.

V.

PROBLEMS PECULIAR TO THE UNITED STATES

In this country many vexing problems stem from our dual Government structure—State and Federal. They relate primarily to taxation, to some public sentiment against further public ownership of land, and to the question of the duration of tenancy rights, which is bounded by the common-law Statute against Perpetuities. Taxation is, perhaps, the greatest of these problems, for it arises out of the removal of valuable properties from the local tax rolls and raises the issue of "enclaves" between the Federal Government and the States. The extreme complexity of these problems must eventually be faced and a thorough study must ultimately be made of the divergencies of State policies and laws. The Committee feels, however, that consideration of the State problems should be deferred until the purely Federal problems have been overcome.

VI.

THE PROPOSED NATIONAL TRUST

1. *The Purpose.* At the outset it is necessary to establish and agree upon the fundamental underlying purpose for which the Trust is to be established. This purpose is stated generally in the By-laws of the National Council as the furtherance of the "preservation and interpretation of sites and structures significant in American history and culture." The Committee on the Organization of the National Trust believes that there are two possibly complementary methods to accomplish this purpose: first, to arrange for the preservation and interpretation of historic properties *by whatever practicable methods may come to hand;* and second, *to acquire* and hold properties so that they may be preserved and interpreted.

These alternatives may appear to present a distinction without a difference. It is the view of the Committee, however, that a fatal difference does exist. The purpose must be preservation and interpretation; acquisition should never become more than a residual means to that end.

It is considered that if the Trust first exhausts all alternatives to acquisition, it can and will accomplish more actual preservation on a larger and more effective scale than it could ever accomplish through acquisition alone. Moreover, the position of the Trust with relation to Congress and the public will be strengthened if it does not appear as an organization whose main purpose is the acquisition of property and the resultant removal of that property from the tax rolls.

To arrange for the preservation and interpretation of historic properties "by any practicable methods" means that the Trust will not actually acquire property in any case where preservation and interpretation can otherwise be accomplished. Varying degrees of protection may be obtained through negotiation of restrictive covenants, custodianship agreements, or other legally satisfactory relationships, as has been done so effectively in England. Thus the owners will continue to own the properties, subject to certain restrictions, and the properties will be preserved.

It is only as a last resort that the Trust will acquire or accept title to properties. And then the property must be acquired from gifts for purchase or by the use of Trust funds otherwise obtained. The essential conditions to accomplish this are discussed in greater detail in a later section.

2. *Legal Status—A Quasi-Public Organization.* The earlier discussion in Section I of this Report indicated why the Committee agreed that the new agency should not be a part of the Federal Government. But it also agreed that the Trust could not be wholly private, largely because of the statutory authority, particularly regarding tax exemptions, it would need for effective operation. The solution was found in the proposed establishment of a quasi-public body, chartered by Congress, responsible to it and prepared to submit financial statements and reports annually—a solution for which there are historical precedents in other lands.

3. *Legal Authority — Congressional Charter.* An alternative to a Congressional charter is incorporation under the laws of the District of Columbia or of some State. Careful study and considerable discussion, however, indicated that there would be no advantage, and perhaps considerable disadvantage in the form of later legal complications, in first organizing under State or District of Columbia law and subsequently by Congressional charter. Until a Congressional charter can be secured, it is possible for the National Council for Historic Sites and Buildings to receive properties under the terms of its present charter, if deemed necessary or advisable. The Council can set up a small Operating Committee to administer such properties, if acquired, until such time as title might be vested in the United States through the National Trust.

The Committee therefore recommends that it would be best to proceed at once to seek a charter for the National Trust from the next Congress, relying meanwhile on the existing legal provisions of the By-laws of the Council to receive properties in danger.

4. *Scope of Coverage.* The Committee has dealt at length with the case made out for the inclusion of scenic sites within the purview of the proposed National Trust. It has concluded that the Trust should be concerned primarily with historical properties, but that it should also be authorized to assist in the temporary preservation of scenic sites in jeopardy. It recommends that as a legal matter the Trust be empowered to accept scenic sites pending further disposition into sympathetic hands. To insure favorable consideration in Congress, it is recommended that total acreage of any such scenic area shall not exceed 500 acres.

The scope of coverage shall specifically not include any of the conservation fields already covered by existing Federal or other agencies, such as wild life preserves or recreational areas.

5. *Scope of Authority.*

a. *Conformance with Established Public Policy.* By reason of the quasi-public nature of the Trust and of its consequent obligations to Congress, its activities and the nature of the legal transactions into which it shall be empowered to enter must conform with established public policy. Mr. Huntington Cairns, a member of the Committee, has prepared a legal brief dealing with certain questions that arise in this connection. Among the questions dealt with are these: In cases of acquisition of title, shall legal title to Trust properties be taken in the name of the United States or in the name of the Trust? Or shall it be taken by way of some combination of the kind, such as a beneficial interest in the United States subject in all other respects, including disposition, to the authority of the Trust? What problems of Federal and State taxation must be met? What are the problems of limited tenancy arising out of the Statute against Perpetuities? What are the various statutory requirements involving Government processing of legal details?

"It has been suggested that title to the property acquired by the Trust should be vested in the United States rather than in the Trust. States frequently exempt the property of charitable corporations from real estate taxation, but they do so with varying degrees of liberality.[1] The Government's property interests, however, are not taxable by the states in the absence of a Congressional waiver of immunity.[2] While bequests to the United States may be within a State's taxing power,[3] it is quite possible that a State may have exempted bequests to the United States from death duties on a more liberal basis than it has exempted bequests to non-local charities like the Trust. In any event placing title in the United States would increase the chances that a given bequest is within the exemption provisions of the relevant State statute. Donations probably would be deductible as charitable contributions for State income tax purposes even though title were taken in the name of the Trust rather than the United States. It is probable likewise that the exemptions for Federal tax purposes will not depend on

---

[1] Note "Exemption from Taxation of Property of Charitable Institutions," 36 Harv. Law Rev., 733.

[2] Rottschaefer's *Constitutional Law*, p. 99, and cases cited in footnote 66; 1 Willoughby on the *Constitution of the United States* (2d ed., 1929), sec. 88; cf. U. S. v. County of Allegheny (1944), 322 U. S. 174.

[3] U. S. v. Perkins (1896), 163 U. S. 625.

[4] Cf. S.R.A. v. Minnesota (1946), 327 U. S. 558, which upheld the state taxation of property to which the United States held title for security purposes only.

[5] 2 Bogert, *Trusts and Trustees*, sec. 352.

whether title is taken as above suggested or by the Trust. If the courts should hold that title were only nominally in the United States, the rule exempting property of the United States from State real estate taxation might be inapplicable.[4] Perhaps it would be practicable, however, to draft a plan which would satisfy Congress and the courts and yet would not subject the Trust to unduly restrictive governmental controls.

"As a general rule charitable trusts may be created to endure forever or for an indefinite period.[5] The Rule against Perpetuities may, however, have more force in those instances in which property is not bequeathed directly to the Trust upon the death of a testator, but follows upon one or more intermediate dispositions. Since other charitable foundations operate without much fear of the Rule against Perpetuities, the Rule should not cause undue concern among the organizers of the Trust nor be permitted to govern the manner in which title is taken.

"If the title is to be taken in the name of the United States (through the Trust), it will be necessary of course to have a special act of Congress incorporating the Trust. If, on the other hand, the title to property acquired by the Trust is to be taken in the name of the Trust, new legislation would not be required."

The Committee recommends that the National Council empower the Executive Board to take such action as may be necessary in this connection.

A further question in this phase of the discussion was, whether the Trust should seek exemption from the Constitutional power of eminent domain of the Federal Government to preempt property for public use? After careful consideration, the Committee recommends that such an exemption should not be sought, on the grounds that to do so would constitute so exceptional a request as possibly to incur substantial, if not overwhelming, Congressional or Administrative opposition. If, however, titles to Trust properties be taken in the name of the United States, solution of problems arising out of the preemptive powers of the States and municipalities with respect to such properties would, it is believed, be materially simplified.

b. *Coordination with other Federal Agencies, primarily the National Park Service Advisory Board.*

i. The Committee recommends that the Trust be authorized and empowered to call upon the National Park Service Advisory Board, already established by the Act of August 21, 1935, for assistance, as desired, with respect to any problems with which it may be faced. This relationship should be of inestimable value to the Trust throughout its operations and would provide continuity in Federal legislation. It should be noted particularly, however, that the Trust would not be in any way under the supervision or direction of this Advisory Board and that the assistance of the Board would be forthcoming only upon request of the Trust.

ii. The Trust, it is felt, should be generally empowered to obtain advisory assistance in general from any appropriate agency, whether Federal, State, or private.

c. *General Operating Powers.* It is proposed that the Trust shall seek to obtain the general, flexible, and comprehensive operating powers usually accorded similar organizations.

These will include, of course, power to acquire and dispose of properties by purchase, gift or devise, loan, or any other basis desired, to hold property so obtained in perpetuity from States, municipalities, corporations, and individuals, and to enter into any non-acquisitive arrangement for the preservation of the property as may be suitable. It will include the power to accept from Departments or Agencies of the United States any property, including real estate, no longer needed by the Department or

Agency for the purpose for which it was acquired and of such nature or character as to be properly held or administered by the Trust. It will also include the power to enter into appropriate contractual arrangements with State or local preservation organizations to operate, manage, and maintain any such properties.

d. *The Adoption and Application of Criteria.* A major aspect of the Trust's operational functions will be the application to historic properties of criteria for qualification as proper subjects for Trust action. For the protection both of the Government and of the Trust it is essential that the criteria be so drawn as to permit, at the same time, both desirable inclusions and necessary exclusions. The time may come when the Trust is offered an embarrassment of riches; it must therefore have some limits behind which it can retreat in case of necessity.

e. *Finances.* There remains one further element of the proposed scope of authority of the National Trust: finances. In England, Government funds now match private contributions—a development which took place by action of the Chancellor of the Exchequer in 1946.

The Committee recommends in this connection, however, that the Trust seek no direct Governmental financial assistance, support, or contribution whatever. It is believed that the absence of such a request will enhance the chances for obtaining Congressional approval and will, furthermore, tend to strengthen the Trust as a quasi-public, non-Governmental body in the public mind. It is believed, moreover, that the tax advantages under which it will be proposed that the Trust operate will and should, at this time, constitute the full extent of financial assistance to be obtained from the Government. Later on, corresponding advantages should be sought as needed from the several States as well.

6. *Character of the Internal Organizational Structure.* There are certain important but rather mechanical details which, in the interests of most effective accomplishment, should be left to the technicians to work out along relatively standard lines. These involve the specific provisions of the proposed charter and By-laws or Constitution of the Trust. The Committee, however, would like to make several recommendations:

a. The Trust should be governed by Trustees, nine in number (corresponding to the governing body of the National Gallery, for example), of which four would be ex officio members as follows, and so designated by reason of the potential assistance which their offices could afford in the later operations:

Attorney General of the United States
Secretary of the Treasury
Secretary of the Interior
Director of the National Gallery

Each ex officio member should be empowered to designate an official of his Department to act for him.

The remaining five Trustees would be elected by the membership of the National Council from among its members. The Chairman of the Board of Trustees would be elected from among these five non-ex officio members. Three Trustees would constitute a quorum for the transaction of business. While nine Trustees are at present recommended by the Committee, it is proposed that authority be sought to change this number from time to time.

b. *The executive officers* of the Trust would be: a President and a Vice President, selected by the Trustees from among the non-ex officio members of the Board; a Treasurer, selected by the Trustees either from among its non-ex officio members or from the general membership of the National Council; an Executive Secretary, who shall serve under compensation and who shall be selected by the Board whether or not a member thereof or of the Council. The Committee suggests that as a matter of practice this office and that of Executive Secretary of the National Council be filled by one individual, with his compensation shared between the two organizations.

7. *Means of Preservation.*

a. *Flexible Arrangements.* There are at least six different arrangements under which the preservation work of the Trust can be accomplished:

   i. By restrictive covenants against demolition or against harmful alterations. It is probably important to note that the Secretary of the English National Trust in 1945 stated in connection with restrictive covenants that "In the case of buildings of historic interest covenants will in any event continue to be of some value, though they may prove difficult to enforce effectively. They will not insure that the buildings are kept in repair, but only that they are not demolished or so altered as materially to diminish their historical interest."

   ii. By custodianship contract or similar trusteeship arrangement whereby the owner retains the beneficial interest or the actual title, as the case may be.

   iii. By gift of property.

   iv. By devise of property (left by will).

   v. By purchase of property by the Trust from funds contributed generally or specifically by an individual or group of individuals.

   vi. By receipt of properties from Government agencies, State or Federal.

b. *Other Arrangements.* There may be others. As has been stated before, however, the Trust should have maximum flexibility to enter into such arrangements as it considers expedient, the objective being at all times preservation as such rather than acquisition.

8. *Conditions for Acquisition.* The first of two essential conditions which the Committee feels should govern any arrangements is that in every possible case of acquisition the property be accepted only with an endowment adequate for its upkeep or, alternatively, on a basis where the property is or can be made self-supporting. Endowment or self-support are mandatory conditions in England. Here the Committee feels that more latitude is desirable in the interests of preservation but that nonetheless every possible effort be made short of loss of the property, to obtain maintenance funds.

The second condition is that the public should be admitted for certain minimum prescribed periods annually. The Committee believes that one of the basic objectives of preservation is interpretation and the educational opportunities which the properties afford. Their exhibition to the public, under reasonable conditions, seems essential also not only with regard to Congressional acceptance of the Trust proposals but as a general public relations matter. Certainly the educational dividends of preservation would be lost, and with it one of the principal objectives of the Trust, were the public excluded from the properties.

9. *Advantages and Inducements to Donors.*

a. The Committee, as stated before, advocates maximum flexibility in the Trust in order to negotiate on the facts of each case such arrangements as will be most advantageous. Bearing in mind, however, that the main objective is preservation, and through preservation, education and interpretation, the Committee believes that, to the extent practicable, these arrangements should provide for the continued tenancy of the property by its owners. In this way, problems of maintenance and custody are simplified; more important, in certain cases the continuity of living, the way of life represented by the property may be preserved. Finally, if a donor can be sure that he and his family and even perhaps his heirs after him can, if they so elect, continue their residence, at the same time as estate, inheritance, and real estate tax advantages are obtained, the inducement to the gift of the property becomes considerable. This is particularly true when substantially the only price he would have to pay for these assurances, plus the assurance that the property will be preserved intact, is to accept the public at convenient times during each year.

VII.
RELATIONSHIP OF THE TRUST TO THE COUNCIL

In considering what relationship should exist between the National Council and the National Trust, the Committee first considered the possibility of absorption of the Council by the Trust. But the consequences of such an arrangement seemed too complicated—particularly perplexing were the questions of internal government and membership —and the idea was abandoned.

Ultimately after careful study the Committee decided that the Trust should be an entirely separate organization, although closely related to and coordinated with the Council. The Trust will thus serve, in effect, as the operating agency of the Council in the actual preservation work, while the advantages of the already organized National Council will be retained. The Council, through its broad membership, will serve admirably as the public relations and the fund raising agency of the Trust. Around it will center the interests of the groups and individuals who are anxious to help in the work of preservation. Where the Trust cannot appropriately appear in its own behalf, such as before Congress and before State Legislatures, the Council, as such and through its constituent member organizations and affiliates, can admirably and far more effectively serve as the principal advocate. And yet the link between the two organizations would be direct, for, as was pointed out earlier, the majority of the Trustees of the National Trust will be elected from and by the Council membership, and thus the policy of the Council will become that of the Trust.

VIII.
RECOMMENDATION

The Committee recommends that this Report be adopted by the National Council for Historic Sites and Buildings at its annual meeting on November 4-5; that a bill to charter the National Trust for the Preservation of Historic Sites in the United States be prepared on the basis of the general principles and provisions enunciated in the foregoing Report, for submission to the next session of Congress; that the Executive Board of the National Council be empowered to exert every effort to secure the necessary charter from Congress in the shortest possible time; that the Executive Board be empowered to take such action as it may deem advisable in furtherance of the foregoing, including, in its discretion, such modification or substantial departure from any and all of such principles or provisions as may be necessary; and that in the interim the Executive Board may be empowered to act as an Emergency Operating Committee to receive in the name of the proposed National Trust gifts or properties fulfilling the requirements of the Trust, but with the proviso that all gifts or properties so received shall be transferred to the new organization after its charter is secured.

PUBLIC LAW 81–408, ESTABLISHING THE NATIONAL TRUST, AND PUBLIC LAW 83–160, AMENDING PUBLIC LAW 81–408

[Public Law 408—81st Congress]
[Chapter 755—1st Session]
[H. R. 5170]

AN ACT

To further the policy enunciated in the Historic Sites Act (49 Stat. 666) and to facilitate public participation in the preservation of sites, buildings, and objects of national significance or interest and providing a national trust for historic preservation.

Be it enacted by the Senate and House of Representatives of the United States of America in Congress assembled, That, in order to further the policy enunciated in the Act of August 21, 1935 (49 Stat. 666), entitled "An Act to provide for the preservation of historic American sites, buildings, objects, and antiquities of national significance, and for other purposes," and to facilitate public participation in the preservation of sites, buildings, and objects of national significance or interest, there is hereby created a charitable, educational, and nonprofit corporation, to be known as the National Trust for Historic Preservation in the United States, hereafter referred to as the "National Trust." The purposes of the National Trust shall be to receive donations of sites, buildings, and objects significant in American history and culture, to preserve and administer them for public benefit, to accept, hold, and administer gifts of money, securities, or other property of whatsoever character for the purpose of carrying out the preservation program, and to execute such other functions as are vested in it by this Act.

Sec. 2. The National Trust shall have its principal office in the District of Columbia and shall be deemed, for purposes of venue in civil actions, to be an inhabitant and resident thereof. The National Trust may establish offices in such other place or places as it may deem necessary or appropriate in the conduct of its business.

Sec. 3. The affairs of the National Trust shall be under the general direction of a board of trustees composed as follows: The Attorney General of the United States; the Secretary of the Interior; and the Director of the National Gallery of Art, ex officio; and not less than six general trustees who shall be citizens of the United States, to be chosen as hereinafter provided. The Attorney General, and the Secretary of the Interior, when it appears desirable in the interest of the conduct of the business of the board and to such extent as they deem it advisable, may, by written notice to the National Trust, designate any officer of their respective departments to act for them in the discharge of their duties as a member of the board of trustees. The number of general trustees shall be fixed by the Executive Board of the National Council for Historic Sites and Buildings, a corporation of the District of Columbia, and the general trustees first taking office shall be chosen by a majority vote of the members of the Executive Board from the membership of the National Council. The respective terms of office of the first general trustees so chosen shall be as prescribed by the said Executive Board but in no case shall exceed a period of five years from the date of election. A successor to a general trustee shall be chosen in the same manner as the original trustees and shall have a term expiring five years from the date of the expiration of the term for which his predecessor was chosen, except that a successor chosen to fill a vacancy occurring prior to the expiration of such term shall be chosen only for the remainder of that term. The chairman of the board of trustees shall be elected by a majority vote of the members of the board. No compensation shall be paid to the members of the board of trustees for their services as such members, but they shall be reimbursed for travel and actual expenses necessarily incurred by them in attending board meetings and performing other official duties on behalf of the National Trust at the direction of the board.

Sec. 4. To the extent necessary to enable it to carry out the functions vested in it by this Act, the National Trust shall have the following general powers:

(a) To have succession until dissolved by Act of Congress, in which event title to the properties of the National Trust, both real and personal, shall, insofar as consistent with existing contractual obligations and subject to all other legally enforceable claims or demands by or against the National Trust, pass to and become vested in the United States of America.

(b) To sue and be sued in its corporate name.

(c) To adopt, alter, and use a corporate seal which shall be judicially noticed.

(d) To adopt a constitution and to make such bylaws, rules, and regulations, not inconsistent with the laws of the United States or of any State, as it deems necessary for the administration of its functions under this Act, including among other matter, bylaws, rules, and regulations governing visitation to historic properties, administration of corporate funds, and the organization and procedure of the board of trustees.

(e) To accept, hold, and administer gifts and bequests of money, securities, or other personal property of whatsoever character, absolutely or on trust, for the purposes for which the National Trust is created. Unless otherwise restricted by the terms of the gift or bequest, the National Trust is authorized to sell, ex-change, or otherwise dispose of and to invest or reinvest in such investments as it may determine from time to time the moneys, securities, or other property given or bequeathed to it. The principal of such corporate funds, together with the income therefrom and all other revenues received by it from any source whatsoever, shall be placed in such depositories as the National Trust shall determine and shall be subject to expenditure by the National Trust for its corporate purposes.

(f) To acquire by gift, devise, purchase, or otherwise, absolutely or on trust, and to hold and, unless otherwise restricted by the terms of the gift or devise, to encumber, convey, or otherwise dispose of, any real property, or any estate or interest therein (except property within the exterior boundaries of national parks and national monuments), as may be necessary and proper in carrying into effect the purposes of the National Trust.

(g) To contract and make cooperative agreements with Federal, State, or municipal departments or agencies, corporations, associations, or individuals, under such terms and conditions as it deems advisable, respecting the protection, preservation, maintenance, or operation of any historic site, building, object, or property used in connection therewith for public use, regardless of whether the National Trust has acquired title to such properties, or any interest therein.

(h) To enter into contracts generally and to execute all instruments necessary or appropriate to carry out its corporate purposes, which instruments shall include such concession contracts, leases, or permits for the use of lands, buildings, or other property deemed desirable either to accommodate the public or to facilitate administration.

(i) To appoint and prescribe the duties of such officers, agents, and employees as may be necessary to carry out its functions, and to fix and pay such compensation to them for their services as the National Trust may determine.

(j) And generally to do any and all lawful acts necessary or appropriate to carry out the purposes for which the National Trust is created.

Sec. 5. In carrying out its functions under this Act, the National Trust is authorized to consult with the Advisory Board on National Parks, Historic Sites, Buildings, and Monuments, on matters relating to the selection of sites, buildings, and objects to be preserved and protected pursuant hereto.

Sec. 6. The National Trust shall, on or before the 1st day of March in each year, transmit to Congress a report of its proceedings and activities for the preceding calendar year, including the full and complete statement of its receipts and expenditures.

Sec. 7. The right to repeal, alter or amend this Act at any time is hereby expressly reserved, but no contract or individual right made or acquired shall thereby be divested or impaired.

Approved October 26, 1949.

Public Law 160—83rd Congress
Chapter 255—1st Session
H. R. 3581

AN ACT

All 67 Stat. 228.

To further the policy enunciated in the Act of October 26, 1949 (63 Stat. 927), to facilitate public participation in the preservation of sites, buildings, and objects of national significance or interest by providing for a National Trust for Historic Preservation in the United States.

Be it enacted by the Senate and House of Representatives of the United States of America in Congress assembled, That, in order to further the policy of historic preservation in the United States as enunciated in the Act of October 26, 1949 (63 Stat. 927), the third, fourth, and fifth sentences of section 3 of that Act are hereby amended to read as follows: "The number of general trustees shall be fixed by the Board of Trustees of the National Trust and shall be chosen by the members of the National Trust from its members at any regular meeting of said National Trust. The respective terms of office of the general trustees shall be as prescribed by said board of trustees but in no case shall exceed a period of five years from the date of election. A successor to a general trustee shall be chosen in the same manner and shall have a term expiring five years from the date of the expiration of the term for which his predecessor was chosen, except that a successor chosen to fill a vacancy occurring prior to the expiration of such term shall be chosen only for the remainder of that term."

Approved July 28, 1953.

National Trust for Historic Preservation in U. S. General trustees. 16 USC 468b.

SPONSORING ORGANIZATIONS
OF THE NATIONAL TRUST

American Anthropological Association
American Association for State and Local History
American Association of Museums
American Historical Association
American Historical Association, Pacific Coast Branch
American Institute of Architects
American Institute of Decorators (now American Institute of Interior
  Designers)
American Planning and Civic Association (now National Urban Coalition)
American Scenic and Historic Preservation Society
American Society of Landscape Architects
Archaeological Institute of America
Association for the Preservation of Virginia Antiquities
California Historical Society
Carolina Art Association
Cincinnati Historical Society
Colonial Williamsburg, Inc.
Columbia Historical Society
Garden Club of America
Gore Place Society
Mississippi Valley Historical Association (now Organziation of American
  Historians)
Monterey Foundation
National Conference on State Parks
National Society Sons of the American Revolution
New York State Historical Association
North Carolina Society for the Preservation of Antiquities
Ohio Historical Society
Oregon Historical Society
Pennsylvania Historical and Museum Commission
Society for American Archaeology
Society for the Preservation of Maryland Antiquities
Society for the Preservation of New England Antiquities
Society of Architectural Historians
Society of the Cincinnati
Southern Historical Association
The Trustees of Public Reservations (now The Trustees of Reservations)
United Daughters of the Confederacy

BOARD OF TRUSTEES, 1950–73

Name	Elected	Reelected	Termination of Service	Notes
*Abell, Mrs. Irvin, Jr.	1971			
Adler, Leopold, II	1971			
Albright, Horace Marden	1950	1953, 1958	1963	1970 elected Trustee emeritus
Aldrich, Winthrop W.	1950		1953	1953 resigned
Allen, Mrs. William S.	1961	1966, 1969	1972	1972 elected Trustee emeritu
Astor, Mrs. Vincent	1969		1971	1971 resigned
*Baker, Robert Calhoun	1962	1965, 1968	1970	1963–70 treasur 1970 resigned; elected Trustee emeritus
Bannister, Turpin C.	1952	1956	1961	1970 elected Trustee emeritu
Barrett, John D.	1958		1963	
Beinecke, Walter, Jr.	1972			
Bingham, Barry	1962	1963	1968	
Bird, Charles Sumner	1950	1953	1958	
Black, Eugene R.	1950		1955	
Bliss, Robert Woods	1950	1953, 1958	1962	1956–62 vice chairman 1959 elected honorary Truste 1962 deceased
Bolton, Mrs. Frances P.	1955	1957	1959	1959 elected honorary Truste
Brown, Mrs. Constance M.	1971			
Brown, John Nicholas	1950	1954	1956	1956 resigned
Bruce, David K.E.	1955		1957	1957 resigned
Bullis, Harry A.	1950	1954	1959	
Burgess, Carter L.	1967		1970	
Burgess, Mrs. W. Randolph	1953	1958, 1963	1968	1970 elected Trustee emeritu

* Is or was a member of the Executive Committee.

Name	Elected	Reelected	Termination of Service	Notes
Hofheimer, Henry Clay, II	1957	1962, 1967	1970	Trustee emeritu 1970 elected
Hollister, Mrs. John B.	1964	1967, 1970	1973	1973 elected Trustee emeritu
Homans, Mrs. Robert	1966	1967, 1970, 1973		
Hoover, Herbert	1950	1955	1959	1959 elected honorary Truste 1964 deceased
Houghton, Arthur A., Jr.	1952		1957	
*Humelsine, Carlisle H.	1961	1966, 1969	1972	1972 elected Trustee emeritu
Irwin, John N., II	1962		1963	
*Jacobsen, C. F.	1950	1955, 1960	1962	1950–62 treasur 1962 resigned
Jenrette, Richard H.	1972			
Johnson, Mrs. J. Lee, III	1968	1969, 1972		
Johnson, Philip C.	1968		1971	1971 resigned
Knott, Lawson B., Jr.	1969		1972	
Kornfeld, Albert	1952		1957	
Lane, Mills B., Jr.	1967		1968	1968 resigned
*Lee, Ronald F.	1950	1952, 1957, 1962	1967	1970 elected Trustee emeritu 1972 deceased
Leland, Austin P.	1963	1968, 1971		
Lewis, Mrs. Wilmarth S.	1955		1959	1959 deceased
Macondray, Mrs. Atherton (now Mrs. Armistead Peter, III)	1959	1964, 1967	1970	1970 elected Trustee emeritu
*Manigault, Peter	1963	1968, 1971		1965– vice chairman
Marshall, George C.	1950		1954	1954 resigned
McAneny, George	1950		1953	1950–53 vice chairman 1953 deceased
McCone, Mrs. John A.	1968	1971		
McGee, Joseph H.	1972			
McGhee, George C.	1970	1973		
McLaughlin, H. Roll	1972			
Merrill, Keith	1952		1955	1955 resigned

HONORARY AND EX-OFFICIO TRUSTEES

Honorary Trustees

Robert Woods Bliss	1959–62
Frances P. Bolton	1959–
David E. Finley	1964–
Herbert Hoover	1959–64

Honorary Members

Mrs. Harry S. Truman
Mrs. Dwight D. Eisenhower
Mrs. Aristotle Onassis
Mrs. Lyndon B. Johnson
Mrs. Richard Nixon

Ex-Officio Trustees

ATTORNEY GENERAL OF THE UNITED STATES

J. Howard McGrath	May 1950—April 1952
James P. McGranery	May 1952—January 1953
Herbert Brownell, Jr.	January 1953—November 1957
William P. Rogers	November 1957—January 1961
Robert F. Kennedy	January 1961—September 1964
Nicholas deB. Katzenbach	February 1965—October 1966
Ramsey Clark	March 1967—January 1969
John N. Mitchell	January 1969—March 1972
Richard G. Kleindienst	June 1972—May 1973
Elliot L. Richardson	May 1973—October 1973

Representative:

Patricia H. Collins	1952–
	(1965– secretary)

SECRETARY OF THE INTERIOR

Oscar Littleton Chapman	May 1950—January 1953
Douglas McKay	January 1953—April 1956
Fred Andrew Seaton	June 1956—January 1961
Stewart L. Udall	January 1961—January 1969
Walter J. Hickel	January 1969—November 1970
Rogers C. B. Morton	January 1971–

Representatives:

Newton B. Drury	May 1950—March 1951
Arthur E. Demaray	April 1951—December 1951
Conrad L. Wirth	December 1951—January 1964
George B. Hartzog, Jr.	January 1964—December 1972
Ronald H. Walker	January 1973–

DIRECTOR OF THE NATIONAL GALLERY OF ART

David E. Finley	May 1950—June 1956
John Walker, III	July 1956—June 1969
	(1970 elected Trustee emeritus)
J. Carter Brown	July 1969–

Representative:

W. Howard Adams	July 1969–

ADVISORY COMMITTEES
TO THE BOARD, 1972–73

Awards
Mrs. Irvin Abell, Jr.,
    chairman
Robertson E. Collins
Mrs. Lammot du Pont
    Copeland
Carlisle H. Humelsine
Robert H. Murphy
Charles van
    Ravenswaay

Officers Nominating
George M. Elsey,
    chairman
Mrs. John B. Hollister
Austin P. Leland

Trustees Nominating
Mrs. Robert Homans,
    chairman
Robert B. Rettig
Samuel Wilson, Jr.

Education
Robert C. Giebner,
    chairman
Mrs. J. Carter Brown
Leonard Carmichael
Ernest A. Connally
Virginia Daiker
Frank B. Evans
Carl Feiss, FAIA, AIP
Joan Hull
J. Hurst Purnell, Jr.
Barnes Riznik

Field Services
F. Blair Reeves, AIA,
    chairman
Robertson E. Collins
Mrs. James F. Dreher
Richard C. Frank, AIA
Lawrence O.
    Houstoun, Jr.

Thomas W. Leavitt
Thomas G. McCaskey
Dorn C. McGrath,
    Jr., AIP
William J. Murtagh
Robert B. Rettig
Frederick Schmid
George H. Shirk
Albert B. Wolfe
Russell Wright, AIP
Western Regional
Subcommittee
Robertson E. Collins,
    chairman
Elizabeth Hay Bechtel
Raymond Girvigian,
    FAIA
Mrs. Robert Homans
Mrs. John A. McCone
Dennis McCarthy

Finance and Investment
George M. Elsey,
    chairman
Charles L. Booth
Henry C. Hofheimer, II
Richard H. Jenrette
George C. McGhee
Peter Manigault
W. Jarvis Moody
Macon G. Patton
Julian Robertson, Jr.
Samuel Reid Sutphin
Charles H. Woodward

Historic Properties
Committees
Walter Beinecke, Jr.,
    chairman
Frederick H. Nichols,
    FAIA, vice chairman

Curatorship,
Interpretation and
Use Subcommittee
Frederick D. Nichols,
    FAIA, chairman
Ernest A. Connally
John M. Dickey, AIA
Mrs. George E.
    Downing
Mrs. John B. Hollister
Mrs. George M. Morris
William Pfeiffer
Barbara Wriston
Property Management
Subcommittee
Walter Beinecke, Jr.,
    chairman
Constance M. Greiff
Ralph P. Hanes
Mrs. Henry P. Hoffstot,
    Jr.
Nancy N. Holmes
Joseph H. McGee
H. Roll McLaughlin,
    FAIA
S. K. Stevens

International Relations
Robert H. Thayer,
    chairman
Mrs. W. Randolph
    Burgess
Mrs. Frederick
    Frelinghuysen
Richard H. Howland
Mrs. J. Lee Johnson, III
Mrs. John A. McCone
Henry P. McIlhenny
Mrs. Armistead
    Peter, III
Robert E. Stipe

NATIONAL TRUST BYLAWS, 1950–73

Bylaws Adopted in 1950

Article I—Membership

Section 1. The members of the Corporation shall be the Board of Trustees and shall consist of the Attorney General of the United States; the Secretary of the Interior; and the Director of the National Gallery of Art, ex officio; and not less than six General Trustees, who shall be citizens of the United States. The number of General Trustees shall be fixed by the Executive Board of the National Council for Historic Sites and Buildings.

Article II—Limitations

Section 1. No part of the net earnings of the Corporation shall inure to the benefit of any member or individual. The Corporation shall not devote any substantial part of its activities to carrying on propaganda, or otherwise attempting to influence legislation.

Article III—Officers

Section 1. The officers of the Corporation shall be a Chairman, two Vice Chairmen, a Secretary and a Treasurer, an Administrator, a Director, a General Counsel and such other officers as the Board of Trustees may from time to time determine. The Chairman and the Vice Chairman shall be elected by the Board of Trustees triennially from among their number. The other officers shall be elected in like manner and may or may not be chosen from among the Trustees. All officers shall hold office for three years and until their successors are elected and assume office.

Section 2. Any vacancy in any office, however arising, shall be filled by the Board of Trustees for the unexpired term. In the case of a vacancy in the offices of Administrator, Secretary, Treasurer, Director, or General Counsel, the Chairman may temporarily appoint a substitute, who shall serve until such office is filled by the Board of Trustees. One or more offices may be held by a single individual.

Section 3. The Chairman shall preside at all meetings of the Board of Trustees and, ex officio, shall be a member and chairman of the Executive Committee. He shall act in an advisory capacity to all other officers.

Section 4. The Chairman shall exercise general supervision over the affairs of the Corporation and shall enforce the provisions of the Charter and By-laws, with discretionary power and authority in all cases not specifically provided for therein. He shall be ex officio a member of all committees of the Board of Trustees, except the Nominating Committee.

Section 5. In case of a vacancy in the office of Chairman or during his absence or inability to act, the powers and duties of the Chairman shall be exercised by the senior Vice Chairman present and able to act, or in case of the unavailability of both Vice Chairmen then by the senior member of the Executive Committee in length of service present and able to act. Any action taken by the Vice Chairman or senior member of the Executive Committee pursuant to this section shall be conclusive evidence of the absence or inability to act of the Chairman or of an officer of preceding rank and authority.

Section 6. The Secretary shall cause notice to be issued of all meetings of the Board of Trustees at least ten days in advance thereof and of all committees and a record to be made of all proceedings. He shall have custody of and preserve the corporate seal and the archives and shall affix the seal under the direction of the Chairman or the Board of Trustees.

Section 7. The Treasurer shall receive and disburse the funds of the Corporation under the direction of the Board of Trustees and shall deposit all funds in the name of the Corporation and all securities in such depository or depositories as the Board of Trustees may, from time to time, designate or approve. He shall also have custody of and preserve all records and documents relating to the property of the Corporation, keep proper books of accounts which shall be open at all times to inspection by the Board of Trustees, and render to the Board of Trustees upon request, a report of all his activities as Treasurer. At least once a year he shall submit to the Board of Trustees a statement of the financial condition of the Corporation, certified by independent accountants if required by the Executive Committee, consisting of a balance sheet and related statements of income and expenses and of changes in all funds for the fiscal year then ended. The Board of Trustees may in its discretion require the Treasurer to give bond in such amount and with such surety or sureties as they shall determine. Each disbursement over $100.00 in amount shall be made by check signed by him and countersigned by the Administrator.

Section 8. The other officers shall have such responsibilities and perform such duties as the Board of Trustees shall in its discretion prescribe in the By-laws or by resolution.

Section 9. Honorary officers may be elected by the Board of Trustees in its discretion.

ARTICLE IV—Trustees

Section 1. The Board of Trustees shall administer, preserve, and protect the property of the Corporation and shall have full and exclusive power to administer and conduct its affairs. The General Trustees first taking office shall be chosen by majority vote of the members of the Executive Board of the National Council for Historic Sites and Buildings, a corporation of the District of Columbia. The terms of membership of the said Trustees so chosen shall be as prescribed by the said Executive Board but in no case shall exceed a period of five years from the date of election. A successor to a General Trustee shall be chosen in the same manner as the original trustees and shall have a term expiring five years from the date of the expiration of the term for which his predecessor was chosen, except that a successor chosen to fill a vacancy occurring prior to the expiration of such term shall be chosen only for the remainder of that term.

Section 2. The Attorney General and the Secretary of the Interior when it appears desirable in the interest of the conduct of the business of the Corporation and to such extent as they deem it advisable, may by written notice to the Corporation designate any officer of their respective departments to act for them in the discharge of their duties as a member of the Board of Trustees.

Section 3. No compensation shall be paid to the members of the Board of Trustees for their services as such members, but they may be reimbursed for travel and actual expenses necessarily incurred by them in attending Board meetings and performing other official duties on behalf of the Corporation at the direction of the Board.

Section 4. The Board of Trustees shall determine the manner and form of its proceedings and may appoint an Executive Committee and such other committees as it may deem advisable for the administration of the Corporation. The other committees shall have and exercise such powers as the Board of Trustees may delegate to them.

Section 5. At all meetings of the Board of Trustees 5 members shall constitute a quorum, but the concurrent vote of a majority of the members shall be necessary for the election of the Chairman of the Board of Trustees.

Section 6. Any action in which a majority of the existing trustees shall concur in writing shall be binding and valid although not authorized or approved at any meeting of the Board.

Section 7. The Board of Trustees may adopt rules and regulations consistent with the By-laws for the administration of the affairs of the Corporation and may alter, amend, or repeal any such rule or regulation adopted by it.

Section 8. The Board of Trustees shall meet on a day in October of each year specified by the Executive Committee. Special meetings of the Board shall be called at any time by the Secretary upon the order of the Chairman or either of the Vice Chairmen or written request of three members of the Board. All meetings of the Board shall be held at the offices of the Corporation in Washington, D. C., unless otherwise designated in the notice by the authority of the person or persons calling the meeting.

Article V—Executive Committee

Section 1. The Executive Committee shall consist of the Chairman, and four Trustees. A majority of the existing members shall constitute a quorum.

Section 2. The Executive Committee shall have and exercise all the powers of the Board of Trustees during all intervals between meetings of the Board of Trustees subject to the general policies from time to time established by the Board, and shall determine the manner and form of its proceedings and the time, place, and notice to be given of its regular or special meetings.

Section 3. Any vacancies in the Executive Committee shall be filled by the Board of Trustees.

Section 4. Any action in which a majority of the existing members of the Executive Committee shall concur in writing shall be binding and valid, although not authorized or approved at any meeting of the Executive Committee.

Article VI—Administrator

Section 1. The Administrator shall be the chief administrative officer of the Corporation, subject to the general control of the Board of Trustees and shall report directly to them; he shall devote such time to the affairs of the Corporation as the Board of Trustees may determine and shall be responsible generally for the performance by all employees of their respective duties and for the execution of all orders of the Board of Trustees. He shall attend all meetings of the Board of Trustees. He shall supervise the administration of the property of the Corporation, and shall prescribe and publish rules for the conduct of administrative affairs of the Corporation subject to the approval of the Executive Committee. He shall have power to appoint and remove employees subject to the prior approval of the Executive Committee, provided that any expenses incurred for additional personnel shall have been provided for in the budget. He shall supervise and approve all administrative and operating expenditures of the Corporation and matters of personnel. He shall have such other responsibilities and perform such other duties as may be assigned to him by the Board of Trustees.

Article VII—The Director

Section 1. The Director shall be the chief officer of the Corporation, with regard to all matters of history, culture, research, education, techniques and methods of preservation of historic sites, buildings and objects, and corporate policies in respect of such matters, and shall represent the Corporation in all such regards. He shall be in charge of all educational, historical, research and cultural activities of the Corporation and shall be responsible only to the Board of Trustees or the Executive Committee in those respects.

Article VIII—The General Counsel

Section 1. The General Counsel shall be the chief law officer of the Corporation, and shall have responsibility for all legal matters of the Corporation, and shall represent the Corporation in all such matters and shall exercise general supervision over local counsel who may have to be retained from time to time to represent the Corporation. He shall advise the Board of Trustees, the Executive Committee, standing committees, and all other officers on all questions of law that may arise in the business or administration of the Corporation or in carrying out its purposes. He shall review all letters and other documents signed by any officer of the Corporation which involve any legal matter.

Article IX—Tenure of Office

Section 1. Unless otherwise provided, all officials and employees of the Corporation shall hold their positions during the pleasure of the Board of Trustees.

Section 2. No official or employee of the Corporation shall be entitled to or shall receive any compensation for service rendered to the Corporation other than his salary, except by special resolution of the Board of Trustees.

Article X—Fiscal Year

Section 1. The fiscal year of the Corporation shall run from September 1 to August 31.

Article XI—Budget

Section 1. Not later than August 1 of each year, the Administrator in consultation with the Treasurer shall prepare a budget, showing estimated operating income and operating expenses of the Corporation for the ensuing fiscal year, and shall submit it to a meeting of the Executive Committee for consideration and adoption.

Section 2. Any budget so adopted shall without further action authorize the Treasurer to advance the amounts included in the budget from time to time on request or pursuant to a fixed schedule. The Treasurer shall make no advancements and no officers or employees shall incur any expenses in addition to the amounts specified in the budget as approved without prior approval of the Executive Committee.

Section 3. The Budget as adopted by the Executive Committee and as amended from time to time shall be reported to the Board of Trustees at its October meetings for ratification.

Article XII—Amendments

Section 1. These By-laws may be amended in whole or in part only upon the affirmative vote of a majority of the members present at a regular or special meeting of the Board of Trustees, provided that notice in writing of the proposed change shall have been mailed by the Secretary to each member of the Board of Trustees at least thirty days in advance of the meeting at which such change is to be considered.

May 1, 1950

BYLAWS ADOPTED IN 1973

ARTICLE I—Name and Office of the Corporation

Section 1. *Name.* This Corporation is a charitable, educational, and non-profit corporation and shall be known as the "National Trust for Historic Preservation in the United States," hereinafter referred to as the National Trust or the Corporation.

Section 2. *Office of the Corporation.* The National Trust shall have its principal office in the District of Columbia and shall be deemed, for purposes of venue in civil actions, to be an inhabitant and resident thereof. The National Trust may establish offices in such other place or places as it may deem necessary or appropriate in the conduct of its business.

ARTICLE II—Purposes

The purposes of the National Trust, as stated in its Charter, consisting of the Act of October 26, 1949 (Public Law 408), as amended, and related Acts, shall be:

(a) to further the policy enunciated in the Act of August 21, 1935, and related Acts, for the preservation of Historic American sites, buildings, objects, and antiquities of national significance,

(b) to facilitate public participation in the preservation of sites, buildings, and objects of national significance or interest,

(c) to receive donations of sites, buildings, and objects significant in American history and culture and preserve and administer them for public benefit,

(d) to accept, hold, and administer gifts of money, securities, or other property of whatsoever character for the purpose of carrying out the preservation program, and

(e) to execute such other functions as are vested in it by the Act of October 26, 1949, as amended, and by related Acts.

ARTICLE III—Powers

To the extent necessary to enable it to carry out the functions vested in it by the Act of 1949, as amended, and related Acts, the National Trust shall have the following general powers:

(a) to have succession until dissolved by Act of Congress, in which event title to the properties of the National Trust, both real and personal, shall, insofar as consistent with existing contractual obligations and subject to other legally enforceable claims or demands by or against the National Trust, pass to and become vested in the United States of America,

(b) to sue and be sued in its corporate name,

(c) to adopt, alter, and use a corporate seal which shall be judicially noticed,

(d) to adopt a constitution and to make such bylaws, rules, and regulations, not inconsistent with the laws of the United States or of any State, as it deems necessary for the administration of its functions under the Act of 1949, as amended, and related Acts, including among other matters, bylaws, rules, and regulations governing visitation to historic properties, administration of corporate funds, and the organization and procedure of the board of trustees,

(e) to accept, hold, and administer gifts and bequests of money, securities, or other personal property of whatsoever character, absolutely or on trust, for the purposes for which the National Trust is created. Unless otherwise restricted by the terms of the gift or bequest, the National Trust is authorized to sell, exchange, or otherwise dispose of and to invest or reinvest in such investments as it may determine from time to time the moneys, securities, or other property given or bequeathed to it. The principal of such corporate funds, together with the income therefrom and all revenues received by it from any source whatsoever, shall be placed in such depositories as the National Trust shall determine and shall be subject to expenditure by the National Trust for its corporate purposes,

(f) to acquire by gift, devise, purchase, or otherwise, absolutely or on trust, and to hold and, unless otherwise restricted by the terms of the gift or devise, to encumber, convey, or otherwise dispose of, any real property, or any estate or interest therein (except property within the exterior boundaries of national parks and national monuments), as may be necessary and proper in carrying into effect the purpose of the National Trust,

(g) to contract and make cooperative agreements with Federal, State, or municipal departments or agencies, corporations, associations, or individuals, under such terms and conditions as it deems advisable, respecting the protection, preservation, maintenance, or operation of any historic site, building, object, or property used in connection therewith for public use, regardless of whether the National Trust has acquired title to such properties, or any interest therein,

(h) to enter into contracts generally and to execute all instruments necessary or appropriate to carry out its corporate purposes, which instruments shall include such concession contracts, leases, or permits for the use of lands, buildings, or other property deemed desirable either to accommodate the public or to facilitate administration,

(i) to appoint and prescribe the duties of such officers, agents, and employees as may be necessary to carry out its functions, and to fix and pay such compensation to them for their services as the National Trust may determine,

(j) and, generally, to do any and all lawful acts necessary or appropriate to carry out the purpose for which the National Trust is created.

In carrying out its functions under the Act of 1949, the National Trust is authorized to consult with the Advisory Board on National Parks, Historic Sites, Buildings, and Monuments, on matters relating to the selection of sites, buildings, and objects to be preserved and protected pursuant to the Act of 1949. The right to repeal, alter or amend the Act of 1949 at any time is expressly reserved to the Congress, but no contract or individual right made or acquired shall thereby be divested or impaired.

The Corporation is not organized, nor shall it be operated, for pecuniary gain or profit, and it does not contemplate the distribution of gains, profits or dividends to the members thereof and is organized solely for the nonprofit purposes. Any property, assets, profits and net income of the Corporation located within the State of California are irrevocably dedicated to charitable, religious, scientific and/or hospital purposes as that term is defined and interpreted for the purposes of California law. No part of the profits or net income of the Corporation shall ever inure to the benefit of any Trustee, officer, or member thereof or to the benefit of any private shareholder or individual. Upon the dissolution or winding up of the Corporation, which shall be by Act of Congress, title to its properties, both real and personal, shall, insofar as consistent with existing contractual obligations and subject to all other legally enforceable claims or demands by or against the National Trust, pass to and become vested in the United States of America. No part of the activities of the Corporation shall involve attempts to influence legislation by propaganda or lobbying, and the Corporation shall not participate in any way in any political campaign.

ARTICLE IV—Membership

Section 1. *Members.* The members of the National Trust shall be such individuals, organizations, institutions and corporations as may be accepted from time to time in accordance with procedures established by the Board of Trustees.

Section 2. *Voting.* Each member shall be entitled to one vote on each matter submitted to a vote of the members.

Section 3. *Transfer of Membership.* Membership in this Corporation is not transferable or assignable without the written consent of the Board of Trustees or of the Executive Committee.

Section 4. *Termination of Membership.* The Board of Trustees may request the resignation, or terminate the membership of, any member, whether an individual, organization, institution or corporation, for any act or omission which is deemed by the Board of Trustees to be inconsistent with or harmful to the accomplishment of the purposes and objectives of the National Trust or which it deems would interfere with the accomplishment of said purposes and objectives.

Section 5. *Dues.* Each member shall pay such annual dues as may be from time to time fixed by the Board of Trustees.

Section 6. *Honorary Members.* Honorary members of the National Trust may be elected by the Board of Trustees at any time and shall hold such position at the pleasure of the Board of Trustees. Honorary members may attend meetings of the members, but shall not be entitled to vote and shall have no duties, liabilities or responsibilities of any kind.

ARTICLE V—Membership Meetings

Section 1. *Regular and Special Meetings.* The members of the National Trust shall meet annually, at a time and place to be determined by the Board of Trustees or by the Executive Committee. Other regular or special meetings of the members shall be held at the direction of the Board of Trustees or the Executive Committee.

Section 2. *Business of Annual Meeting.* The business of the Annual Meeting shall include the election of Trustees and such other business as may be laid before the members by the Chairman of the Board of Trustees who shall preside at the meeting.

Section 3. *Voting.* Any person attending a membership meeting in the capacity of an individual member and also in the capacity of a delegate of a member organization shall be entitled to one vote on behalf of the member organization and one vote on his own behalf as an individual member.

Section 4. *Alternate Delegates.* If the delegate of a member organization is absent from a meeting of the members of the National Trust, an alternate delegate duly appointed by the member organization shall be entitled to vote in his place.

Section 5. *Proxies.* Any member of the National Trust may vote at any meeting of the members of the National Trust in person or by written proxy.

Section 6. *Quorum.* At any regular or special meeting of the members of the National Trust, 25 members in person or by written proxy shall constitute a quorum for the transaction of business.

Section 7. *Notices.* Written notice of the time and place of the Annual Meeting of the members of the National Trust shall be sent to all such members not less than 30 days in advance of the date of such meeting. Written notice of the time and place of all other regular or special meetings of the members shall be sent to all such members not less than 14 days in advance of the date of such meetings. Such notices may be given in a publication that goes to all members of the National Trust.

ARTICLE VI—Trustees

Section 1. *Authority.* The affairs of the National Trust shall be under the general direction of a board of trustees which shall administer, manage, preserve and protect the property of the Corporation and shall have full power to administer, direct, manage, and conduct its affairs.

Section 2. *Number.* The Board of Trustees shall be composed as follows: The Attorney General of the United States, the Secretary of the Interior and the Director of the National Gallery of Art, ex-officio, and not less than six general trustees who shall be citizens of the United States, to be chosen as hereinafter provided. The number of general trustees shall be fixed by the Board of Trustees of the National Trust.

Section 3. *Election.* The general trustees shall be chosen by the members of the National Trust from its members at any regular meeting of the National Trust as hereinafter provided in Article VII.

Section 4. *Vacancies.* The Board of Trustees shall have the power to appoint members of the National Trust to fill temporary vacancies in the Board of Trustees. The appointment of a successor trustee by the Board of Trustees shall be subject to confirmation by the members of the National Trust at the next regular meeting of the members following the date of such appointment. The Trustees Nominating Committee shall submit the name of any such appointee, together with the names of any other members of the National Trust who are candidates for election as trustees, to the members at the next regular meeting of the members.

Section 5. *Term of Office.* The respective terms of office of the general trustees shall be as prescribed by the Board of Trustees but in no case shall exceed a period of five years from the date of election. Any trustee who has served three consecutive full terms shall, unless serving as Chairman, be ineligible for re-election as a trustee until one year has elapsed following the date of expiration of the third consecutive term of office. A successor trustee appointed by the Board of Trustees shall, if confirmed by election of the members at a regular meeting of the National Trust serve for the remainder of the unexpired term and such service shall not count as a full term for purposes of the three-term limitations imposed herein.

Section 6. *Termination of Office.* Failure to attend three consecutive meetings of the Board of Trustees shall, except for good cause shown, terminate the term of office of any trustee. Prior to the conclusion of the meeting at the end of which such termination becomes effective, the Board of Trustees shall be notified thereof. As promptly as feasible after such termination, the Secretary shall notify the trustee of such termination.

Section 7. *Delegation.* The Attorney General, and the Secretary of the Interior, when it appears desirable in the interest of the conduct of the business of the Board and to such extent as they deem it advisable, may, by written notice to the National Trust, designate any officer of their respective departments to act for them in the discharge of their duties as a member of the Board of Trustees.

Section 8. *Honorary Trustees.* Honorary trustees may be elected by the Board of Trustees at any time and shall hold such position at the pleasure of the Board of Trustees. Honorary trustees may attend meetings of the Board of Trustees at the discretion of the Board, but shall have no duties, liabilities or responsibilities of any kind.

Section 9. *Trustees Emeriti.* A trustee who has served three consecutive full terms shall be eligible for election by the Board of Trustees as a Trustee Emeritus. Trustees Emeriti may attend meetings of the Board of Trustees at the discretion of the Board but shall have no duties, liabilities or responsibilities of any kind.

Section 10. *Compensation.* No compensation shall be paid to the members of the Board of Trustees for their services as such members, but they shall be reimbursed for travel and actual expenses necessarily incurred by them in attending Board meetings and performing other duties on behalf of the National Trust at the direction of the Board.

Section 11. *Meetings.* The Board of Trustees shall meet at least three times a year on dates prescribed by the Executive Committee. One of these meetings, which will be the Annual Meeting of the Board, shall be held at the time and place of the Annual Meeting of the membership. Special meetings shall be called at any time by the Secretary upon the order of the Chairman or at the written request of six members of the Board. All meetings of the Board shall be held at the principal office of the Corporation unless otherwise designated in the notice at the request of the person or persons calling the meeting.

Section 12. *Quorum.* At all meetings of the Board of Trustees five members shall constitute a quorum. Any lawful action on which a majority of the entire Board of Trustees shall concur in writing shall be binding and valid although not authorized or approved at any regular or special meeting of the Board.

Section 13. *Voting.* Each member of the Board of Trustees, including each ex-officio member, shall be entitled to one vote on each matter submitted to a vote of the trustees.

Section 14. *Committees.* The Chairman of the Board of Trustees may establish such standing and ad hoc committees, not specifically provided for in these Bylaws, as the Chairman may deem advisable in the administration and conduct of the affairs of the National Trust. Such committees appointed by the Chairman shall advise and consult with the Board and staff of the National Trust to the extent authorized by the Chairman. The Executive Committee is authorized in its discretion to approve reimbursement for travel and actual expenses necessarily incurred by members of committees in attending committee meetings and in performing other official duties as such. The Chairman and Vice Chairmen of the Board of Trustees and the President of the National Trust are ex-officio members of all Trust committees except the Trustees Nominating Committee, the Officers Nominating Committee and the Awards Committee. The Chairmen of all Board Committees shall be invited to participate, but without a vote, in all meetings of the Executive Committee of the Board of Trustees. The Chairman of the Board of Trustees shall appoint all Chairmen and members of the committees and the number of Trustee members and non-Trustee members (each of whom shall be a member of the National Trust) of each committee shall be determined by the Chairman of the Board after consultation with the President and the Chairmen of the Committees. The composition of such committees shall, to the extent practical, be changed or rotated at regular intervals by the Chairman of the Board to the end that wide membership participation in the affairs of the National Trust may be attained and expertise be drawn upon. The Chairman of each committee shall determine the date and place of all committee meetings, each committee shall adopt its own rules of procedure, and the President of the National Trust, after consultation with the Chairman of each committee, shall assign one or more members of the staff of the National Trust to serve as staff for each committee.

Section 15. *Rules and Regulations.* The Board of Trustees may adopt rules and regulations not inconsistent with these Bylaws for the administration and conduct of the affairs of the Corporation and may alter, amend or repeal any such rules or regulations adopted by it.

Section 16. *Annual Report.* The Chairman of the Board of Trustees shall cause an Annual Report to be prepared with respect to the activities of the National Trust for submission to the members. A summary of the financial status of the Corporation shall be included in that report with a notice that a full financial report is available at the principal office of the National Trust.

Section 17. *Notices.* Written notice of the time and place of all meetings of the Board of Trustees shall be sent to all Trustees not less than 10 days in advance of the date thereof.

ARTICLE VII—Trustees Nominating Committee and Elections

Section 1. *Composition, Term, and Duties.* The Board of Trustees at its Annual Meeting shall designate a Trustees Nominating Committee consisting of two individual non-Trustee members of the National Trust and one general trustee, who shall serve as Chairman. Such committee shall serve continuously until designation by the Board of Trustees of a successor Trustees Nominating Committee. It will be the responsibility of the Trustees Nominating Committee to present its nominations of general trustees to be elected, or confirmed at the Annual Meeting held during the calendar year following the year in which the Trustees Nominating Committee is designated, and to advise the Board of Trustees of its nominations to fill any vacancies which may occur on the Board of Trustees prior to said Annual Meeting. A vacancy in the Trustees Nominating Committee may be filled by the Chairman for the unexpired term of the committee member unable to serve.

Section 2. *Criteria for Nominations.* In selecting nominees for general trustees the Trustees Nominating Committee shall give due but not necessarily controlling weight to geographical considerations to the end that the Board of Trustees shall be representative of the various regions of the United States.

Section 3. *Nominations by Members.* Nominations for general trustees may be made by a petition signed by not less than 15 members of the National Trust, provided that any such petition is sent to the Trustees Nominating Committee addressed to the Chairman thereof at the principal office of the National Trust, not less than two weeks in advance of the Annual Meeting at which the election is to be held. The Trustees Nominating Committee shall advise the members of the National Trust at said Annual Meeting of the names of candidates nominated pursuant to this section.

Section 4. *Elections.* Election of general trustees shall be by secret ballot except that this requirement may be waived by the unanimous consent of all members present at the Annual Meeting. The candidates receiving a plurality of the votes cast shall be elected or confirmed, as the case may be.

Article VIII—Executive Committee

Section 1. *Composition.* The Executive Committee of the Board of Trustees of the National Trust shall consist of the Chairman and the two Vice-Chairmen of the Board of Trustees, the Secretary and the Treasurer of the Corporation, and three non-officer trustees who shall be elected by the Board of Trustees at each Annual Meeting of the Board and who shall serve for a period of one year, but shall continue in office until their successors have been elected and qualified.

Section 2. *Powers.* The Executive Committee shall have and exercise all the powers of the Board of Trustees between the meetings of the Board of Trustees subject to general policies established by the Board.

Section 3. *Proceedings.* The Board of Trustees shall designate one of the members of the Executive Committee as Chairman of said committee and another as Vice-Chairman thereof. In the event of the inability of the Chairman of the Executive Committee to act for any reason, the Vice-Chairman of the Executive Committee shall act in the Chairman's stead. The Chairman of the Board of Trustees may also be Chairman of the Executive Committee. Three members of the Executive Committee shall constitute a quorum. The Executive Committee may determine the manner and form of its proceedings and the time, place and notice to be given of its regular or special meetings. Any lawful action in which a majority of the entire Executive Committee shall concur in writing shall be binding and valid although not authorized or approved at any regular or

special meeting of the Executive Committee but such action shall be reported to the next meeting of the Board of Trustees.

Article IX—Officers

Section 1. *Officers.* The officers of the Corporation shall be a Chairman and two Vice-Chairmen of the Board of Trustees, a Secretary, a Treasurer, a President, an Executive Vice-President, and such assistant secretaries and treasurers and other officers as the Board of Trustees may from time to time designate.

Section 2. *Terms.* The Chairman and the two Vice-Chairmen of the Board of Trustees and the Secretary and the Treasurer shall be elected by the Board of Trustees at the Annual Meeting thereof and shall hold office for a term of one year. The President shall be appointed by and serve at the pleasure of the Board of Trustees and the Executive Vice-President shall be appointed by the President with the approval of the Board of Trustees and shall serve at the pleasure of the President.

Section 3. *Qualifications.* The Chairman and the two Vice-Chairmen of the Board of Trustees must be trustees, and their term of office shall not in any event extend beyond such date as they for any reason cease to be trustees. The Secretary and the Treasurer need not be trustees. The President, the Executive Vice-President, and any assistant secretaries and treasurers shall not be trustees.

Section 4. *Selection.* The Chairman and the two Vice-Chairmen of the Board of Trustees and the Secretary and the Treasurer shall be selected and presented to the Board at its Annual Meeting by an Officers Nominating Committee appointed by the Chairman of the Board of Trustees before the close of the previous Annual Meeting. The Officers Nominating Committee shall be comprised of three members selected from the membership of the Board and shall serve for one year. A vacancy in the Officers Nominating Committee may be filled by the Chairman of the Board by the appointment of another member to serve the unexpired term.

Section 5. *Vacancies.* Any vacancy

in the office of Chairman or Vice-Chairman of the Board of Trustees or of Secretary or Treasurer shall be filled by the Board of Trustees for the unexpired term of the office. The Chairman of the Board may, however, temporarily fill vacancies in the office of Secretary, Treasurer, or any other office designated by the Board of Trustees until such vacancy is filled by the Board of Trustees.

Section 6. *The Chairman.* The Chairman of the Board of Trustees shall be elected by a majority vote of the members of the Board. The Chairman shall preside at all meetings of the members and of the Board of Trustees of the National Trust and shall act in an advisory capacity to all other officers of the Corporation. The Chairman shall be an ex-officio member of all committees of the Board of Trustees except the Trustees Nominating Committee, the Officers Nominating Committee and the Awards Committee.

Section 7. *The Vice-Chairman.* In the event of a vacancy in the office of Chairman of the Board of Trustees or during the Chairman's absence or inability to act for any reason, the powers and duties of this office shall be exercised by one of the Vice-Chairmen as designated by the Executive Committee. If the offices of both Vice-Chairmen are vacant or they are absent or unable to act, the powers and duties of the Chairman shall be exercised by a member of the Executive Committee who shall be selected by said Committee at a special meeting called for that purpose. The Vice-Chairman shall perform such other appropriate duties as the Board of Trustees, the Executive Commitee or the Chairman of the Board may assign to them.

Section 8. *The Secretary.* The Secretary shall make or cause to be made a record of all meetings of the members of the National Trust, the Board of Trustees, the Executive Committee and all other committees of the National Trust. The Secretary shall be responsible for the timely mailing or delivery of all notices of meetings of the National Trust and of its committees and shall have custody of the corporate seal and shall affix it at the direction of the Chairman of the Board of Trustees or a majority of the members of the Board. The Secretary may call upon the President of the National Trust to assign one or more staff members of the National Trust to assist.

Section 9. *The Treasurer.* The Treasurer shall receive and disburse the funds of the Corporation under the direction of the Board of Trustees. The Treasurer shall deposit all funds in the name of the Corporation and all securities in such depository or depositories as the Board of Trustees may, from time to time, designate or approve, and shall have custody of all records and documents relating to the property of the Corporation, keep proper books of account which shall be open at all times to inspection by the Board of Trustees, and shall render to the Board of Trustees upon request a report of all activities executed as Treasurer. At least once a year the Treasurer shall submit to the Board of Trustees a statement of the financial conditions of the Corporation, certified by independent accountants if required by the Board of Trustees, consisting of a balance sheet and related statements of income and expenses, and of the status of and changes in, all funds for the preceding fiscal year. The Board of Trustees may in its discretion require the Treasurer and any assistant treasurer to give bond in such amount and with such surety or sureties as the Board shall determine. Every disbursement of $1,000 or more shall be made by check, signed by the Treasurer and countersigned by such other officer of the National Trust or member of the Executive Committee as the Executive Committee may from time to time designate in writing. The Treasurer may call upon the President of the National Trust to assign one or more staff members of the National Trust to assist.

Section 10. *The President.* The President shall be the chief executive officer of the Corporation. The President shall exercise general supervision of the affairs of the Corporation and shall see to it that such affairs are conducted in accordance with the charter and bylaws of the Corporation and pursuant to the direction of the Board of Trustees. The President shall select all employees of the Corporation and they shall serve at the President's pleasure. The President shall be responsible for carrying out the budget as approved by the Board of Trustees.

Section 11. *The Executive Vice-President.* The Executive Vice-President shall perform such appropriate duties as may be assigned by the President. In the event of a vacancy in the office of the President or in the President's inability to act for any reason, the powers and duties of this office shall be exercised by the Executive Vice-President.

Section 12. *Other Officers.* All other officers of the Corporation shall have such responsibilities and perform such duties as may be prescribed by the Board of Trustees or by the Executive Committee.

Article X—Budget

The fiscal year for the Corporation shall be July 1 through June 30. A budget for each fiscal year shall be prepared by the President and submitted for the consideration of the Finance Committee before being submitted to the Board of Trustees at its spring meeting in the preceding fiscal year. Any budget adopted by the Board shall, without need for further action, authorize the Treasurer to advance the amounts included in the budget from time to time upon receipt of appropriate vouchers. The Treasurer shall make no advancements and no officer or employee shall incur any obligation or expense for any item not included in the budget or in excess of the amount specified therein without prior approval of the Executive Committee. The budget may be amended by the Executive Committee but any amendment must be reported to the Board of Trustees at its next meeting.

Article XI—Board of Advisors of the National Trust

Section 1. *Name.* There shall be a Board of Advisors of the National Trust hereinafter referred to as the Board of Advisors.

Section 2. *Purpose.* The purpose of the Board of Advisors is to assist the National Trust in facilitating public participation in the performance of the mission of the National Trust.

Section 3. *Membership.* The Board of Advisors shall consist of two or more members from each State, the District of Columbia, the Commonwealth of Puerto Rico, the Virgin Islands, Guam and American Samoa. They shall be appointed from the National Trust membership by the Chairman of the Board of Trustees with the approval of the Board of Trustees. Qualification for membership will be evidence of leadership ability and interest in the work of the National Trust.

Section 4. *Term.* Individual members shall serve for three years with one-third of the members appointed each year. Members shall be eligible for reappointment at the completion of a first term but may serve no more than two consecutive terms.

Section 5. *Officers.* The officers of the Board of Advisors shall be a Chairman, two Vice-Chairmen, a Secretary and such other officers as the Chairman of the Board of Advisors may from time to time designate. Such officers shall be elected by the members of the Board of Advisors for one year and the election thereof shall take place at the time of the National Trust annual meeting.

Section 6. *Committees.* An Administrative Committee shall be organized by the Chairman of the Board of Advisors to carry on the work of the Board between annual plenary sessions, and other committees shall be organized as required by the affairs and activities of the Board of Advisors.

Section 7. *Functions.* The functions of the Board of Advisors shall be to:

(a) advise the National Trust on citizen thinking and interest in historic preservation,

(b) serve as a direct channel for the expansion of citizen concern,

(c) provide a network of key leaders whose interest and leadership resources may be mobilized in behalf of the preservation movement,

(d) act as liaison between the National Trust headquarters and individuals or organizations seeking practical advice, assistance, support or sponsorship for preservation projects.

Section 8. *Activities.* The Board of Advisors shall engage in appropriate activities in accordance with its authorized functions. It shall emphasize the citizen participation and educational aspects of the National Trust's preservation program. The Board of Advisors shall meet in plenary session once a year at the time of the Annual Meeting of the National Trust. It may meet at other times upon call of the Chairman of the Board of Advisors. The Board of Advisors shall be represented on the appropriate committees of the Board of Trustees of the National Trust. The Chairman of the Board of Advisors or his designee among the other officers of the Board of Advisors may be invited to attend meetings of the Board of Trustees and the Executive Committee of the National Trust.

Section 9. *Reports.* The Board of Advisors shall maintain appropriate records and report to the Board of Trustees of the National Trust at least once a year. Its activities shall be briefly recorded in the annual report of the National Trust.

ARTICLE XII—Amendments

These bylaws may be amended by the Board of Trustees by an affirmative vote of not less than two-thirds of the members in attendance at any meeting of the Board of Trustees.

August 21, 1973

APPENDIX 7

ANNUAL MEETINGS OF THE NATIONAL COUNCIL FOR HISTORIC SITES AND BUILDINGS AND THE NATIONAL TRUST, 1947–73

NATIONAL COUNCIL FOR HISTORIC SITES AND BUILDINGS

1947	Washington, D.C.
1948	Washington, D.C.
1949	Williamsburg, Va.

NATIONAL COUNCIL FOR HISTORIC SITES AND BUILDINGS AND THE NATIONAL TRUST FOR HISTORIC PRESERVATION

1950	Washington, D.C.
1951	Philadelphia, Pa.
1952	Washington, D.C.
1953	Newport, R.I.

NATIONAL TRUST FOR HISTORIC PRESERVATION

1954	Chicago, Ill.
1955	Nashville, Tenn.
1956	Washington, D.C.
1957	Swampscott, Mass.
1958	New Orleans, La.
1959	Washington, D.C.
1960	Pittsburgh, Pa.
1961	New York, N.Y.
1962	San Francisco, Calif.
1963	Washington, D.C.
1964	San Antonio, Tex.
1965	Raleigh, N.C.
1966	Philadelphia, Pa.
1967	St. Louis, Mo.
1968	Savannah, Ga.
1969	Denver, Colo.
1970	Charleston, S.C.
1971	San Diego, Calif.
1972	Washington, D.C.
1973	Cleveland, Ohio

NATIONAL TRUST STAFF AND ORGANIZATION

Full-Time Staff Members, 1948–June 30, 1973*

Wendy J. Adler 1972–

Worth Bailey 1951–54
Anthony D. H. Baker 1973–
Mark N. Beach 1972–
Ellen Beasley 1966–70
Pierre G. T. Beauregard, III 1967–73
Patricia McK. Beckington 1967–69
Helen M. Benson 1967–
Joy Berghaus 1971–73
Angela Berzeg 1970–72
J. William Bethea 1966–68
James Biddle 1968–
Brigitta R. Billings 1958–
Dorothy D. Blaska 1973–
John J. G. Blumenson 1971–73
Kathryn Bottorff 1967–68
Margaret Bouslough 1970–71
Ruth P. Brandt 1969–
Helen Duprey Bullock 1950–73
Helen B. Byrd 1970–

Berman Chang 1968–70
E. Blaine Cliver 1972–
Jane A. Coughlin 1966–
Elizabeth B. Cunningham 1968–70

Millicent Dew 1971–
Ruth L. Dillon 1964–73
Dennis Doornekamp 1969–72

Martha L. Easter 1972–73
Lynn M. Emerich 1972–

Gerald L. Fiedler 1968–71
Cecil E. Finn 1963–66
Abigail H. Ford 1970–72
Gail C. Freeman 1968–72
Robert Frick 1951–55
Susan Frisch 1973–
John L. Frisbee, III 1967–

Letitia G. Galbraith 1971–
Robert R. Garvey, Jr. 1960–67
Katherine Gessford 1951–66
Marguerite B. Gleysteen 1968–70
Doris Godsey 1951–60
Lillian A. Goetz 1971–72
Raymond P. Gott 1967–
Isabella H. Grant 1966–69
Anne E. Grimmer 1969–72
Eleanor N. Hamilton 1966–68
Charlotte Hatton 1953–56
Frederick Haupt, III 1968–
Richard W. Haupt 1973–
Inez V. Hebert 1956–
Lynne L. Herman 1971–
Marva J. Heywood 1966–67
April M. Hockett 1970–
Richard H. Howland 1956–60

Paul W. Ivory 1971–

Sandra D. Jackson 1972–
Loretta J. Jamieson 1973–
Arthur Johnson 1948–70
Isabel F. Johnson 1959–61
Meredith Johnson 1954–62
Constance Jones 1970–71

Anthea M. Keane 1972–73
Richard K. Kearns 1970–73
Alan Keiser 1973–
Russell V. Keune 1969–
Lee Ann Kinzer 1971–
Carleton Knight, III 1971–
Laura F. Knox-Dick 1970–71
Patricia A. Kobel 1972–
Cheryl I. Kreiger 1973–
Roland E. Kuniholm 1972–

Barbara B. Lusby 1965–68

*This list includes only permanent, full-time employees who worked at the Trust for a year or more. A few Trust properties staff employed before 1970 may have been omitted due to incomplete personnel records at some Trust properties before 1970.

Kathleen B. McCurdy 1961–68
Maryann Macdonald 1972–
Linda H. Macpherson 1972–73
Diane R. Maddex 1968–72
Kaye Maggard 1973–
Madeleine L. Marcouyeux 1969–71
Shirley M. Markley 1973–
James C. Massey 1972–
William U. Massey 1972–
Mary C. Means 1973–
Hans Meier 1965–72
Georgene R. Menk 1969–71
Louise McA. Merritt 1967–71
Mimi Micheline 1967–69
Mary Christine Miller 1972–73
Margaret M. Missar 1961–65
Lucy M. L. Morgan 1966–68
Terry B. Morton 1956–
Betty Walsh Morris 1948–53
Virgil M. Mullins 1966–69
William J. Murtagh 1958–67

George E. Newstedt 1965–
Joann Noblett 1970–72

Barbara M. O'Connell 1972–
Young Kun Oh 1973–
Joan Olshansky 1971–73

Thomas W. Paige 1971–
Imogene Patrick 1972–74
John N. Pearce 1964–70
Floyd L. Pearson 1967–
Mildred M. Pearson 1966–
Mary Clare Shenkir Peden 1966–67
Kenneth Pendar 1969–71
Barbara S. Perry 1971–
Patricia Phelan 1969–73
Eugenia Porter 1963–64
Joseph Prendergast 1967–73
Theresa M. Profilet 1972–

Miriam G. Rabb 1968–
Brigid Rapp 1973–
Frederick L. Rath, Jr. 1948–56
Marjorie G. Recinos 1969–
Alida E. Ruesch 1963–
Claudia S. Ritter 1972–
Sabin Robbins, IV 1969–
Homer E. Rollins 1966–70
Margaret L. Rombousek 1965–67
Jessie F. Rowlands 1967–
Laurie Ryan 1968–70

Virginia Salzman 1965–67

Radmilla Savic 1967–69
Mary Ann Schilling 1972–73
Ralph G. Schwarz 1970–72
Hardinge Scholle 1952–61
Kathleen R. Schroeder 1968–72
Gyla B. Seal 1957–61
Alice A. Sharpe 1969–
Sandra G. Sharpe 1969–72
Martha Jane Shay 1967–69
Raymond V. Shepherd, Jr. 1971–
Willie Shepherd 1967–72
Brinton E. Sherwood 1964–66
Suzanne B. Sherwood 1973–
Doris M. Simmons 1967–
Thomas M. Slade 1972–
Daniel Sleeper 1971–72
George M. Smith 1970–
Leila J. Smith 1969–71
Nancy L. Smith 1973–
Peter H. Smith 1971–
Carola Southers 1952–54
Ruby R. Stefansson 1962–66
Robert G. Stewart 1961–64
Virginia Strahan 1947–51
Hazel Z. Stuart 1963–
Henry H. Surface 1950–56
Jean L. Swarts 1970–

William C. Taggart 1971–
Phyllis Talley 1966–67
Elizabeth Terry 1971–
Charles W. Thomas 1972–
Glenn E. Thompson 1963–73
Jennie Thompson 1973–
Pearl D. Thompson 1960–73
Rose Z. Thorman 1968–70
Richard J. Thorpe 1951–61
Sharon W. Timmons 1973–
Robert E. Tourville 1969–73

Josephine Van Fossen 1953–58
Ruth Vest 1970–
George Vetterman 1961–69

Linda E. Ward 1964–67
Dorothy Watson 1969–72
Charles Way 1956–73
Samuel G. Welsh 1972–
Michael F. Wiedl, III 1972–
Mabel B. Willey 1959–67
Patricia E. Williams 1966–
Leroy Wise, Jr. 1970–
Tony P. Wrenn 1962–66

ORGANIZATION OF THE NATIONAL TRUST, 1953–73*

1953–54
Director: Frederick L. Rath, Jr.
Administrator: Henry H. Surface
Historian: Helen Duprey Bullock

1955
Director: Frederick L. Rath, Jr.
Administrator: Henry H. Surface
Consultant: Hardinge Scholle
Historian: Helen Duprey Bullock

1956
President: Richard H. Howland
Consultant: Hardinge Scholle
Historian: Helen Duprey Bullock

1957
President: Richard H. Howland
Historian: Helen Duprey Bullock
Properties officer: Hardinge Scholle
Managing editor: Terry Brust (Morton)
Assistant to the president:
  George Worthington, III

1958–59
President: Richard H. Howland
Historian: Helen Duprey Bullock
Assistant to the president:
  William J. Murtagh
Properties officer: Hardinge Scholle
Managing editor: Terry B. Morton

1960–61
Executive director: Robert B. Garvey, Jr.
Consultant: Hardinge Scholle

Department of Education
Director: William J. Murtagh

Department of Information
Director: Helen Duprey Bullock

Department of Properties
Director: Robert G. Stewart

1962–65
Executive director: Robert R. Garvey, Jr.

Fiscal Department
Administrative assistant:
  Mabel B. Willey

Department of Education
Director: William J. Murtagh

Department of Information
Director: Helen Duprey Bullock

Department of Membership
Director: Glenn E. Thompson

Department of Properties
Director: Brinton E. Sherwood

1966–67
Executive director: Robert R. Garvey, Jr.
Senior editor and historian:
  Helen Duprey Bullock

Department of Administration
Director: George E. Newstedt

Department of Program
Director: William J. Murtagh
  Membership Services—
    Glenn E. Thompson, *director*
  *Publications—*Terry B. Morton, *director*
  *Properties—*John N. Pearce, *curator*

Department of Public Affairs
Director: J. William Bethea
Press officer: Eleanor N. Hamilton

1968–69
Office of the President
President: James Biddle
Executive director: Joseph Prendergast
Administrator: George E. Newstedt

Department of Historic Properties
Curator: John N. Pearce

Department of Programs and Services
Correspondence and Consultation
  *Services—*Helen Duprey Bullock,
  senior editor and historian

Education and Training Services—
  Glenn E. Thompson, *director*
*Field Services—*Russell V. Keune, *director*
*Publications—*Terry B. Morton, *director*

Department of Public Affairs
Director: Frederick Haupt, III

1970–71
Office of the President
President: James Biddle
Executive director: Joseph Prendergast
Administrator: George E. Newstedt
Senior editor and historian:
  Helen Duprey Bullock
Special assistant to the president:
  Helen B. Byrd

Department of Education
Director: Glenn E. Thompson

Department of Field Services
Director: Russell V. Keune
Western field office representative:
  John L. Frisbee, III

Department of Plans and Development
Interim director: Frederick Haupt, III

Department of Properties
Interim director: Ralph G. Schwarz

Department of Public Affairs
Director: Frederick Haupt, III

Department of Publications
Director: Terry B. Morton

National Historic Preservation Fund
Director: Ralph G. Schwarz

1972
Office of the President
President: James Biddle
Executive director: Joseph Prendergast
Administrator: George E. Newstedt
Senior editor and historian:
  Helen Duprey Bullock
Special assistant to the president:
  Helen B. Byrd

Department of Education
Director: Glenn E. Thompson

Department of Field Services
Director: Russell V. Keune
West Coast field services representative:
  John L. Frisbee, III

Department of Historic Properties
Director: James C. Massey

Department of Plans and Development
Interim director: Frederick Haupt, III

Department of Public Affairs
Director: Frederick Haupt, III

Department of Publications
Director: Terry B. Morton

National Historic Preservation Fund
Director: Ralph G. Schwarz

1973
Office of the President
President: James Biddle
Executive director: Joseph Prendergast
Administrator: George E. Newstedt
Senior editor and historian:
  Helen Duprey Bullock
Special assistant to the president:
  Helen B. Byrd

Department of Education
Director: Richard W. Haupt

Department of Field Services
Director: Russell V. Keune
Western field services representative:
  John L. Frisbee, III
Midwest field services representative:
  Mary C. Means

Department of Historic Properties
Director: James C. Massey
Property manager:
  Pierre G. T. Beauregard, III

Department of Plans and Development
Director: Mark N. Beach

Department of Public Affairs
Director: Frederick Haupt, III

Department of Publications
Director: Terry B. Morton

* The National Council and the Trust merged in October 1953; therefore the staff
organization listing begins in 1953.

NATIONAL TRUST MEMBERSHIP, 1950–73

Fiscal Year	Individual	Organizations	Corporations	Complimentary*	Total
1950	267	63			330
1951	374	96			470
1952	486	104			590
1953	884	136			1,020
1954	1,100	150			1,250
1955	1,300	160	1		1,461
1956	1,477	182	2		1,661
1957	2,118	234	6		2,358
1958	2,270	264	6		2,540
1959	2,487	293	6		2,786
1960	2,696	336	5		3,037
1961	2,829	341	6		3,176
1962	3,056	395	4		3,455
1963	3,800	443	5		4,248
1964	5,453	538	35		6,026
1965	7,502	531	43	589	8,665
1966	8,570	613	44	1,441	10,668
1967	11,004	758	34	501	12,297
1968	13,963	758	54	1,150	15,925
1969	17,826	1,239	60	1,174	20,299
1970	21,069	1,325	61	1,215	23,670
1971	25,155	1,397	61	1,291	27,904
1972	29,121	1,522	56	1,176	31,875
1973	37,267	1,722	76	1,205	40,270

*Members of Congress and the news media.

NATIONAL TRUST BUDGETS, ENDOWMENTS AND ASSETS, 1956–73

Fiscal Year	Budget	Endowments	Total Assets*
1956	Records	$ 467,111	Records
1957	not	2,967,111	not
1958	available**	2,967,111	available**
1959		3,034,430	
1960		3,034,430	
1961	$ 214,438	3,478,017	$3,598,305
1962	229,890	3,593,453	3,690,340
1963	268,944	3,625,093	3,707,706
1964	368,175	3,630,178	3,706,374
1965	723,937	3,911,026	4,063,175
1966	784,310	5,255,744	5,751,550
1967	1,010,540	5,284,838	5,634,150
1968	1,174,082	5,552,568	6,122,674
1969	1,265,305	5,751,208	6,387,411
1970	1,611,791	5,226,942	5,862,972
1971	2,327,063	5,142,906	6,141,020
1972	2,956,934	5,328,844	6,512,989
1973	3,099,623	5,447,038	6,843,612

*Total asset figures do not include values for Trust historic properties.

**Comprehensive fiscal planning was initiated in 1961. Prior to that time records were not kept on a uniform fiscal year basis.

NATIONAL TRUST PROPERTIES
AND DATES OF ACQUISITION, 1953–73

CASA AMESTI, Monterey, Calif. Bequest of Mrs. Frances Adler Elkins, 1953

DECATUR HOUSE, Washington, D.C. Bequest of Mrs. Truxtun Beale in memory of her husband, Truxtun Beale, 1956

WOODLAWN PLANTATION, Mount Vernon, Va. Deeded by Woodlawn Public Foundation, 1957

THE SHADOWS-ON-THE-TECHE, New Iberia, La. Bequest of William Weeks Hall, 1959

WOODROW WILSON HOUSE, Washington, D. C. Gift of Mrs. Woodrow Wilson as a memorial to President Wilson, 1961

BELLE GROVE, Middletown, Va. Bequest of Francis Welles Hunnewell, 1964

LYNDHURST, Tarrytown, N.Y. Bequest of Anna Gould, Duchess of Talleyrand-Perigord, in memory of her parents, Jay and Helen Gould, 1964

POPE-LEIGHEY HOUSE, Mount Vernon, Va. Gift of Mrs. Robert A. Leighey, 1964

OATLANDS, Leesburg, Va. Gift of Mrs. David E. Finley and Mrs. Eustis Emmet, in memory of their parents, William and Edith Eustis, 1965

CHESTERWOOD, Stockbridge, Mass. Gift of the Daniel Chester French Foundation; endowed by Margaret French Cresson, 1969

CLIVEDEN, Germantown, Pa. Acquired through the generosity of the Chew family, 1972

COOPER-MOLERA ADOBE, Monterey, Calif. Bequest of Frances M. Molera, 1972

All Trust properties are listed in the National Register of Historic Places. As of December 1973, the following had been designated National Historic Landmarks: Belle Grove, Chesterwood, Cliveden, Decatur House, Lyndhurst, Oatlands and the Woodrow Wilson House.

NATIONAL TRUST PROPERTY COUNCILS, 1972–73

BELLE GROVE COUNCIL
Mrs. C. Ridgeley White, *chairman*
Dabney W. Watts, *vice chairman*
Mrs. Roderick Cheeseman, *secretary*
Benjamin Belchic
Malcolm T. Brumback
Mrs. Duncan Gibb
Mrs. Drayton Hite Gordon
Mrs. Paul Hatmaker
Fred R. Painter
George R. Scheulen
Mrs. Lilburn Talley
John A. Washington

Ex Officio
Mrs. John B. Hollister*
William McCoy
Mrs. Will L. Owing
Neil Stallings

CHESTERWOOD COUNCIL
Stephen V. C. Morris, *chairman*
Robert K. Wheeler, *vice chairman*
Stephen B. Hibbard, *secretary*
Ingersoll Cunningham
Donald C. Douglass
Mrs. Charles W. Earnshaw
Mary V. Flynn
Mrs. Douglas Krumbhaar
John S. McLennan
Rosamond Sherwood
Alexander Stoller

Ex Officio
Mrs. William F. Barrett, Jr.
Margaret French Cresson
George E. Emerson, Jr.
Helen D. French
Prentiss French
Stuart Henry
James F. Kiley

Robert G. Williams
Mrs. Stewart C. Woodworth

CLIVEDEN COUNCIL
Nicholas B. Wainwright, *chairman*
R. Damon Childs
Mrs. William T. Coleman, Jr.
Mrs. Anthony N. B. Garvan
F. Otto Haas
Roger W. Moss, Jr.
Margaret Tinkcom
Mrs. John Wintersteen
Thomas Wistar, Jr.
Charles H. Woodward

Ex Officio
Ernesta D. Ballard
Samuel Chew
Harold D. Saylor

DECATUR HOUSE COUNCIL
William J. McManus, *chairman*
Clement E. Conger, *vice chairman*
Mrs. E. P. Moore, *secretary*
Mrs. Loring C. Christie
Mrs. Clarence Dodge, Jr.
Mrs. Alexander B. Hagner
Mrs. Paul Magnuson
Mrs. Thomas C. Musgrave, Jr.
Adm. Jerauld Wright, USN (Ret.)

Ex Officio
Leonard Carmichael*
Mrs. Nicholas Longworth
William F. Machold
Mrs. Thomas H. Moorer

LYNDHURST COUNCIL
Walter K. Sturges, *chairman*
Mrs. Benjamin Ginsburg, *vice chairman*
Robert Hochhauser, *secretary*
Robert Cole

APPENDIX 13

RECIPIENTS OF THE LOUISE DU PONT CROWNINSHIELD AWARD, 1960–73

1960   Mount Vernon Ladies' Association, Mount Vernon, Va.

1961   Henry Francis du Pont, Wilmington, Del.

1962   Katharine Prentis Murphy, New York, N.Y.

1963   Martha Gilmore Robinson, New Orleans, La.

1964   Mr. and Mrs. Bertram K. Little, Brookline, Mass.

1965   Charles E. Peterson, Philadelphia, Pa.

1966   Ima Hogg, Houston, Tex., and Mary Gordon Latham Kellenberger, Greensboro, N.C.

1967   Not awarded

1968   St. Clair Wright, Annapolis, Md.

1969   Mr. and Mrs. Henry N. Flynt, Greenwich, Conn.

1970   Frank L. Horton, Winston-Salem, N.C.

1971   Frances R. Edmunds, Charleston, S.C.

1972   Alice Winchester, New York, N.Y.

1973   Ricardo E. Alegría, San Juan, P.R.

THE PURPOSE OF THE NATIONAL TRUST:
A STATEMENT ADOPTED BY THE
BOARD OF TRUSTEES, MAY 1964

The National Trust for Historic Preservation in the United States is a national association chartered by Congress in 1949 as a charitable, educational and non-profit organization. Its members are individuals, societies and corporations dedicated to guarding the American heritage of historic sites and buildings. It is supported entirely by memberships and voluntary contributions.

The Trust believes in the value to the nation of public awareness of the continuity of our past, present and future. It believes also in the educational value of historic sites and buildings, and views them as a means of public instruction and patriotic inspiration.

The purpose of the Trust is to arouse public interest in the preservation of American monuments; to lead the public interest where it already exists; and to spearhead the American preservation movement on a national scale.

The National Trust itself preserves and exhibits nationally important historic properties entrusted to its care, with adequate endowment, provided that their preservation and restoration are determined to be necessary and desirable. Thus the Trust demonstrates its belief in the principle of trusteeship, whereby historic buildings are preserved, maintained and administered by trustee groups.

The Trust considers that research—historical, architectural and archaeological—provides the soundest foundation for the selection, restoration and interpretation of historic sites and buildings. Recognizing that not all properties are equally valuable and that not all can be saved, the Trust has established criteria for fair and uniform evaluation of sites and buildings of national, regional and local interest so that what is truly worthy may be recognized and preservation efforts begun.

The Trust encourages preserving the function as well as the fabric of historic buildings so that, where appropriate, houses are lived in and public buildings serve as living monuments to our past.

The Trust gives active moral support and, upon request, expert technical advice to preservation organizations for their local projects. Through its work with national, state and local government agencies, professional associations, and civic and patriotic societies in all parts of the country, the Trust is completely familiar with the ways and means of preservation. This knowledge is available to the public at no cost.

The Trust endorses interpretive programs as desirable adjuncts to historic properties, and encourages correct interpretations of history through its own educational programs. It deplores spurious and false presentations which commercialize the nation's heritage and cheapen and vulgarize public taste.

As part of its education program, the Trust conducts workshops, seminars and conferences, and is especially active in training future preservationists and administrators for historic properties.

The Trust's publications serve as a clearinghouse for national preservation information. In them are published endorsements of the preservation work of individuals and organizations, as well as exposures of indiscriminate commercial destruction made in the so-called public interest, whether of a single building or of an entire area.

The Trust's coast-to-coast membership and activities reflect its truly national interest. It is the only non-governmental body operating on a nationwide basis in the preservation field. Its Trustees are private citizens chosen from all parts of the nation, serving without pay in the country's preservation cause.

The Trust is a militant, independent organization, not opposed to necessary and constructive change, and one that seeks to mobilize and channel national sentiment and opinion in support of historic preservation so that we will always have visible embodiments of our nation's past.

EXCERPT FROM ADDRESS BY GORDON GRAY,
1966–67 DECADE OF DECISION,
ANNUAL REPORT OF THE
NATIONAL TRUST FOR HISTORIC PRESERVATION
IN THE UNITED STATES, FISCAL YEAR 1965–66

In the next decade, we will construct more than was built in our first two hundred years.

We're here tonight to vocalize and volatize the age-old mystery of how to live with history—to face the challenge, to inspire and activate ourselves and the nation, to avert an American landmarks tragedy within this next decade, in every little town, big town, old town, new town.

History can be dead or alive—it can be told and retold, but to make it expressive, we will have to live with and in history. To live, to make history live, is to be aware, to feel. How do you feel history? Try living in an old and meaningful structure, working in an old and meaningful structure, teaching in an old and meaningful structure; try to save an old and meaningful structure.

The past belongs not to the limited number of professional historians, teachers, architectural historians, but to anyone who is aware of it—and it grows—lives—by being shared. Everyone can be a collector—if not of American cut glass, arrowheads, covered bridges, mansions—at least a collector in awareness and appreciation.

But Americans were once afraid of their history—or overwhelmed by it. We tried to make it sacred and we called our monuments shrines. They were something to stand back and look at, of our religious, military and political life—something which we consider supernatural, superhuman. Are we able today and will we be better able in ten years—at the end of what we choose to call this Decade of Decision—to accept ourselves as a nation and preserve some of the best of the past of all phases of our lives?

Must we remain simply collectors of facts, microfilm, and museums, or can we live closer with history and in history? By understanding it and translating its best lesson of living and design and taste and style—you might say we would be on the inside of history.

We have begun to call our monuments landmarks. In the very term, we accept them as a part of our environment—we can walk around them, touch them, and live in them—they are everywhere, they are for everybody. If we really accept and understand and live with our past, we will make demands on it, and will take sustenance from it. We will pursue life knowing the meaning of taste, the anatomy of change, the heritage of instinct, and the basics of a sound and prideful nationalism.

In the next decade, we will construct more than was built in our first two hundred years.

Here, practically in the shadow of Independence Hall, we are prompted to think of our origins and the times of celebration of the great events in our national life. I am persuaded that we are mighty celebrants—on anniversaries —if we remember them. Is this to continue to be our focus and compulsion, or can we accept the imperative of on-going evolving history? Ten years from now, national attention will be centered on Philadelphia at the confluence of the Delaware and Schuylkill Rivers as the United States of America celebrates the 200th anniversary of its Independence on July 4, 1976.

STATE OF THE UNION

On July 4, 1976, what will be the status of our landmarks across the country as they relate to the State of the Union? Will we have dealt well with the faith, the vision, the promise of our fathers? Will there be a true confluence of the past and present—a more realistic appreciation of the old and new and our use of them? In the ten years ahead, what we choose to call in the Decade of Decision, we shall have to determine if the answer is "yes."

Economically, by the end of this decade we will be the richest nation on earth, with a predicted Gross National Product of more than one trillion dollars. We must assure that an adequate percentage will be for culture, conservation, recreation; and landmarks, which link all three. Landmarks must be protected as a natural resource, just as openspace, redwoods and wild life. These programs have been generously supported in the past primarily by private philanthropists. There must be more of the same, but there has been a federal recognition of the cultural lag in the state of the humanities in a nation providing vast sums for science and technology. Thus, grants have been made to the performing arts, fine arts, and teaching. But what of the environmental arts? I submit that we, too, must join in the politics of art, or is it in the art of politics?

Scientifically, existing and projected programs will be directed toward solving the problems of water and air pollution, of diminishing natural resources, of disease, of social welfare and of redevelopment, while pushing forward the scientific frontiers of outer space. Some of these programs will work for preservation. Clean air will help keep our buildings and sculpture clean; landmark maintenance will be less costly; new techniques will enable us to make structures more enduring, and rehabilitation and restoration easier, and sometimes feasible in instances where it had been thought impossible.

Other of these programs may seem to work against preservation, but it is up to us to see that each of them, to the extent possible, evaluates and considers its contribution to preservation.

Socially, landmarks must have function as well as aesthetic significance.

They must be made an adventure for everyone, or at least accessible to everyone from our young to the retirement population. The old have memories, but I submit that landmarks are not irrelevant to the problems we feel we have with our young people. Landmarks are still necessary to the teaching of local history where people can best understand their democratic heritage. The saving and use of landmarks will bring back pride in community and a feeling of neighborhood, both so necessary to education for responsible citizenship. Can it not be said that the current revolt of our swinging generation may not be against roots, form, and discipline, but against rootlessness?

We must be wise enough, convinced enough and dedicated enough to put landmarks in our future environment; to identify, evaluate and interpret them into our other national programs for the common good. . . .

As far as the *preservation community* is concerned, I have various suggestions which it seems to me are important in making a total national program viable and coherent. Obviously, all dedicated individual and institutional efforts must continue, but I submit these propositions, recognizing that I run the risk of over-statement:

We must, as preservationists, stop talking simply to each other. On behalf of the National Trust, I plead guilty, for I fear that in our past Annual Meetings and Preservation Conferences we have indulged in that cozy practice which I suggest we now abandon. The Every-Member-Canvass is an accepted American device, but it doesn't go far in spreading the Gospel. I hope that we all might agree that yesterday's government panel discussion will have served to chart a new type of communication, to bring a new dimension to the formal and traditional activities of preservationists.

Hysterical Preservationists

We must learn to help shape events not by simple noisy protest, but by submitting constructive alternatives, recognizing that change is with us and progress persists. Too often we have laid ourselves open to the charge of being "hysterical" preservationists, because we have simply been in blind opposition to some of the imperative necessities of our increasingly complex society.

We must understand that the old is not necessarily the good, and we must embrace the notion that some of the new is worth preserving, including examples of our way of life that will not return again. It is in this area that some of the greatest challenges exist, for otherwise our grandchildren can properly blame us for significant gaps in what will remain of our historical and architectural heritage.

We must, as we too often have not, always be aware of the economic facts and compulsions of life. We must realize that some landmarks will inevitably be lost because of the astronomical funds required to save them, and that many will be preserved only as we find viable economic justification.

And above all, perhaps, as has been pointed out in an exhibit entitled, "New Life for Landmarks," now circulating under the auspices of the American Federation for the Arts, "the best hope of saving our cities' landmarks is to find new uses for them. We have no patience with simply embalming a building that is dead. The job is only worth doing if it creates a more interesting environment than the one that is there now. We come not to buy these buildings, but to bring them back alive. . . . As the cities of Europe prove, it is the surest way of preserving the grace and continuity of urban living."

As far as the National Trust is concerned, in the last year it has been re-examining its own opportunities and responsibilities in the Decade of Decision. Although the chartered reasons for its creation are unchanged since 1949, its role of key leadership in the common effort has been recognized as vastly enlarged.

We believe that we are challenged:

To arouse and coordinate public interest.

To aid local groups. By loans and challenge gifts, we aim to help with the acquisition of significant properties in emergency situations; to help provide qualified staff for preservation organizations; and to permit scholarly and evaluative surveys.

To make field services available to communities and institutions, wherever they may be in America. We visualize being able to send a team of experts in architecture, architectural history, landscape design, publications, public relations, fund raising, to assist those who believe in the accepted American practice of "do-it-yourself."

To serve as a central clearinghouse of information for the many governmental programs affecting preservation directly or indirectly.

To stimulate and in some cases participate in a technical educational program to improve the caliber of those already active professionally in this field. In colleges and graduate schools the Trust must encourage financing of scholarships and internships for students, and chairs of instruction for the faculty.

To establish a comprehensive special library on all the academic disciplines involved in this field, from archaeology and architecture, city planning and political science to the sciences and technologies that it involves.

To enlarge its own membership, its Seminars and Conferences and its awards program.

To operate a placement bureau to aid qualified and trained personnel to find careers in the preservation field.

TRUST BOARD OF ADVISORS

To have an active Board of Advisors to the National Trust. I am happy to report what, in my view, has been an extremely significant development. Our Trustees have authorized, and we have begun to create, such a Board, which will consist of two members from each of the fifty states, territories and possessions. This will give us instant and easy communication with individuals and organizations throughout America and will alleviate one of our most vexing problems arising out of the necessarily inadequate geographic spread of the Board of Trustees. There will be a nation-wide channel of communication from and to our Board which has not heretofore existed.

To broaden its own properties program. It has not yet, as you know, been the policy of the National Trust to acquire properties in competition with local interests, but I am persuaded that it does need to increase the number, variety, and geographic distribution of its holdings. The nine houses now owned by the Trust present a range of period styles. This is, candidly, not a broad representation of America in terms of association, era and culture. Missing from the Trust-owned properties are those associated with science, such as study rooms or laboratories of eminent Americans; those associated with various ethnic backgrounds; those related to the lives and works of artists and writers; sites or buildings related to American business; American labor; and the communications media.

PROPERTIES COME ALIVE!

To make our properties come alive! A symbol of the Trust's new effort in this program, and its conviction of suitable adaptive use of historic structures is the staff's move last week to the remodeled servants' wing and third floor of Decatur House. The House faces on Lafayette Square, known as the President's Square, when it was erected in 1818–19 for the dashing naval hero, Stephen Decatur, and is on the left flank of the White House.

In the coming months other National Trust properties will also find new life. At *Lyndhurst,* nature trails have been marked for tourists, while other areas have been left unmarked for Boy Scouts earning merit badges. A nature training and study center in the recreation hall, and concerts and theater performances in the transformed swimming pool building are planned. The spectacular green house will be reglazed.

The *Oatlands* stables may be used for art exhibits and a ring may be installed for horse shows.

At *Woodlawn Plantation,* the early 19th century mansion and the 20th century *Pope-Leighey House* will be linked with a nature trail. The latter structure, designed by Frank Lloyd Wright, will be used for conferences on contemporary architecture. Experimental school tours were developed at *Woodlawn* last year and will be extended to other Trust properties.

An archaeological dig at *The Shadows-on-the-Teche* will be used for the teaching of young people through their volunteer service, as well as for historical fact finding.

Belle Grove will be the setting for seminars on the study of a working farm, and farm-making—perhaps more importantly an understanding of how the estate was carved from the wilderness.

Lest I become too entranced and enchanted by my own catalogue, I must remind myself that at this precise moment in history I am in the position of a jet airplane landing on its mother carrier. Have I said that we will do all these things? I can only assert that we have the will to try. Some are within our normally growing means. But those which are to make perhaps the greatest contribution will require not only a substantial enhancement of our financial resources, but an augmentation of our staff, in terms of skill, knowledge, and ability.

Your Trustees are prepared—indeed for a year have been prepared—to seek to meet this challenge. A year ago, I think, I told you that we planned to attempt to corral some $7 or $8 million in new money for the Trust. However, as the prospects for a true national program have developed, and as we have reassessed the need, our sights have risen. We now hope that by the end of the Decade of Decision, we will have received in existing and new endowments and operating funds, the total equivalent of $25 million.

This is our staggering, formidable goal. Naturally, this will include such federal funds as may come to us, but I must remind you that they will be on a matching basis, and warn you that they will in every likelihood constitute the smaller part of the total. Private philanthropy must—and should—carry the major burden. Naturally, I bespeak the support of all of you.

As I approach my conclusion, I must confess that deliberately I have until now delayed one of the most important things I have to say. It could, indeed possibly must, be the central core of a truly national program. There is a thrilling opportunity to bring historic preservation—not, I hope, screaming and kicking—into the last half of the 20th century by harnessing technology and science which have, in their own way, helped create many, if not most, of our problems. Advances in information gathering, handling and communications—computer technology—have made us aware that there is a way to identify, catalogue, and categorize by style, period, architect, region, use, association, standards, and almost any other measurement that one can think of, every object of preservation concern in the United States, with ready and instant access. There can be finger-tip availability of information about every important site, structure and object in America. Such an instant archive could provide the basis for a dramatic change in what essentially now must be a more passive attitude into one of complete aggression. It would convert our orientation from one of attacking local problems to that of dealing with a national resource.

THE CHALLENGE

In a way, this notion is awesome to a national leader in the field of preservation. For, indeed, it would not simply be a basis for a change in approach. It would compel a change in approach. Too often we have been there with too little and too late. Too often landmarks have disappeared before our eyes, because we had not the timely means to see them. If we know what is to be saved, what excuse will we have not to move relentlessly to the attack? How could we then avoid the challenge?

However, I must at the same time insist that the simple development of such a resource alone could be meaningless unless we are intelligent enough and determined enough to associate with us people of such high competence and unquestioned professional integrity and ability that we will have the wisdom and energy to use it effectively. Wise standards, sound criteria, and impeccable judgment would necessarily need to be applied to the new data base to make this resource the very heart of the preservation movement.

Thus, we perhaps come full circle with science and technology which, having seemed to conspire to defeat us, may now be our salvation and may, in this field, force us to shock ourselves out of national passivity.

To accomplish our goals in the next decade, the entire nation must move from concept and criteria, from the fine but fragmented programs, from the local to the national, from the defensive to the offensive, to total aggressive and meaningful programs for landmarks. This can be achieved in the partnership now being established among the federal, state and city governments, the preservation community, and the National Trust.

We, in the Trust, must not be timid about accepting the leadership role which events have thrust upon us.

Will we let American landmarks flicker out? or will we make the supreme effort in the Decade of Decision to bring them back alive?

Most of you, I am sure, will remember these few lines by Longfellow:

O, Summer Day, beside the joyous sea!
O, Summer Day, so wonderful and white
So full of gladness and so full of pain
Forever and forever shalt thou be
To some the gravestone of a dead delight
To some the landmark of a new domain.

Shall be not make these 3,650 days in the Decade of Decision our summer days, assuring that the landmarks of our domain remain? Then could it truly be said of us—if you would seek our monument, look about you.

APPENDIX **16**

NATIONAL HISTORIC PRESERVATION ACT OF 1966

Public Law 89–665
89th Congress, S. 3035
October 15, 1966

80 STAT. 915

AN ACT

To establish a program for the preservation of additional historic properties throughout the Nation, and for other purposes.

Be it enacted by the Senate and House of Representatives of the United States of America in Congress assembled,
The Congress finds and declares—

(a) that the spirit and direction of the Nation are founded upon and reflected in its historic past;

(b) that the historical and cultural foundations of the Nation should be preserved as a living part of our community life and development in order to give a sense of orientation to the American people;

(c) that, in the face of ever-increasing extensions of urban centers, highways, and residential, commercial, and industrial developments, the present governmental and nongovernmental historic preservation programs and activities are inadequate to insure future generations a genuine opportunity to appreciate and enjoy the righ heritage of our Nation; and

(d) that, although the major burdens of historic preservation have been borne and major efforts initiated by private agencies and individuals, and both should continue to play a vital role, it is nevertheless necessary and appropriate for the Federal Government to accelerate its historic preservation programs and activities, to give maximum encouragement to agencies and individuals undertaking preservation by private means, and to assist State and local governments and the National Trust for Historic Preservation in the United States to expand and accelerate their historic preservation programs and activities.

TITLE I

SEC. 101. (a) The Secretary of the Interior is authorized—

(1) to expand and maintain a national register of districts, sites, buildings, structures, and objects significant in American history, architecture, archeology, and culture, hereinafter referred to as the National Register, and to grant funds to States for the purpose of preparing comprehensive statewide historic surveys and plans, in accordance with criteria established by the Secretary, for the preservation, acquisition, and development of such properties;

(2) to establish a program of matching grants-in-aid to States for projects having as their purpose the preservation for public benefit of properties that are significant in American history, architecture, archeology, and culture; and

(3) to establish a program of matching grant-in-aid to the National Trust for Historic Preservation in the United States, chartered by act of Congress approved October 26, 1949 (63 Stat. 927), as amended, for the purpose of carrying out the responsibilities of the National Trust.

(b) As used in this Act—

(1) The term "State" includes, in addition to the several States of the Union, the District of Columbia, the Commonwealth of Puerto Rico, the Virgin Islands, Guam, and American Samoa.

(2) The term "project" means programs of State and local governments and other public bodies and private organizations and individuals for the acquisition of title or interests in, and for the development of, any district, site, building, structure, or object that is significant in American history, architec-

ture, archeology, and culture, or property used in connection therewith, and for its development in order to assure the preservation for public benefit of any such historical properties.

(3) The term "historic preservation" includes the protection, rehabilitation, restoration, and reconstruction of districts, sites, buildings, structures, and objects significant in American history, architecture, archeology, or culture.

(4) The term "Secretary" means the Secretary of the Interior.

SEC. 102. (a) No grant may be made under this Act—

(1) unless application therefor is submitted to the Secretary in accordance with regulations and procedures prescribed by him;

(2) unless the application is in accordance with the comprehensive statewide historic preservation plan which has been approved by the Secretary after considering its relationship to the comprehensive statewide outdoor recreation plan prepared pursuant to the Land and Water Conservation Fund Act of 1965 (78 Stat. 897);

(3) for more than 50 per centum of the total cost involved, as determined by the Secretary and his determination shall be final;

(4) unless the grantee has agreed to make such reports, in such form and containing such information as the Secretary may from time to time require;

(5) unless the grantee has agreed to assume, after completion of the project, the total cost of the continued maintenance, repair, and administration of the property in a manner satisfactory to the Secretary; and

(6) until the grantee has complied with such further terms and conditions as the Secretary may deem necessary or advisable.

(b) The Secretary may in his discretion waive the requirements of subsection (a), paragraphs (2) and (5) of this section for any grant under this Act to the National Trust for Historic Preservation in the United States, in which case a grant to the National Trust may include funds for the maintenance, repair, and administration of the property in a manner satisfactory to the Secretary.

(c) No State shall be permitted to utilize the value of real property obtained before the date of approval of this Act in meeting the remaining cost of a project for which a grant is made under this Act.

SEC. 103. (a) The amounts appropriated and made available for grants to the States for comprehensive statewide historic surveys and plans under this Act shall be apportioned among the States by the Secretary on the basis of needs as determined by him: *Provided, however,* That the amount granted to any one State shall not exceed 50 per centum of the total cost of the comprehensive statewide historic survey and plan for that State, as determined by the Secretary.

(b) The amounts appropriated and made available for grants to the States for projects under this Act for each fiscal year shall be apportioned among the States by the Secretary in accordance with needs as disclosed in approved statewide historic preservation plans.

The Secretary shall notify each State of its apportionment, and the amounts thereof shall be available thereafter for payments to such State for projects in accordance with the provisions of this Act. Any amount of any apportionment that has not been paid or obligated by the Secretary during the fiscal year in which such notification is given, and for two fiscal years thereafter, shall be reapportioned by the Secretary in accordance with this subsection.

SEC. 104. (a) No grant may be made by the Secretary for or on account of any survey or project under this Act with respect to which financial assistance has been given or promised under any other Federal program or activity, and no financial assistance may be given under any other Federal program or activity for or on account of any survey or project with respect to which assistance has been given or promised under this Act.

(b) In order to assure consistency in policies and actions under this Act with other related Federal programs and activities, and to assure coordination of the planning acquisition, and development assistance to States under this Act with other related Federal programs and activities, the President may issue such regulations with respect thereto as he deems desirable, and such assistance may be provided only in accordance with such regulations.

SEC. 105. The beneficiary of assistance under this Act shall keep such records as the Secretary shall prescribe, including records which fully disclose the disposition by the beneficiary of the proceeds of such assistance, the total cost of the project or undertaking in connection with which such assistance is given or used, and the amount and nature of that portion of the cost of the project or undertaking supplied by other sources, and such other records as will facilitate an effective audit.

SEC. 106. The head of any Federal agency having direct or indirect jurisdiction over a proposed Federal or federally assisted undertaking in any State and the head of any Federal department or independent agency having authority to license any undertaking shall, prior to the approval of the expenditure of any Federal funds on the undertaking or prior to the issuance of any license, as the case may be, take into account the effect of the undertaking on any district, site, building, structure, or object that is included in the National Register. The head of any such Federal agency shall afford the Advisory Council on Historic Preservation established under title II of this Act a reasonable opportunity to comment with regard to such undertaking.

SEC. 107. Nothing in this Act shall be construed to be applicable to the White House and its grounds, the Supreme Court building and its grounds, or the United States Capitol and its related buildings and grounds.

SEC. 108. There are authorized to be appropriated not to exceed $2,000,000 to carry out the provisions of this Act for the fiscal year 1967, and not more than $10,000,000 for each of the three succeeding fiscal years. Such appropriations shall be available for the financial assistance authorized by this title and for the administrative expenses of the Secretary in connection therewith, and shall remain available until expended.

TITLE II

SEC. 201. (a) There is established an Advisory Council on Historic Preservation (hereinafter referred to as the "Council") which shall be composed of seventeen members as follows:

(1) The Secretary of the Interior.

(2) The Secretary of Housing and Urban Development.

(3) The Secretary of Commerce.

(4) The Administrator of the General Services Administration.

(5) The Secretary of the Treasury.

(6) The Attorney General.

(7) The Chairman of the National Trust for Historic Preservation.

(8) Ten appointed by the President from outside the Federal Government. In making these appointments, the President shall give due consideration to the selection of officers of State and local governments and individuals who are significantly interested and experienced in the matters to be considered by the Council.

(b) Each member of the Council specified in paragraphs (1) through (6) of subsection (a) may designate another officer of his department or agency to serve on the Council in his stead.

(c) Each member of the Council appointed under paragraph (8) of subsection (a) shall serve for a term of five years from the expiration of his predecessor's term; except that the members first appointed under that paragraph shall serve for terms of from one to five years, as designated by the President at the time of appointment, in such manner as to insure that the terms of not less than one nor more than two of them will expire in any one year.

(d) A vacancy in the Council shall not affect its powers, but shall be filled in the same manner as the original appointment (and for the balance of the unexpired term).

(e) The Chairman of the Council shall be designated by the President.

(f) Eight members of the Council shall constitute a quorum.

SEC. 202. (a) The Council shall—

(1) advise the President and the Congress on matters relating to historic preservation; recommend measures to coordinate activities of Federal, State,

and local agencies and private institutions and individuals relating to historic preservation; and advise on the dissemination of information pertaining to such activities;

(2) encourage, in cooperation with the National Trust for Historic Preservation and appropriate private agencies, public interest and participation in historic preservation;

(3) recommend the conduct of studies in such areas as the adequacy of legislative and administrative statutes and regulations pertaining to historic preservation activities of State and local governments and the effects of tax policies at all levels of government on historic preservation;

(4) advise as to guidelines for the assistance of State and local governments in drafting legislation relating to historic preservation; and

(5) encourage, in cooperation with appropriate public and private agencies and institutions, training and education in the field of historic preservation.

(b) The Council shall submit annually a comprehensive report of its activities and the results of its studies to the President and the Congress and shall from time to time submit such additional and special reports as it deems advisable. Each report shall propose such legislative enactments and other actions as, in the judgment of the Council, are necessary and appropriate to carry out its recommendations.

SEC. 203. The Council is authorized to secure directly from any department, bureau, agency, board, commission, office, independent establishment or instrumentality of the executive branch of the Federal Government information, suggestions, estimates, and statistics for the purpose of this title; and each such department, bureau, agency, board, commission, office, independent establishment or instrumentality is authorized to furnish such information, suggestions, estimates, and statistics to the extent permitted by law and within available funds.

SEC. 204. The members of the Council specified in paragraphs (1) through (7) of section 201 (a) shall serve without additional compensation. The members of the Council appointed under paragraph (8) of section 201 (a) shall receive $100 per diem when engaged in the performance of the duties of the Council. All members of the Council shall receive reimbursement for necessary traveling and subsistence expenses incurred by them in the performance of the duties of the Council.

SEC. 205. (a) The Director of the National Park Service or his designee shall be the Executive Director of the Council. Financial and administrative services (including those related to budgeting, accounting, financial reporting, personnel and procurement) shall be provided the Council by the Department of the Interior, for which payments shall be made in advance, or by reimbursement, from funds of the Council in such amounts as may be agreed upon by the Chairman of the Council and the Secretary of the Interior: *Provided*, That the regulations of the Department of the Interior for the collection of indebtedness of personnel resulting from erroneous payments (5 U.S.C. 46e) shall apply to the collection of erroneous payments made to or on behalf of a Council employee, and regulations of said Secretary for the administrative control of funds (31 U.S.C. 665 (g)) shall apply to appropriations of the Council: *And provided further*, That the Council shall not be required to prescribe such regulations.

(b) The Council shall have power to appoint and fix the compensation of such additional personnel as may be necessary to carry out its duties, without regard to the provisions of the civil service laws and the Classification Act of 1949.

(c) The Council may also procure, without regard to the civil service laws and the Classification Act of 1949, temporary and intermittent services to the same extent as is authorized for the executive departments by section 15 of the Administrative Expenses Act of 1946 (5 U.S.C. 55a), but at rates not to exceed $50 per diem for individuals.

(d) The members of the Council specified in paragraphs (1) through (6) of section 201(a) shall provide the Council, on a reimbursable basis, with such facilities and services under their jurisdiction and control as may be needed by the Council to carry out its duties, to the extent that such facilities and services are requested by the Council and are otherwise available for that purpose. To the extent of available appropriations, the Council may obtain, by purchase, rental, donation, or otherwise, such additional property, facilities, and services as may be needed to carry out its duties.

Approved October 15, 1966.

(An amendment to the act on November 3, 1966, enacted as part of the Demonstration Cities and Metropolitan Development Act of 1966 [Public Law 91-243] authorized the Secretary of the U.S. Department of Housing and Urban Development to make grants to the Trust for renovation and restoration costs of Trust-owned historic properties, not exceeding $90,000 for any one structure.

An amendment to the act on May 9, 1970 [Public Law 91-243], authorized United States participation in the International Centre for the Study of the Preservation and Restoration of Cultural Property and increased Advisory Council on Historic Preservation membership from 17 to 20, adding the secretaries of the U.S. Departments of Agriculture and Transportation and the Secretary of the Smithsonian Institution. The council's existence was authorized until 1985, and the additional council members and the chairman of the National Trust were granted the right to appoint officers of their organizations to serve on the council as their designees.)

LEGISLATIVE HISTORY:
HOUSE REPORT No. 1916 (Comm. on Interior & Insular Affairs).
SENATE REPORT No. 1363 (Comm. on Interior & Insular Affairs).
CONGRESSIONAL RECORD, Vol. 112 (1966):
July   11: Considered and passed Senate.
Sept.   19: Considered in House.
Oct.   10: Considered and passed House, amended.
Oct.   11: Senate concurred in House amendment.

GPO 65-139

U.S. DEPARTMENT OF THE INTERIOR
APPORTIONMENTS TO THE NATIONAL TRUST
AND THE STATES, 1968–73*

	1968	1969	1970	Year 1971	1972	1973
National Trust	$300,000.00	$17,500.00	$300,000.00	$1,042,023.00	$1,042,023.00	$1,313,375.00
Alabama		3,784.87	19,434.21	74,749.48	193,567.00	348,978.00
Alaska		6,308.13	9,156.96	49,162.75	85,488.00	49,348.00
Arizona			8,997.21	44,115.86	29,900.00	53,167.00
Arkansas			17,083.85	284,976.72	171,127.00	69,701.00
California			40,567.00	129,190.00	70,535.00	167,197.00
Colorado				34,441.75	29,900.00	73,270.00
Connecticut		1,292.37	12,551.65	52,113.90	29,900.00	47,747.00
Delaware				29,900.00	69,136.00	141,018.00
Florida				174,837.34	135,004.00	182,250.00
Georgia			28,486.71	32,104.90	29,900.00	56,142.00
Hawaii				85,000.00	29,900.00	40,936.00
Idaho				29,900.00	30,676.00	49,932.00
Illinois			26,098.44	227,900.00	76,600.00	84,425.00
Indiana				29,900.00	29,900.00	6,175.00
Iowa				29,900.00	29,900.00	125,372.00

	1968	1969	1970	Year 1971	1972	1973
Kansas		7,044.59	13,842.96	119,028.84	29,900.00	50,182.00
Kentucky				49,000.00	134,992.00	115,482.00
Louisiana				29,900.00	29,900.00	81,672.00
Maine		788.51	4,524.21	32,610.24	50,219.00	46,067.00
Maryland		4,573.39	23,889.10	101,474.00	110,124.00	142,857.00
Massachusetts		2,838.65	19,434.21	69,622.66	115,173.00	97,102.00
Michigan		4,573.39	41,799.21	251,458.90	191,005.00	102,472.00
Minnesota		1,892.43	8,251.71	116,961.39	266,409.00	134,567.00
Mississippi		1,248.37	14,535.21	107,226.52	89,574.00	76,990.00
Missouri		11,745.09	25,298.63	114,876.54	91,617.00	95,780.00
Montana			2,500.00	29,900.00	31,376.72	50,692.00
Nebraska		3,101.23	8,251.71	55,237.66	33,941.00	79,332.00
Nevada				33,463.16	29,900.00	88,582.00
New Hampshire				58,501.53	29,900.00	66,537.00
New Jersey			48,455.46	78,000.00	80,061.00	69,697.00
New Mexico			13,496.83	82,065.20	72,115.08	88,807.00
New York		1,135.46	30,483.59	299,399.90	279,159.00	290,597.00
North Carolina		4,180.70	28,633.15	206,607.72	209,652.00	236,876.00
North Dakota						
Ohio			2,500.00	54,438.78	80,370.00	71,382.00
Oklahoma		1,002.99	7,186.71	30,223.16	33,697.00	82,082.00
Oregon			10,381.71	43,118.00	29,900.00	60,632.00
Pennsylvania			28,486.71	176,541.00	137,312.00	133,962.00
Rhode Island				104,168.88	83,030.00	130,912.00
South Carolina			37,377.86	299,000.00	299,000.00	375,250.00
South Dakota				29,900.00	29,900.00	49,007.00
Tennessee		946.22	8,517.96	42,802.10	75,247.00	106,542.00

			Year			
	1968	1969	1970	1971	1972	1973
Texas		2,407.60		131,462.31	86,286.00	133,102.00
Utah		1,892.43	13,603.34	79,125.03	56,800.00	73,532.00
Vermont		1,090.51	4,998.14	33,765.40	97,535.00	68,582.00
Virginia		6,164.61	49,272.31	144,119.58	86,757.00	194,612.00
Washington		1,261.62	11,979.21	149,141.90	45,550.00	133,907.00
West Virginia		5,992.71	12,245.46	187,055.00	39,372.00	97,702.00
Wisconsin		1,892.43	9,849.21	89,724.40	39,480.00	100,807.00
Wyoming		2,660.76	19,366.18	112,341.09	106,518.00	63,007.00
American Samoa						47,140.00
District of Columbia				45,601.75	83,636.00	122,562.00
Guam						
Puerto Rico		1,892.43	8,251.70			
Trust Territory						
Virgin Islands						

*See *The Historic Preservation Grants-in-Aid Catalogue,* U.S. Department of the Interior, January 1974, for information on how funds were used. The catalogue is updated periodically.

STATE HISTORIC PRESERVATION OFFICERS, 1967–73*
(formerly State Liaison Officers)

Alabama
Milo B. Howard, Jr.

Alaska
Theodore G. Smith

Arizona
Dennis McCarthy

Arkansas
Winston C. Byrd
John Peterson
George M. Reynolds
William E. Henderson

California
William P. Mott, Jr.

Colorado
Stephen H. Hart

Connecticut
Eric Hatch
William J. Morris
Harlan H. Griswold

Delaware
Leon deValinger, Jr.
Rea Wilkie
E. Berkeley Tompkins
Grover A. Biddle

Florida
W. Robert Williams

Georgia
Mary G. Jewett

Hawaii
Sunao Kido

Idaho
Merle W. Wells

Illinois
Daniel L. Malkovich
Henry N. Barkhausen
Anthony Dean

Indiana
John R. Lloyd
S. Donald Durfee
Joseph D. Cloud

Iowa
William J. Peterson
Adrian D. Anderson

Kansas
Nyle H. Miller

Kentucky
Frank J. Groschelle
Joseph M. Gray
Laurel W. True
Mrs. Simeon E. Willis

Louisiana
Lamar Gibson
A. Otis Hébert, Jr.
George M. Leake
Jay R. Broussard

Maine
Lawrence M. Stuart
James H. Mundy

Maryland
Orlando Ridout, IV

Massachusetts
John F. X. Davoren

Michigan
Ralph A. MacMullan
Samuel A. Milstein

Minnesota
Russell W. Fridley

Mississippi
Charlotte Capers
R. A. McLemore
Elbert R. Hilliard

Missouri
Joseph Jaeger, Jr.
James L. Wilson

Montana
Wesley R. Woodgerd
Ashley C. Roberts

Nebraska
Marvin F. Kivett

Nevada
Eric R. Cronkhite

New Hampshire
Russell B. Tobey
Roger J. Crowley, Jr.
George Gilman

*State historic preservation officers as of December 1973 are capitalized and are the last or only entry.

New Jersey
Robert A. Roe
Joseph T. Barber
RICHARD J. SULLIVAN

New Mexico
Arthur L. Ortiz
Elie S. Gutierrez
Keith Dotson
DAVID W. KING

New York
Conrad L. Wirth
Louis C. Jones
ALEXANDER ALDRICH

North Carolina
Christopher Crittenden
H. G. JONES

North Dakota
Ray H. Mattison
JAMES E. SPERRY

Ohio
DANIEL R. PORTER

Oklahoma
GEORGE H. SHIRK

Oregon
Forrest Cooper
Roderick L. Porter
GEORGE M. BALDWIN

Pennsylvania
S. K. Stevens
WILLIAM J. WEWER

Rhode Island
Adolph B. Schmidt
FREDERICK C. WILLIAMSON

South Carolina
CHARLES E. LEE

South Dakota
Oris J. Scherschligt
JAMES E. GILLIHAN

Tennessee
Stephen S. Lawrence
Michael J. Smith
HERBERT L. HARPER

Texas
TRUETT LATIMER

Utah
MILTON L. WEILENMANN

Vermont
WILLIAM B. PINNEY

Virginia
Edward P. Alexander
James W. Moody, Jr.
JUNIUS R. FISHBURNE, JR.

Washington
CHARLES H. ODEGAARD

West Virginia
Dallas B. Shaffer
Carolyn Zinn
MAURICE BROOKS

Wisconsin
Leslie H. Fishel, Jr.
Richard A. Erney
JAMES M. SMITH

Wyoming
Charles R. Rodermel
PAUL H. WESTEDT

American Samoa
John M. Haydon
DONALD F. GRAF

District of Columbia
Thomas W. Fletcher
Graham W. Watt
JAMES G. BANKS

Guam
Paul B. Souder
Frank B. Blas
JOSE D. DIEGO

*Commonwealth of
Puerto Rico*
Ricardo E. Alegría
LUIS M. RODRIGUEZ-
MORALES

*Trust Territory of
the Pacific Islands*
GEORGE V. STATES

Virgin Islands
THOMAS BLAKE

NATIONAL TRUST BOARD OF ADVISORS, 1967–73

Alabama

C. Wilder Watts 1967–69
Albert M. Rains 1967–72
James L. Loeb 1970–
Nancy N. Holmes 1973–

Alaska

Robert B. Atwood 1967–69
Robert A. Frederick 1970–
Norma J. Hoyt 1970–

Arizona

Mrs. Jack D.H. Hayes 1967–71
Robert C. Giebner 1970–72
Mrs. Duane D. Miller 1971–
James E. Ayres 1973–

Arkansas

George M. Reynolds 1967–72
Mrs. George Rose Smith 1967–72
Edwin B. Cromwell 1973–
Melanie H. Speer 1973–

California

Mrs. John A. McCone 1967–69
Thomas H. Kuchel 1969–72
Elizabeth Hay Bechtel 1969–
William Roth, Jr. 1972–

Colorado

James Hopkins Smith 1967–69
Robert L. Stearns 1967–72
Stephen H. Hart 1969–72
Mrs. Stephen H. Hart 1972–

Connecticut

Eric Hatch 1967–71
David Shiverick Smith 1967–72
  (chairman, 1967–69)
Mrs. David B. Findlay, Jr. 1973–

Delaware

Mrs. Thomas Herlihy, Jr. 1967–69
Mrs. Charles L. Terry 1967–69
Mrs. C. Lee Reese, Jr. 1971–73
Robert L. Raley 1971–

Florida

Mrs. Jack T. Dobson 1969–
Thomas S. Kenan, III 1970–73

Georgia

Mills B. Lane, Jr. 1967–68
Mrs. J.L. Roberts 1967–68
  (now Mrs. M. R. Cross)
Leopold Adler, II 1969–72
Henry D. Green 1969–
Paul Muldawer 1972–

Hawaii

William F. Quinn 1967–72
Mrs. H. Alexander Walker 1967–72
Charles M. Black 1973–
Mrs. Allyn Cole, Jr. 1973–

Idaho

Mrs. Steele Barnett 1967
H.F. Magnuson 1967–69
Mrs. Louis F. Lesser 1969–
Julie J. Hyslop 1972–

Illinois

Mrs. C. Phillip Miller 1967–70
Mrs. Charles Deere Wiman 1967–70
Edmund B. Thornton 1971–
Michael D. Newsom 1972–

Indiana

Samuel R. Sutphin 1967–69
Thomas S. Emison 1967–72
H. Roll McLaughlin 1969–72
John T. Windle 1973–

Iowa

Mrs. C. Maxwell Stanley 1967–72
William J. Wagner 1969–

Kansas

M. Phyllis Steinkirchner 1972–
Paul E. Wilson 1972–

Kentucky

Mrs. Floyd Wright 1967–69
Mrs. Irvin Abell, Jr. 1967–72
    (chairman, 1969–71)
Thompson Willett 1970–
Richard S. DeCamp 1972–

Louisiana

Mrs. Robert G. Robinson 1967–69
Mrs. John P. Manard 1969–
Walter C. Peters 1970–

Maine

L. Kinvin Wroth 1968–71
Dorris A. Isaacson 1968–
Donald Shepard 1971–72
Susan T. Sewall 1973–

Maryland

Charles E. Scarlett, Jr. 1967–69
St. Clair Wright 1967–72
J. Hurst Purnell, Jr. 1971–
Mrs. Coleman duPont 1973–

Massachusetts

William B. Osgood 1967–69
William Harvey Pierson, Jr. 1967–72

Charles R. Strickland 1971–
Barnes Riznik 1973–

Michigan

Jordan Sheperd 1969–71
Richard C. Frank 1969–72
Weldon D. Frankforter 1972–
Donald M.D. Thurber 1972–

Minnesota

Mrs. Fredrick K. Weyerhaeuser
    1970–73
Richard B. Dunsworth 1972–

Mississippi

Mrs. William Pratt Thomas 1967–72
Mrs. Robert E. Ivy 1970–

Missouri

Chapin S. Newhard 1967–69
Raymond R. Tucker 1967–69
Philip C. Brooks 1970–71
James H. Williams 1970–

Montana

Mrs. Ivan Small, Sr. 1971–
David E. Nelson 1972–

Nebraska

Fred A. Seaton 1967–69
Mrs. William T. Utley 1970–

Nevada

Thomas A. Cooke 1969–
Howard Hickson 1972–

New Hampshire

Mrs. Perkins Bass 1967–69
Robb H. Sagendorph 1967–70
G. Peter Guenther 1972–
Robbins Milbank 1972–

New Jersey

Mrs. Frederick Frelinghuysen 1967–72
W. Howard Adams 1968–69
Raymond Dey 1970–73
Constance M. Greiff 1973–

Washington

Richard D. Daugherty 1969–72
Robert D. Ashley 1972–
Susan H.L. Barrow 1972–

West Virginia

Bradley Nash 1967–72
Clifford M. Lewis 1969–73

Wisconsin

Robert B. Murphy 1967–72
Richard W.E. Perrin 1970–73
Eleanor C. Bell 1973–

Wyoming

Thomas B. Muths 1973–

American Samoa

Mrs. John M. Haydon 1972–

District of Columbia

Mrs. Robert Low Bacon 1967–69
Francis D. Lethbridge 1967–72
Constance M. Green 1971
Channing Phillips 1972–

Guam

Paul J. Bordallo 1972–

Puerto Rico

Francisco Javier Blanco 1972–

Virgin Islands

Frederik C. Gjessing 1970–
Edward I. Williams, Jr. 1973–

RECIPIENTS OF NATIONAL TRUST MATCHING CONSULTANT SERVICE GRANTS, 1969–73

Alabama

Marengo County Historical Society, Inc., Demopolis, July 1969, $1,000
Mobile Historic Development Commission, July 1971, $500
Tuscaloosa County Preservation Society, Tuscaloosa, July 1970, $700

Alaska

Kodiak Historical Society, Kodiak, January 1972, $1,000

Arizona

Arizona Historical Society, Tucson, January 1973, $350

California

County of Riverside, Riverside, July 1970, $650
Foundation for San Francisco's Architectural Heritage, July 1973, $500
Tuolumne County Historical Society, Sonora, January 1973, $500

Connecticut

Southeastern Connecticut Arts Council, New London, July 1971, $600
Society of the Founders of Norwich, July 1971, $800
Noah Webster House Foundation, West Hartford, January 1971, $500

District of Columbia

Howard University, January 1973, $800
Jewish Historical Society of Greater Washington, January 1971, $300
Joint Committee on Landmarks, July 1970, $1,000
Ledroit Park Historical District, July 1973, $700
National Firefighting Museum, January 1973, $800

Florida

National Society of Colonial Dames of America in the State of Florida, Jacksonville,
    July 1971, $500
Monticello Musical Theater, Tallahassee, July 1973, $500

Georgia

Old Capital Historical Society, Milledgeville, January 1970, $1,200
Historic Savannah Foundation, Inc., January 1970 and August 1973, $800 and $1,300
Save-the-Bay Committee, Inc., Savannah, July 1971, $900

Hawaii

Kalahikiola Congregational Church, Kapaau, July 1973, $400
Lahaina Restoration Foundation, Lahaina, Maui, July 1973, $600

Idaho

Idaho State Historical Society, Boise, November 1973, $1,000
Owyhee County Historical Society, Murphy, January 1972, $800

Illinois

St. Clair County Historical Society, Belleville, July 1972, $300
Chicago School of Architecture Foundation, January 1970, $1,100
Commission on Chicago Historical and Architectural Landmarks, July 1971, $500
Intercontinental Steel Corporation, Chicago, July 1973, $700
Open Lands Project, Chicago, July 1973, $500
Frederick Law Olmsted Society of Riverside, January 1970, $500

Indiana

Junior League of Evansville, July 1970 and January 1973, $200 and $300
Howard Steamboat Museum, Jeffersonville, July 1972, $400

Iowa

Dubuque County Historical Society, Dubuque, January 1971, $500
North Lee County Historical Society, Fort Madison, January 1973, $400
Midwest Old Settlers and Threshers Association, Inc., Mount Pleasant, January 1972, $500

Kansas

Harvey County Arts Council, Inc., Newton, July 1971, $900

Kentucky

Neighborhood Development Corporation, Louisville, January 1971, $800
Stone Conservation Center, Louisville, January 1973, $1,000

Louisiana

Kent Plantation House, Alexandria, July 1973, $500
Shreveport Beautification Foundation, Shreveport, July 1973, $700

Maine

Maine State Museum, Augusta, January 1973, $800
Sagadahoc Preservation, Inc., Bath, July 1973, $700
Greater Portland Landmarks, Inc., January 1970, $400

Maryland

Historic Annapolis, Inc., January 1971, $400
Historic District Commission, Annapolis, January 1972, $400
Maryland Commission on Negro History and Culture, Annapolis, July 1973, $800
Historic Fells Point and Federal Hill Fund, Inc., Baltimore, July 1972, $500
Allegheny Beverage Corporation, Baltimore, July 1973, $1,000
Preservation Society of Allegany County, Inc., Cumberland, January 1971, $500
Union Mills Homestead Foundation, Inc., Westminster, October 1970, $400

Massachusetts

Beverly Historical Development Foundation, Inc., Beverly, July 1971, $600
National Conference on Architectural Review, Landmarks and Historic Districts, Boston, February 1970, $1,000

Society for the Preservation of New England Antiquities, Boston, January 1972 and July 1973, $1,000 and $1,000
Gloucester Community Development Corporation, Gloucester, July 1973, $1,000
Lexington Historical Society, Lexington, October 1970, $500
Hoosuck Community Resources Corporation, North Adams, January 1973, $1,000
French Cable Museum in Orleans, Inc., Orleans, July 1972, $300
The Springfield Armory Museum, Inc., Springfield, January 1970, $800
Worcester Heritage Society, Worcester, January 1973, $700

Michigan

Old West Side Association, Inc., Ann Arbor, July 1969 and October 1970, $1,000 and $600
Berrien County Historical Commission, Inc., Berrien Springs, January 1971, $500
Save Orchestra Hall, Inc., Detroit, January 1973, $600
Woodward East Project, Detroit, October 1973, $1,000
Heritage Hill Foundation, Grand Rapids, January 1970, $1,500
Marshall Historical Society, Marshall, January 1971, $800

Mississippi

Friends of Jefferson College, Inc., Washington, January 1972, $500

Missouri

Cole County Historical Society, Jefferson City, October 1970, $500
Landmarks Commission of Kansas City, July 1972, $300
St. Joseph Historical Society, Inc., St. Joseph, January 1972, $400
Arts and Fountains Fund Committee, St. Louis, July 1971 and January 1973, $500 and $500
Landmarks Association of St. Louis, Inc., January 1971, $1,500

Nebraska

Lincoln-Lancaster Historical Society, Lincoln, July 1971, $800

New Hampshire

Canaan Street Historic Commission, Canaan, January 1972, $500
New Hampshire Farm Museum, Exeter, July 1972, $500
Save the Mills Society, Laconia, July 1970, $500
Planning Department and Chamber of Commerce, Portsmouth, July 1973, $1,000

New Jersey

Princeton Battlefield Area Conservation Society, Princeton, July 1973, $500

New Mexico

White Oaks Historical Association, Carrizozo, July 1971 and January 1973, $1,000 and $500

New York

Valley Development Foundation, Inc., Binghamton, January 1971, $600
Society for the Preservation of Weeksville and Bedford-Stuyvesant History, Brooklyn, July 1970, $600
Town of Ellicottville, January 1970, $1,000
Historic Ithaca and Thompson Counties, Ithaca, July 1973, $700

Saint Catherine Greek Orthodox Church, Ithaca, July 1972, $400
Queens Institute of Anthropology, Jackson Heights, January 1971, $500
Historic Landmarks Preservation Commission of Kingston, July 1970, $400
Little Falls Historical Society, Little Falls, October 1970, $300
Greater Newburgh Arts Council, Newburgh, January 1970, $1,000
Town of Oyster Bay American Revolution Bicentennial Committee, January 1973, $350
Hudson Valley Philharmonic Society, Inc., Poughkeepsie, January 1972, $300
Landmark Society of Western New York, Inc., Rochester, January 1970 and January 1972, $900 and $700
Hudson-Mohawk Industrial Gateway, Troy, January 1972, $700

North Carolina

Chapel Hill Preservation Society, Chapel Hill, January 1973, $400
North Carolina Society for the Preservation of Antiquities, Inc., Raleigh, January 1973, $600
Shaw University, Raleigh, July 1972, $400

Ohio

Chillicothe Restoration Foundation, Chillicothe, January 1970, $800
Ohio Historical Society, Columbus, January 1970, $500
Montgomery County Historical Society, Dayton, January 1970, $900
Community Design Committee of Medina, January 1973, $700
Miami University, Oxford, July 1971, $500
Landmarks Committee, Maumee Valley Historical Society, Toledo, January 1970, $600

Oklahoma

Lincoln-Terrace Historical Preservation Area, Oklahoma City, July 1973, $300

Oregon

City of John Day, January 1972, $800

Pennsylvania

Tri-County Conservancy of the Brandywine, Inc., Chadds Ford, July 1971, $700
Yellow Springs Association, Chester Springs, January 1971, $500
Lancaster Mennonite Conference Historical Society, Lancaster, January 1970, $600
The Episcopal Academy, Merion, July 1973, $750
The Athenaeum of Philadelphia, July 1971, $800
The Free Library of Philadelphia, July 1972, $400
Philadelphia Architects Charitable Trust, July 1973, $800
Preservation Committee, Society of Architectural Historians and Save the Upper School Committee, Philadelphia, December 1973, $5,500
French and Pickering Creeks Conservation Trust, Pottstown, July 1973, $500

Rhode Island

Rhode Island Bicentennial Commission, Providence, January 1971, $400

South Carolina

Historic Beaufort Foundation, Beaufort, January 1970, $800

Greenville County Historic Preservation Commission, Greenville, January 1972, $500
Newberry County Community Hall Commission, Newberry, January 1971, $300

South Dakota

South Dakota Historic Preservation Program, Deadwood, July 1973, $1,000

Tennessee

Heritage Foundation of Franklin and Williamson County, Franklin, July 1969, $1,500
Association for the Preservation of Tennessee Antiquities, Memphis Chapter, January 1972, $500
Citizens to Preserve Overton Park, Memphis, July 1970, January 1971 and January 1972, $500, $500 and $1,000

Texas

State Historic Preservation League, Dallas, January 1973, $500
Galveston Historic Foundation, Inc., Galveston, January 1970, $800

Utah

Utah Heritage Foundation, Salt Lake City, January 1973, $500

Vermont

Barre Historical Society, Barre, July 1973, $700
Jericho Historical Society, Jericho, July 1972, $400
McCullough-Park Foundation, Inc., North Bennington, January 1971, $600
Orleans County Historical Society, Inc., Orleans, July 1969 and July 1972, $300 and $400
American Precision Museum, Windsor, October 1970, $500

Virginia

St. James Episcopal Church, Accomac, July 1969, $300
Historic Green Springs, Inc., Gordonsville, January 1972 and July 1973, $500 and $1,200
Historic Lexington Foundation, Inc., Lexington, October 1970, $500
Historic Lynchburg Foundation, Lynchburg, January 1971, $500
Museum of the Confederacy, Richmond, July 1973, $300
Waterford Foundation, Inc., Waterford, January 1973, $800

Washington

Whitman County Historical Society, Pullman, July 1973, $600
City of Seattle, January 1973, $2,000

West Virginia

Municipal Planning Commission of Sistersville, July 1970 and July 1971, $600 and $200
West Virginia Independence Hall Foundation, Inc., Wheeling, January 1970, $1,000

Wisconsin

Rock County Historical Society, Janesville, January 1971, $550
Land Ethics, Inc., Milwaukee, January 1970 and July 1971, $1,000 and $400

NATIONAL HISTORIC PRESERVATION FUND
LOAN AND GRANT RECIPIENTS, 1971–73

Grants

HISTORIC LANDMARK SOCIETY, New York, N.Y., January 1972, $20,000
GREATER PORTLAND LANDMARKS, INC., Portland, Maine, December 1972, $1,350
UTAH HERITAGE FOUNDATION, Salt Lake City, Utah, December 1972, $2,210

*Loans**

HISTORIC HARRISVILLE, Harrisville, N.H., April 1971, $10,000
HISTORIC ANNAPOLIS, INC., Annapolis, Md., June 1972, $15,000
WESTERN MONTANA GHOST TOWN PRESERVATION SOCIETY, Missoula, Mont., June 1972, $2,500
HERITAGE HILL FOUNDATION, Grand Rapids, Mich., December 1972, $25,000
HISTORIC FREDERICKSBURG FOUNDATION, INC., Fredericksburg, Va., December 1972, $25,000
PITTSBURGH HISTORY & LANDMARKS FOUNDATION, Pittsburgh, Pa., December 1972, $85,000
HISTORIC AUGUSTA, INC., Augusta, Ga., April 1973, $25,000
LAFAYETTE SQUARE RESTORATION COMMITTEE, INC., St. Louis, Mo., June 1973, $25,000

*In December 1973, two additional loans were approved: Yellow Springs Foundation, Inc., Chester Springs, Pa., $50,000; and Historic Delaware County, Inc., Swarthmore, Pa., $5,000. However, official notification of this action was not made until January 1974.

APPENDIX **22**

1972 SPECIAL STUDY COMMITTEE MEMBERS AND STAFF

MEMBERS

Leopold Adler, II
Mrs. A. Lewis Bentley
Robertson E. Collins
Mrs. George E. Downing
Richard C. Frank
John Hope Franklin
Mrs. Robert Homans
Carlisle H. Humelsine
Richard H. Jenrette
Peter Manigault
Joan Maynard
H. Roll McLaughlin
Charles E. Peterson
William Harvey Pierson, Jr.
S. K. Stevens
Robert E. Stipe
Charles van Ravenswaay
Carl B. Westmoreland
Robert Williams
St. Clair Wright

STAFF

Thomas W. Richards, director
Samuel N. Stokes
Jane A. Hale
Ann Satterthwaite
Robert Rice

APPENDIX **23**

EXCERPT FROM *GOALS AND PROGRAMS,*
A Summary of the Study Committee
Report to the Board of Trustees,
The National Trust for Historic Preservation, 1973

Today, the National Trust has more than 40,000 members, 12 properties, a $3.5 million annual budget and a headquarters staff of 70 persons. This staff is organized into the Office of the President and the Departments of Education, Field Services, Historic Properties, Plans and Development, Public Affairs and Publications. This is far from the organization that started 25 years ago in two rented rooms with a professional staff of one and $6,000 in assets.

New Concerns

If the National Trust changed greatly in the quarter century after World War II, so did the United States. The nation changed physically, as suburbs made possible by increased use of the automobile sprawled over millions of acres of what once were woods and farms, as city centers crumbled and as freeways cut indiscriminately through urban neighborhoods and countryside. For many, this period marked an improvement in the quality of housing and physical comforts. But such uncontrolled growth has also meant the loss of other qualities and has raised many questions. As the recent report on land use sponsored by the Rockefeller Brothers Fund states:

There is a new mood in America. Increasingly, citizens are asking what growth will add to the quality of their lives. . . . The new attitude toward growth . . . appears to be part of a rising emphasis on humanism, on the preservation of natural and cultural characteristics that make for a humanly satisfying living environment.

The lowered quality of life is responsible for this new concern far more than is the great quantitative loss of structures and land of historical, cultural or aesthetic importance. It is not merely suburban sprawl, urban renewal, highways, poor housing design or lack of planning that cause dismay. The concern arises from the ways the country has dealt with change, growth and development and how it has missed the mark in providing, along with growth, a stimulating and healthy environment. Even, or perhaps particularly, the programs planned to achieve an improved quality of life seem to have failed that goal.

The new concern in America is for the enhancement of the total environment and its amenities. "Amenity," as defined by Sir William Holford, the

English architect and planner, "is not a single quality; it is a whole catalog of values. It includes the beauty that an artist sees and an architect designs for; it is the pleasant and familiar scene that history has evolved; in certain circumstances, it is even utility—the right thing in the right place—shelter, warmth, light, clean air . . . and comfort stations." Today, many Americans are interested in preserving areas and architecture that add to the quality of life by improving the visual order. If historic preservationists are to attract a broad commitment from the American public, they must emphasize the amenity value of preservation.

The new concern presents an unusual opportunity not only to historic preservationists but to environmentalists and all those concerned with the development process and with land use. Preservationists need no longer talk only to themselves. They have a broad range of new allies, tools and programs dedicated to improvement of the environment or the quality of American life.

Preservation of the Historic and Cultural Environment

We recommend that the National Trust regard historic preservation as the protection and use of the historic and cultural heritage, conducted in the context of the broad environmental and land use movement aimed at the overall improvement of the quality of life. The National Trust's central focus should continue to be the preservation of sites, buildings, structures, objects and districts, referred to in this report as *historic properties* or *properties*. *Significant places* will be used in a more limited sense, to indicate those historic properties that are of national importance. While continuing its concern with our nation's architecture and the skills necessary to preserve and interpret it, the Trust must also focus on the broader concerns of the historic and cultural environment.

The historic environment comprises areas where significant events have taken place; the cultural environment, areas where distinctive activities and patterns of life have occurred or remain. The two are clearly interrelated. In both, man and nature have interacted and changed one another. Many historic areas have cultural significance and likewise many cultural areas historical significance. An example is the Concord-Lexington area of Massachusetts where "the shot heard round the world" was fired and where, at the same time, a distinctive cultural life was emerging. Another example is the Amish country of Pennsylvania, where the way of life and the land have interacted and have helped to mold one another, but where there have been few nationally significant historic events or individuals.

Historic preservation is a qualitative factor for instilling a feeling of place and time in a rootless, mobile and standardized society. It involves the natural environment as well as the man-made, because they are closely interwoven. The National Environmental Policy Act of 1969 stated the need to "preserve important historic, cultural, and natural aspects of our national heritage, and maintain, wherever possible, an environment which supports diversity and variety of individual choice." The personal and social disorientation produced by unnecessary destruction of the cultural and material heritage has merged with the more commonly identified symptoms of the environmental crisis, noise, smoke, traffic and so forth.

The diversity of America's peoples and activities is a key factor in the dynamics of historic preservation. This diversity has always been one of the most distinctive characteristics of the United States. For example, the mansion on the hill was an important part of American life, but so were the workers' houses, transportation system, factory, churches and all else that made up the town. The plantation house is understandable only with the slave quarters, the dependencies and the fields. Cultures of ethnic groups have given not only life and color but a rich history to the country.

A concern for the quality of life is common to all people. The hearts of the cities as well as the remote hamlets of the country are part of the historic and cultural environment requiring careful attention of historic preservationists.

Protection of the historic and cultural environment will involve six factors:

Public Decision Making

Historic preservation has changed vastly from the time when its isolated, private organizations were struggling to be heard. Today, several federal programs are concerned specifically with preservation and each state has a state preservation officer. The use of easements, historic districts, local landmarks designation and zoning have increased greatly in the last 25 years as a result of public actions.

As interest in the environment and in urban and rural preservation increases so will the role the public decision makers play in their protection. Decisions on freeway alignments or sewer systems can be critical for historic preservationists. Vital decisions do not only concern land developers. For example, choices involving federal tax depreciation on new construction could be critical to the advocates of the historic and cultural environment.

Often, less obvious public decisions have the most profound impact—for example, the public utility commission's finding or the tax assessment technique. Until now, the economic, social and political systems have not been oriented toward enhancement of the historic and cultural environment, but with new interests and pressures, historic preservationists have an opportunity to redirect the system so that it reflects the new concern for protection of the quality of life.

Total Fabric of an Area

As historic preservation comes to encompass a broad environmental concern, it is clear that preservation activities must consider inter-relationships between people and architecture, buildings and activities, space and buildings, decisions and budgets, public and private investments, culture and commerce. History and culture, integrally intertwined, are not elements that can be isolated and individually preserved. Thus, consideration of preservation must be woven into physical, economic and social plans and programs. For example, efforts to maintain varied income levels and to avoid massive relocations in historic districts are high-priority community concerns involving all such plans. In short, the preservation movement must strive for the recognition of preservation as an integral part of local, state and federal planning.

In dealing with the broad fabric of a community, efforts to protect the historic and cultural environment must have a different nature than in the past. No longer can they be solely desperate battles, but must take the form of continuous, on-the-scene negotiations. The crisis orientation of the past, the race to beat the wrecking ball, should give way to a positive approach to the decisions that shape the environment. Decisions on building permits, zonings, road alignments, sewer trunks are often decisions that quietly and incrementally pave the way for major changes. Environmental impact statements now include historical and cultural considerations concerning federally funded projects. Historic preservationists should insist that the impact of local decisions also undergo similar evaluation.

GEOGRAPHIC DIVERSITY

The historic and cultural environment is "man-made America." Historic preservation efforts must be undertaken in all parts of the country. Preservation is the domain of no individual locale and must represent all peoples in all geographic areas.

TIME SPAN

History is an ongoing process. A broad spectrum of time as well as of people and place is essential if the vitality of the historic and cultural environment is to be preserved. For example, the significant places of the civil rights movement and the space age should be of particular interest to future generations.

VARIETY OF BUILDING TYPES

In the past, historic preservation efforts have focused primarily on major buildings and properties whose owners or uses may have influenced the course of the nation. Preservation tended to overlook the industrial and commercial activities and less dramatic buildings which may also be significant because of design or construction or because they represent a way of life once common.

PRESERVATION CONSTITUENCY

The broadening understanding of historic preservation to include concern for the quality of the environment is, in turn, broadening the ranks of those interested in preservation. The new constituents not only increase the number of preservation advocates but they alter the character of the movement and add to its strength. Urban residents are cooperating to preserve the vitality and viability of inner-city neighborhoods. Rural inhabitants, distraught over threatened changes in their lives, are being drawn to the preservation field. The preservation movement is attracting these groups and individuals as allies. It must adapt programs to their interests and tastes. They can form a new, broad network of advocates who, when joined by the existing core of experienced preservationists, will make up a coalition of diverse groups working toward a common goal.

Toward a New National Trust Program

We recommend that the National Trust assert its leadership in the field of historic preservation, operating with broadened strategies and more clearly defined operational programs than it has in the past. We suggest the following strategy guidelines:

The National Trust's role should remain that of leader and catalyst—encouraging, guiding, assisting, setting standards and stimulating state and local organizations and individuals to undertake the basic work of historic preservation. It is on the local level that preservation battles are won and lost and it is there that the Trust should direct its attention. Those closest to a situation usually can understand and control it far better than can a distant national organization.

To efficiently assist local organizations, the National Trust needs to determine strategies and priorities to guide its operation. All aspects of the Trust programs have suffered from lack of policy strategy. Through all its programs, the Trust must try to work within a total institutional policy framework, reorganizing priorities to reflect changing demands and needs. An organization's activities should not be guided primarily by unsolicited requests or bequests.

The National Trust must be realistic about what it can and cannot accomplish. It must recognize its capabilities and limitations. A realistic assessment of the potentials of the Trust—its objectives, funding, staffing and effectiveness—must be made in the light of changing demands and opportunities. Thus, it is essential for the Trust to understand both itself and its challenges and to identify high-priority goals accordingly.

The National Trust must recognize the ever-present need to aggressively seek excellence in everything it does. In addition to their program responsibilities, the departments are experimental laboratories and all of their programs should be models.

Its properties present the National Trust with its single most vexing problem: how to diminish their relative dominance in the Trust's overall program and, at the same time, how to increase their substantive contribution to that program.

The programs we believe the National Trust can and should engage in now are described in the chapters that follow. Here we mention only those we believe are of highest priority.

The National Trust must develop an education program for decision makers, historic preservation professionals, craftsmen and the public at large. It must conduct the research necessary to further preservation.

In recent years, the National Trust has done little in the education field. It must develop a number of new and imaginative programs. It should greatly increase its efforts to inform local decision makers about the importance of historic preservation. It should originate, help finance and monitor programs for the institutional and in-service training of historic preservation professionals and craftsmen. It should promote the inclusion of preservation in the formal education of all Americans, thereby seeking to increase public awareness of the importance of preservation.

The National Trust must provide relevant and substantive technical services through advice, easement depository, publications, revolving funds and other mechanisms.

There is a growing need for on-the-spot technical advice. More regional offices are needed and the services available both at headquarters and in the regional offices must be expanded. More and better technical bulletins and reports are required to satisfy a growing audience. Many historic preservation groups now need help from the National Trust's revolving and grant funds. A Trust depository for easements is needed by local preservationists.

National Trust properties must be models and demonstrations of exemplary and innovative historic preservation action.

The preservation, restoration, interpretation, management and public relations of National Trust properties should provide models for preservation organizations throughout the country. Each property should be a model of some aspect of museum administration: acquisition techniques, community relationships, interpretation techniques, overall quality of restoration.

Through demonstration projects in areas with problems requiring special attention, the National Trust must take the initiative in pointing to new directions in historic and cultural preservation.

New historic preservation problems will emerge continuously, and it will be the responsibility of the National Trust to select high-priority problems for special treatment. Two current opportunities for Trust demonstration projects are inner-city rehabilitation and the preservation of rural historic and cultural landscapes.

The National Trust must strengthen its public relations program in order to broaden the ranks and to increase the effectiveness of those working to improve the historic and cultural environment.

The new challenges of the historic and cultural environment will require new responses, attitudes, skills and supporters. The National Trust will find it necessary to make concerted efforts to assure that the appropriate organizations and individuals are introduced to the dynamics of environmental protection.

Index

National Trust properties are set in boldface.
Illustration page numbers are set in italic.